THE FIRST CENTURY

The

TEXAS BANKERS ASSOCIATION

THE FIRST CENTURY

1885–1985

By T. HARRY GATTON

This publication is a part of the Centennial Observance of the
Texas Bankers Association as a project of its Historical Committee.
Published by the TEXAS BANKERS ASSOCIATION, Austin, Texas, *1984*.

First Edition
Copyright © 1984
The Texas Bankers Association
203 West Tenth Street
Austin, Texas 78701

Library of Congress Catalogue Card Number 83-51799
International Standard Book Number
0-86701-015-0 (regular edition)
0-86701-016-9 (special edition)

Design and Production by Whitehead and Whitehead, Austin, Texas

Manufactured in the United States of America

Contents

PREFACE   *xi*
FOREWORD   *xiii*
INTRODUCTORY NOTE   *xv*

PART ONE: The Founding Year—1885

CHAPTER 1   Issues and Leaders—Grandiloquent Rhetoric   *1*
2   Banking Structure in Texas: Capital Deficiency, Grievances   *4*
3   The Big Idea and the Colorful Pacesetter Founders   *8*
4   The Year of the TBA Founding: Texas on a Track of Bigness   *10*
5   Shaping an Institution—The First State Bankers Association   *14*
6   The Gentleman from Gonzales   *26*
7   Going First Class at the Park Hotel and Spa in 1885   *27*

PART TWO: Banking in Texas—Merchant Princes to National Charters

CHAPTER 1   A Texan Will Trade Anything   *31*
2   The Mexican Period—First Bank Charter   *33*
3   The Republic of Texas—Banking Overlooked   *37*
4   Sam Houston—Jackson's Protégé   *40*
5   Private Banks Expand—Bankers, Dry Goods and Scissors   *43*
6   Texas and the Confederacy   *45*
7   Union and the New System—National Banks   *46*
8   Reconstruction, Bank Expansion and the Reign of Private Banking   *47*

PART THREE: The TBA Crusade for Equity through Constitutional Reform

CHAPTER 1   Bank Issue Joined: TBA Provides a Forum for Action   *53*
2   Development of TBA Convention Issues and Traditions   *57*
3   The Innovator Points the Way   *60*

THE FIRST
CENTURY

CHAPTER 4   The TBA's First Major Assignment—Amend the Constitution   62

5   Critical Decade of the 1890s—Gaining Political Clout   65

6   Texas Bankers on the Go—and a TBA Yell!   76

7   The TBA and the Turn of the Century   77

8   Inching Along—Momentum for State Banking and the Role of the TBA   81

9   Boll Weevil Blues—Bugs on the Square   84

PART FOUR: Watershed Years for Banking and the TBA

CHAPTER 1   Victory at the Polls—TBA Wins Its Major Goal   87

2   Structuring a State Banking System   88

3   Charter Proliferation—The Line Formed Early   89

4   Prosperity and Panic   93

5   Deposit Guaranty a Reality: Dissension in the TBA Ranks   94

6   The TBA Thrives as Issue-Oriented Bankers Support a Broader Involvement   96

7   *Texas Bankers Record* Established   101

8   Currency Control: Wilson Gets Support from Texas   105

9   Texas Women Bankers Association—Another First for the TBA   106

PART FIVE: Monetary Control and the Federal Reserve System

CHAPTER 1   Wilson Prevails: Congress Approves the Fed   109

2   The Big Push—Texas Seeks Regional Bank   112

3   Dallas Selected: Gold Pens for the Signers   114

4   Join the Fed, the TBA Urges   115

5   TBA Moves Headquarters to Dallas: The Philpott Era Begins   116

6   Par Clearance and Strong Dissent   118

PART SIX: World War I and a Turbulent Postwar Era

CHAPTER 1   Patriotism and Performance   121

2   Drought, Victory and Postwar Problems, Some New and Some Old   123

3   Decade of the Twenties—Readjustment, Contraction and the Guaranty Fund Law Terminated   126

4   TBA Bank Robbery Reward Program is Dead Serious   130

5   The "Santa Claus Bank Robbery" in Cisco   136

PART SEVEN: The Great Depression, Banking and the TBA in a Period of Financial Crisis

CHAPTER 1   Disarray in the Marketplace   139

2   How about Service Charges?   143

CHAPTER 3   The Roosevelt Era Begins   *145*
        4   Texas and the Banking Holiday   *147*
        5   Congressional Action, Alphabet Agencies and Golden Jubilee   *150*

    PART EIGHT: World War II—America, an Arsenal of Democracy

CHAPTER 1   Financing Global Conflict—Texas Banking on the Line   *157*
        2   The TBA Convention Is Canceled for the First Time   *159*
        3   Peace and Prosperity   *159*

    PART NINE: A New TBA Era—The Movers and Shakers

CHAPTER 1   Leaders, Issues and Involvement   *161*
        2   Fiesta Time for the Old TBA—The Diamond Jubilee   *166*
        3   A Decisive Action—State Bankers Organize   *168*
        4   The TBA: Change to Meet New Expectations, New
             Challenges   *169*

    PART TEN: The TBA and the Philpott Era

CHAPTER 1   More than Half a Century—The Major Domo   *173*
        2   Humor and Philosophy—The Creative Mind of "Mr. Phil"   *175*

    PART ELEVEN: Consolidation and Expansion: A New TBA Vigor

CHAPTER 1   Beginning the Kimberlin Era—The Right Combination for a New
             TBA Thrust   *179*
        2   TBA Goes to Washington—Emphasis on Legislative and Regulatory
             Issues and on Education   *181*
        3   Remembering History—TBA Historical Marker for Lampasas   *184*
        4   The TBA and Political Involvement   *187*

    PART TWELVE: Miracle on Tenth Street: The TBA Gets a Permanent Home

CHAPTER 1   Ideas and Action   *189*
        2   The TBA Council Approves the Committee Report   *193*
        3   The Miracle on Tenth Street Dedicated—Without Debt   *206*

    PART THIRTEEN: The TBA Rounds Out the Last Decade of the First Century:
        From the Colorado to the Potomac, Banking Reform and Equity

CHAPTER 1   The Art of Consensus and a Level Playing Field   *209*
        2   Financial Reform: No Tranquility for Banking and the TBA   *213*
        3   Preparing for the TBA Centennial—A Published History and a
             Museum   *215*
        4   Front-Burner Issues and the Deregulatory Splash   *217*

PART FOURTEEN: The Gallery of Presidents of the Texas Bankers Association

(Artist's sketch of each President)   *223*

PART FIFTEEN: Traditions, Bankers and Nostalgia

CHAPTER 1   The Flying Squadron—Pilgrims in the Club Car   *235*
2   The "Memwas" of Preacher Knight   *238*
3   Nail Up the Passageway to the Saloon   *240*
4   Hurrah for a Living Wage!   *240*
5   Carter Glass and His Two-Minute Speech   *241*
6   The Last Roundup of a Loser   *241*
7   Texas Ranger Opens a Bank—Shotgun Basic Equipment   *242*
8   Who Can Play the Arithmometer?   *242*
9   Is an Automobile Necessary?   *243*
10   Hotel Rates in San Antonio   *243*
11   Goodbye to Circulation   *244*
12   An "Itchy Rash"—Ration Coupons   *244*
13   Pioneer Woman Banker Brought Her Bank through the Depression   *245*
14   Another First for Texas—Transit Numbers   *245*
15   Regional Bankers Associations and the TBA—Panhandle Organized in 1904   *246*
16   State Banking Department Organized in 1904—To Date, Twenty-Six Commissioners   *248*

PART SIXTEEN: The Second Century

CHAPTER 1   The TBA in a World of Change—How the Association Will Lead in a New Century—By Glen E. Lemon   *249*
2   The Centennial Year—A Benchmark History and a Permanent Museum—By A. W. (Dub) Riter, Jr.   *250*
APPENDIX   A Presidents of the TBA   *252*
B Treasurers of the TBA   *255*
C Texas Bankers Association   *256*
D Managing Officers of the TBA   *257*
E Historical Committee of the TBA   *258*
INDEX   *259*

Preface

THE FIRST
CENTURY

WHILE MAKING THIS study of the history of the Texas Bankers Association and the relationship of the association to the banking history of Texas, it became obvious to me how contrasts often produced colorful leaders and diverse issues.

John Jay Knox noted the uniqueness of the banking history of Texas in his classic study in 1900. Other writers and researchers have documented the dramatic record. This history, issued as a part of the centennial of the Texas Bankers Association, attempts to identify many of the issues, rhetoric and economic conditions which motivated Texas bankers to form the first state banking association in the United States in 1885. While it took 20 years to achieve the main goal of the association—constitutional change to permit state chartering of banks—the association was innovative in other areas, such as in forming the first bankers' association for women.

This history is essentially anecdotal by design and often portrays the lighter side of the people and issues, but I hope that the reader will find it a valuable and readable source of information about an important organization, its founders, its leaders and the banking institutions of Texas. The total of their contribution to Texas and the nation through the association is a major one.

It is appropriate for the Texas Bankers Association to document and publish its history. Any institution that serves people—and banking is certainly at the vortex of vital service—does well to preserve the story of its birth and development.

To acknowledge appropriately the splendid cooperation from a broad spectrum of institutions and individuals in the hospitable state of Texas is impossible. I have enjoyed learning new and interesting facts about the people and institutions of the Lone Star State. These reinforce the many good things I already knew. No doors have been closed by individuals, libraries, public archives, banks or private collections. Indeed, efforts to cooperate and to linger at length talking about the past and pondering the future have cemented new friendships.

Although Texas now ranks among the leaders in population, finance and economic development, it has not lost the uniqueness that is "peculiarly Texan," as Knox put it. This is good; it augurs well for the future.

During the research and writing of this centennial history, I have incurred a debt of gratitude to many people and institutions that I can never repay. My particular thanks go to the Texas Bankers Association and its Historical Committee headed by

Gene Edwards of Amarillo and to Sam O. Kimberlin, Jr., managing officer, and the highly professional staff of the association. The officers and board of directors, along with the membership, have given total support and have continued to put the observance of the TBA centennial and its projects foremost. They have maintained the high quality of leadership for the margin of excellence in service.

Research has been pleasant, aided by various facilities, including The Institute of Texan Cultures in San Antonio, under the direction of Jack R. Maguire; The University of Texas Eugene C. Barker Texas History Center at Austin; the Rosenberg Library in Galveston; the Library of the Federal Reserve Bank of Dallas; the North Carolina State Library, Raleigh; the Archives and Library of the State of Texas, Austin; and the Banking Department, Austin. Many banks and bankers furnished archival material to the TBA for its museum collection, including several bank histories. Former TBA presidents and other banking leaders in the various sections of Texas granted interviews. The present TBA leaders gave unstinted cooperation in the production of this volume.

The invaluable assistance of Sandra H. Carr in editing the manuscript is gladly acknowledged. As an editor at The Institute of Texan Cultures in San Antonio, she was ever ready to make valuable suggestions. Others at The Institute coordinated the museum project with the manuscript in a very professional manner.

Fred and Barbara Whitehead of Austin cooperated to make the book design and illustrations, along with the layout, an artistic gem.

The archives of the TBA, including the *Texas Bankers Record*, provided a wealth of information. Bill Philpott of Cisco, nephew of the longtime TBA secretary, made available many family items related to his uncle. I studied several published histories and manuscripts, including *The Development of State-Chartered Banking in Texas* by Joseph M. Grant and Lawrence L. Crum.

My wife Mary, who assisted in the research and traveled extensively with me, I am pleased to include in my long and special list of supporters.

As one of the founders of the TBA predicted, the association has been instrumental in the development of the state and the "enlargement of the banking mind."

T. HARRY GATTON

Foreword

WITH MORE THAN ten percent of the banks in the United States located within Texas's borders, it is appropriate that the Texas Bankers Association, serving these banks as their trade association, is both the oldest and largest among the 50 states. From a modest beginning in Lampasas in 1885 it drew its strength through the following century from the support of bankers in all kinds of communities. This diversity has been stimulating and wholesome. Its service to these banks has always been rendered, regardless of state or national charters, large or small communities or, in recent years, independent or holding companies.

The Texas Bankers Association moved into its own headquarters building in Austin in 1976. At the time that plans were formulated for this first building of its own, space was approved and left unfinished for a future banking museum. This advance planning presents the opportunity now to dedicate and open a banking museum on the Association's 100th birthday. With professional aid coming from The Institute of Texan Cultures in San Antonio, the museum will provide a pictorial history of Texas banking with memorabilia and artifacts furnished by various banks throughout the state. The practical uses of the museum for future bankers, student groups and others are almost unlimited.

As a companion project the Historical Committee, established in 1979 and made up of former TBA presidents plus senior staff members, also embarked on another project—the writing and publishing of an appropriate history of the Texas Bankers Association. This was also scheduled to appear in the Association's centennial year 1984–1985. The author is Harry Gatton, well-known banking historian and former executive vice president of the North Carolina Bankers Association. The book will be read with interest by bankers and non-bankers alike. It is a readable illustrated history of the Texas Bankers Association and is in context with the growth of banking itself in Texas. It will recall many interesting and difficult days of the past and will be helpful in acquainting younger bankers and the public in general with facts about the development of banking and its own Association during a colorful century in Texas.

Both of these projects are exciting, and the Historical Committee is enthusiastic about the progress which has been made as of this writing. We, the committee members, are convinced that an institutional history of banking, both depicted in a museum and as described in a book, is a valid and important contribution to Texas history.

GENE EDWARDS
Chairman
Historical Committee
Texas Bankers Association

Introductory Note

THIS IS A CHRONICLE OF TEN DECADES, tilted naturally towards events in which the people involved with the Texas Bankers Association played their roles, but flavored with the essence of their times of activity in the affairs of banking and their communities and state. It is a sequential record of happenings many of which not only were noteworthy in their day but are remarkably similar to occurrences of the present day. History does indeed repeat itself.

Harry Gatton, the author, has a varied and distinguished background, including experience with newspaper and radio media, service with former United States Senator Sam Ervin and with the North Carolina Bankers Association. In the latter capacity, he became well acquainted with bankers from throughout his state and the nation. Harry has been chairman of the North Carolina Historical Commission, and he served for fourteen years as a member of the American Battle Monuments Commission which oversees the construction and preservation of monuments throughout the world to historic battles and wars in which Americans fought. He drew upon his rich background of experience combined with his native interest in and enthusiasm for history in researching and writing the pages which follow.

This is an appropriate place to express sincere appreciation and abiding gratitude to the men and women of Texas banking whose voluntary service to the Texas Bankers Association through the years made the publication of this volume possible. From the beginning, bankers have given of themselves willingly and unhesitatingly to improve the association and through the association to improve banking services for the public. Carrying the mantle of service through the next 100 years with the dedication, fidelity and style of all of the bankers who served their banks, communities, state and nation during the past century will be a challenge. Today's bankers are, however, clearly worthy of meeting the challenge and continuing to carry the mantle with distinction and honor.

SAMUEL OWEN KIMBERLIN, JR.
Executive Vice President
Texas Bankers Association

THE FIRST CENTURY

Proceedings of the First Convention of the
Texas Bankers Association.

PART ONE

The Founding Year—1885

1

ISSUES and LEADERS— GRANDILOQUENT RHETORIC

A banker is like Caesar's wife, he should be above every suspicion.
COLONEL HENRY EXALL, July 23, 1885

COLONEL HENRY EXALL SPOKE as a disciple of a bigger and better Texas as he welcomed bankers from 22 cities and towns to Lampasas Springs on a warm July Thursday.

The 31 banker-delegates, most of them under age 35, were the founders of the Texas Bankers Association, the first state banking association in the United States, established July 23, 1885.

Colorful rhetoric by the former Confederate officer, bank director and political leader set the tone for the three-day meeting to launch the Big Idea proposed by a fellow townsman and bank cashier, Frank R. Malone of the First National Bank, aided by E. M. Longcope, assistant cashier of the same bank.

Applause greeted his extravagant enthusiasm. Warming to his task, Colonel Exall stirred the bankers and guests assembled in the concert room of the impressive new Park Hotel in the young town of Lampasas Springs, now simply Lampasas. Also an advocate of the Big Idea, the colonel graciously rolled out the red carpet.

"It is my pleasant duty to tender to you, in behalf of the citizens of Lampasas, the hospitality and freedom of our city; to welcome you as individuals, and as a body assembled for the laudable purpose of organizing a permanent association, directly for the benefit of the bankers of the State of Texas, and indirectly for the general or public good. We welcome you to our sweet South breezes; to our live oak shades; to our sulphur baths; to our rock-ribbed hills and grassy slopes; and at last, but not least, to the hearts and homes of our people," he said.

"We welcome you as representatives of the life blood of the commerce of our great state, as conservators of the peace and protectors alike of the interests of every department of business. Your prosperity is intimately and indissolubly connected with every legitimate enterprise. You must guide the strong; protect and foster the weak; stimulate honest endeavor; and curb the speculative tendencies of the rash. You must oil the wheels of trade; but keep the brake well in hand, that action and industry may have full vent, that disasters may be averted, that public and private confidence may, as it were, be grounded upon a rock."

The colonel turned to exhortation:

"A banker is like Caesar's wife, he should be above every suspicion.

"Guard well against every appearance of unfair or dishonorable action, as our financial equilibrium, facility and freedom of trade, depends more upon the public faith in banks than upon any other one thing. Guard with zealous eye the reputation of every banking institution. Expose fraud; but do not allow an honestly managed bank to fail for want of a little timely aid. In estimating the liabilities of a customer, with a view of extending credit, it may be well to class his endorsement with his liabilities. These suggestions are made with the hope that they may call to mind such investigations as will cause the proper safeguards to be placed around our every institution, protecting alike banks, individuals and the communities," he said.

The applause told the orator that his words were having an impact. With grandiloquent logic Colonel Exall established the articles of faith for the founders of the permanent organization and for succeeding generations of Texas bankers and the leaders of their association.

The colonel struck the main proposition early, the public faith in banks that had all too often been shattered in other years. Banking in 1885 was making a slow climb on a rocky road to the high ground of public acceptance, to convince the public that banks were needed to serve a diversified and progressive civilization.

The same theme was cited nearly a century later by the executive vice president of the Texas Bankers Association in a thesis for the Stonier Graduate School of Banking of the American Bankers Association. Sam O. Kimberlin, Jr., writing on "The Competitive Structure Within Which the Commercial Banking System Operates in Texas," put the idea in 20th century words:

"Filling a public need! Probably any business or industry prospers or declines in relationship to the increase or decrease of the demand by people for its products or services. Banking, however, begins and ends with how it serves public needs. Usually a bank is born only after a clear public demand for its exclusive services exists or is obviously coming into existence. In the State of Texas, the creation of this demand usually is a product of population growth," Kimberlin pointed out in the introduction to his 1972 thesis.

Colonel Exall, expressing the need for growth in banking, stated the reason:

"Our banking facilities must be increased to keep pace with our growing population, and to furnish the motive power to develop the untold riches of our mines; to build factories, furnaces and machine shops in our cities; to utilize our water power; to manufacture at home the products of our soil, giving profitable employment to

Banking, however, begins and ends with how it serves public needs.

2

thousands of those thrifty toilers, who will bring order out of chaos, and make this state blossom and bloom with the happy homes of industry."

No public relations expert wrote his address. The colonel was his own engine of persuasion and promotion.

This was his high-powered clincher:

"And when we hear the ring of the hammer, with the hum of machinery, and see the smoke of the factory and furnace, as our artisans shape the crude resources into tangible wealth, then with the teeming millions of happy, prosperous people will Texas be, in commercial wealth and importance, what she is in area—the empire state of the Grand Union."

Comfort and prosperity could be the happy plight of millions in the Texas of the future! The audience cheered even more loudly.

The idea for the Texas Bankers Association originated here in the First National Bank of Lampasas as it looked in 1885.

The colonel was almost through with his moving message—the first recorded remarks of a Texas Bankers Association meeting.

Concluding, he said, "You can be instrumental in bringing about these results. Then, indeed, will this be the garden spot of the earth, and we will invite the industrious and honest of every land and clime to come and abide with us, and enjoy to the fullest, the freedom of our institutions."

Colonel Exall had finished his brief but effective welcoming remarks. After the applause ceased he added, "With the brightest hopes for the future of this Association, I now ask for the nomination of your temporary president."

He suggested James Francis Miller of Gonzales, incumbent member of the U.S. House of Representatives, banker and lawyer, and a strong advocate of the organization, for the office. The delegates put down their cigars, applauded again the man, his remarks and his suggestion. His impeccable performance in elocution, marked by Victorian courtesy, civility and common sense, had been powerfully presented.

Colonel Exall, one of the godfathers of the TBA, born in 1848, was a native of Richmond, Virginia. He served as an officer in the 10th Virginia Cavalry and came to Texas by way of Kentucky. He gave up the practice of law for business and cattle raising near Fort Worth in 1877. Living in Lampasas at the time of the TBA meeting, he later moved to Dallas. He was chairman of the Texas State Democratic Committee for two years, 1886 to 1888, and was president of the Texas Industrial Conference.

2
BANKING STRUCTURE in TEXAS: CAPITAL DEFICIENCY, GRIEVANCES

Human history is in essence a history of ideas.
H. G. WELLS

N OW THE DELEGATES settled down to the work at hand, establishing the first of a kind, a state bankers association.

Why?

The past was impressive. The future by all odds appeared to promise even better opportunities, assuming a balanced progression of economic development. To assure this progression, it is anticipated that in each generation an idea large enough to capture the forces of human progress will emerge. Texas expected a future that would harness their burgeoning and vigorous enthusiasm, a resolute future to equate its development with its size. For bankers the Big Idea was in line with the appraisal of history by H. G. Wells—ideas.

With most of the tumult of earlier years behind—and the passing of the old frontier to the expanding Texas of diversified development of farming, ranching, manufacturing, commerce, finance, transportation and other viable aspects of a solid base for growth—the enthusiasm of Texas a century past is understandable. There were few dampening restraints. Not even the cotton boll weevil had crossed the Rio Grande from Mexico. Cotton liked Texas and Texans liked cotton. Cotton was "money in the bank." Cotton was king.

Forces for cultural and educational development and a better life-style were in motion. The traditional eastern and Gulf part of the state had the remnants of Old South traditions and customs and the heritage of the Anglo-Americans such as Stephen F. Austin. The Hispanic heritage was a cherished aspect of Texas social and cultural life over a large area. From El Paso to Brownsville relations with Mexico were peaceful on the long Rio Grande frontier. And in various sections there were pockets of other ethnic groups which gave Texas of 1885 its interesting mix of peoples. To the north the people of the Indian Territory, yet to become a state, were on the move. In the Panhandle and the vast areas west of the Pecos, Texans picked up the theme of stability and progress. They gave the vast land the uniqueness that became its hallmark. Moreover, the merger of traditions and ethnic heritages gave the state and its people a positive image with an indelible brand symbolic of cattlemen and cowboys, merchant princes, railroad developers, plantation and ranch owners, manufacturers, lumbermen, financiers and bankers. The era of oil was yet to come.

In all of this, a serious flaw was obvious.

Banking to a large extent had been cut out of the herd.

A victim of old, politically enshrined prejudices, banking development had been restrained as far back as 1845, when the Texas constitution was adopted. The restrictions against state chartering of banks were carried forward through each succeeding constitution with the exception of a brief period after the Civil War when a few state banks were chartered. The prohibition against banks was reinstituted and reaffirmed in the Constitution of 1876. To free-spirited entrepreneurs of 1885 this was clearly discriminatory, and passing strange that Texas was the only state to retain the restriction. The political stew in banking's pot had been simmering a long time. It was soon to boil over. Action was needed to develop a new menu and a new beginning.

Banking needed a Big Idea to remove effectively the yoke of restriction, and the logical way to accomplish this, reasoned young Lampasas banker Frank R. Malone, was to organize the bankers into an association.

The Big Idea found fertile ground. The Texas Bankers Association was the result.

Texas had been served since 1865 by national banks, a creation of Congress in the Abraham Lincoln administration, the Civil War days of 1863—a bright idea of Secretary of the Treasury Salmon P. Chase to provide war financing for the hard-pressed Union and to remove the arm-lock of state banking.

Although without state banks, Texas did have a form of dual banking system that was performing under adversity to support the financial base for state development. There were the national banks. A system of private banks, unchartered and unregu-

Banking to a large extent had been cut out of the herd.

5

lated, was the other leg of the dual system. The latter were an outgrowth of the pre-Civil War days, when no banks existed except those started largely by merchant houses and commission brokers.

The absence of state banks created an unnatural configuration of financial institutions. Credit facilities to fuel the engine of development were seriously limited by the regressive anti-bank provision. The formation of national banks was seriously limited because of the $50,000 capital needed as a prerequisite for a national charter. That kind of investment capital was not to be found everywhere in Texas. In many places, Texas no exception, money was scarce and costly to use when available.

Expansion of farming produced a host of problems and serious shortages of production credit, especially for the small farmers, tenants and sharecroppers. Production credit was limited, uncertain, expensive—not to mention difficult to acquire on a long-term basis. Too, the risk to lenders was in many instances dangerously high.

The damage resulting from the rigid anti-bank feeling, seemingly etched in granite, was obvious. The passage of time had not eroded the provision that had its Jacksonian imprimatur as practiced by Sam Houston and his colleagues in the formation of the Republic of Texas in 1836 and again in 1845 at statehood.

Farmers felt they were losing out all the way around. They understood full well that "money made the mare trot," but the impasse was there. Bankers, for the most part, were not involved in agricultural credit in 1885 as they were later on.

The issues were there, obvious to all, and crying for a solution.

Aroused farmers wanted organization and united action. They sought governmental solutions for the conditions as they saw them. They vented their wrath, often raised to a fever pitch by emotional stimulation from their leaders, against the protective tariffs, corporations, monopolistic trusts, time merchants, middlemen, railroads and banks, which to them symbolized the perceived evils of "Wall Street," the "money trusts" and "money power" in America. Theirs was a laundry list of grievances. Many of the small farmers and sharecroppers felt they were "not dead or down, but had been badly cussed."

Conditions in Texas were aggravated by the instability of prices for agricultural products, by frequent drought, by recessions. Many viewed the crop lien system as a one-way road to perdition.

Corporate and financial power, in conjunction with large farming and ranching operations and politicians, were to the small farmers sinister forces with undue influence in the legislative halls of Austin and Washington.

The paradox—bankers feeling that the political power in Texas was imposed against them through heavy banking restrictions, and the farmers demanding relief through government—contained the seeds of a collision course. The small farmers, supported by the growing power and sympathy of unions, were joining the militants in the vanguard of Populism which threatened free enterprise banking.

The early agrarian militancy was fanned by stirring editorials from some farm journals which outlined the depth of the charges against corporate and moneyed powers. Wrote the editor of the *Progressive Farmer*: "It struts into and out of halls of legislation and by bribery or intimidation controls and shapes legislation in its favor." The van-

Frank R. Malone, cashier, First National
Bank, Lampasas, the young banker with the
idea for an association of bankers.

E. M. Longcope, assistant cashier of the same
bank, who cooperated in developing the idea.

guard group of Populism and the People's Party—the Farmers' Alliance—listened,
read and believed.

The organized agrarian movement started in Lampasas County in 1877, beginning
and spreading as the Farmers' Alliance. It urged the power of government to change
the credit system, advocated restrictions against banking, railroading and business. Its
agenda for achieving victory was a long one. And in 1885 the militant movement
meant to achieve success.

Bankers felt the charges were largely demagoguery, riddled with untruths, ruthless
and undeserved. After all, the banks were for the most part very small local organizations, acquainted with community needs; money was hard to come by, and as financial institutions they were subject to failure when unwisely managed. The past, they
observed, was littered with failed banks, and depositors demanded conservative lending practices to prevent failure. Regulators followed with close scrutiny their practices
by examinations of the regulated institutions.

Bankers had a stake in community development, they acknowledged, but that role
in 19th century America had many limiting factors—and in Texas the anti-bank restrictions kept the brakes on. Bankers argued also that the banking climate had
changed with improvements brought about by the national system in which stringent
regulations were imposed and strong capital bases required before charters were issued.

Bankers had a stake
in community develop-
ment, they acknowl-
edged, but that role in
19th century America
had many limiting fac-
tors—and in Texas the
anti-bank restrictions
kept the brakes on.

Simply put, 1885's private enterprise ethic was based on the fundamentals of rugged individualism, thrift and prudence. There was little evidence of excessive federal or state controls. This suited most of the people and the time and place. Ben Franklin's wise saying, "He that riseth late must trot all day," was generally accepted. Some folks, the power structure of the day held, were poor managers, idle-natured and, no matter what opportunity was available, would somehow fail.

No doubt about it, the pot was boiling in Texas and the nation. The gold-silver question, antitrust sentiment, tariffs were all national issues, too. Associations and groups were organizing to give muscle, understanding and competitive positioning to the contending forces.

3

THE BIG IDEA and the
COLORFUL PACESETTER
FOUNDERS

Americans of all ages, all stations in life . . . are forever forming associations.
ALEXIS DE TOCQUEVILLE

THE FOUNDING OF THE TEXAS BANKERS ASSOCIATION in 1885 as the first state banking association was not an accidental action, nor was its formation unnoticed in Texas and the nation.

It was a benchmark year, the otherwise fairly uneventful 1885, for getting bankers together, following the good record of the American Bankers Association formed ten years earlier. Too, the bankers, farmers, educators, ranchers, cattlemen, cotton growers, timber producers, miners, manufacturers, laborers—to name only a few groups—liked to get together. Conventions had become necessary and popular. Nobody, it seemed, wanted to stand alone. The successes of the earlier associations produced a grand rush to organization, a practice which has resulted in the high standing of associations in the United States today.

The discerning mind of Frenchman Alexis de Tocqueville glimpsed the American tradition of associations on his visit in 1830. Unlike Europeans, he said, "Americans of all ages, all stations in life . . . are forever forming associations." In his *Democracy in America* he gave a ringing endorsement of the value of association to a free society through voluntary and cooperative action.

Said the observant Frenchman, "In countries where such associations do not exist, if private people do not . . . create something like them, I see no other dike to hold back tyranny of whatever sort, and a great nation might with impunity be oppressed by some tiny faction or by a single man."

8

It is doubtful that the founders of the Texas Bankers Association in Lampasas were thinking of their creation of a voluntary association as an instrument of freedom and the maintenance of a free society with free political institutions. That was the philosophical and net contribution to the American system when they joined for voluntary action. They sought the wisdom and power of numbers in a voluntary association.

How did the Texas Bankers Association (TBA) do it?

This narrative history is not intended as a detailed documentary of the world of banking history. It aims to tell a story, to keep its anchors solidly based, using an anecdotal history approach. To do this requires a presentation of people, issues and events.

Texas in 1885?

The voters of the Lone Star State were voting for Democratic candidates. It was no surprise that Grover Cleveland swept the state and was elected with enough electoral votes to be the first president from his party since 1861. This whiff of political reality set the stage for change in 1885. To the amazement of many supporters in the Midwest and elsewhere—"free silver" advocates who held that silver coinage was the best answer to the nation's monetary problems—the new president supported the "hard money" or gold advocates of the Eastern financial centers. His action polarized the silver issue; a schism of substantial magnitude resulted.

As the days of July dragged along, the illness of the former Union general and president, Ulysses S. Grant, was in the news. Writing with all the ebbing strength he could muster to finish his memoirs, the 63-year-old Grant was slowly succumbing to throat cancer in Mount McGregor, New York. As a young lieutenant Grant saw service in Texas on the way to the war with Mexico, and he remembered with pleasure his duty in the state, a positive impression he documented although in principle he opposed the war.

Needing funds, he raced with impending death to complete the manuscript which was to become a best seller and bring his family $500,000. The work completed, Grant breathed his last on Thursday, July 23, 1885.

Thursday, July 23, 1885—the very day the Texas Bankers Association was organized in a remote Texas town called Lampasas Springs. Appropriate reports of Grant's demise were carried in the press of Texas, and in the same issues word of the founding of the Texas Bankers Association was published.

4
THE YEAR of the TBA FOUNDING:
TEXAS on a TRACK of BIGNESS

Young, middle-aged and old people have turned their backs upon their ancestral homes and set their faces toward the State (Texas) where wealth is to be had without labor and life is a perpetual picnic.

EDITORIAL IN A STATESVILLE, N.C., NEWSPAPER, 1883

Hᴉsᴛᴏʀʏ ɪs ғᴜʟʟ ᴏғ ᴄᴏɴᴛʀᴀsᴛs—examples of this are the doldrums of one generation and the prosperity of another. History directs the forces which result in marked progress or virtual stagnation. Sometimes these forces and events are difficult to chart in the flight of time which is the standard of measurement.

The banking history of Texas, unique in many aspects and fraught with contrasts, is without parallel in this country.

With the encouragement of Sam Houston, the 1845 Texas Constitution provided for a specific exclusion of banking. It said: "No corporate body shall hereafter be created, renewed, or extended, with banking or discounting privileges. Corporations shall not be created in this State, by special laws, except for political or municipal purposes; but the Legislature shall provide, by general laws, for the organization of all other corporations, except corporations with banking or discounting privileges, the creation of which is prohibited."

Writing in his classic *History of Banking* in 1900, John Jay Knox, former U. S. Comptroller of the Currency, stated Texas's uniqueness: "The existence of Texas under so many different kinds and conditions of government, and the environments of country and of people, have been such as to leave upon every characteristic an impress peculiarly Texan, and among others, to make its banking history unique. The Texas we know today represents the growth of the inherent spirit of independent statehood through the intermediate conditions of Spanish dependence, Mexican statehood, Texas independence, and final coalition with the United States."

From a small and scattered population of earlier years, Texas had climbed to the rank of 11th in the nation in population in 1880. The census showed 1,591,749 inhabitants, nearly double the 1870 total. Immigrants swarmed to the state—and more were wanted and were welcomed. Confirming this attitude was a news item from Erin, Jasper County, in 1885: "We would be glad to have immigrants come and look at our country." The Erins were repeated everywhere as the old frontier was fading in the westward march.

The Old South plantation economy of the east Texas cotton empire was giving way to a full-blown tenancy system. Sharecropping was a way of life for many. Ranching and the legendary cowboy, bearing a Texas brand, advanced. The new railroads opened eastern United States markets to Texas cattle. The ports of the southeast

10

coast of Texas facilitated rapidly expanding exports of agricultural and manufactured products.

By 1885 the threats of political insurgency by militant agrarians against the business community were not to be minimized. Grass-roots Texas, through the Farmers' Alliance, took on the establishment. Its 1,600 subchapters had a simple ritual; dues were 6 cents per month for men, nothing for women. It claimed to be the first secret society without a privileged class. The cooperative crusade had the fervor of a religious revival; it touched nearly all bases in the socio-economic life of Texas. It promoted statewide prohibition to eliminate the evils of liquor, in addition to the group's fight against the state's establishment as represented by business, finance and industry. From its bases in Lampasas, Coryell, Hamilton, Parker, Wise and Jack counties, it enveloped the state and spread gingerly through the South.

With the crisis of Civil War and Reconstruction far behind, Texas and the nation were in a burgeoning industrial revolution in 1885. How broadly based were banks in Texas to support the rapid expansion and credit needs of the people and business?

There were 68 national banks in operation with total resources of $25,237,000. Private banks had no reporting requirements because they were unchartered and unincorporated. For the most part, these institutions kept their business unreported, although some did report voluntarily. From these reports it appears that there were approximately 116 private banks from the largest urban areas to the small crossroads towns and villages. It is estimated that their resources in 1885 were not less than $5,000,000 and not in excess of $10,000,000. There were a few of the holdover state banks chartered in the interim period of seven years before the Constitution of 1876.

The Merchants and Farmers National Bank in the north Texas town of Sherman claimed to be the largest in Texas, its paid-up capital at $600,000; in 1885 it was said to have four times the resources of any other bank in the state. Galveston, however, remained the financial center.

Texas, on the move up the population and economic ladder in 1885, was the largest state in land area and boasted a wide range of natural resources.

The following are other events of 1885, the founding year of the Texas Bankers Association:

Haskell, Midland and Val Verde counties were organized.
The XIT Ranch was established in the Texas Panhandle.
The IOA Ranch was established in Lubbock County.
The first creamery was established at Terrell.
The American Economic Association was formed at Saratoga Springs, New York.
The U.S. Post Office established a special delivery service, and postal rates were reduced to 2 cents per ounce.
Promoted by railroads, standard time became widely used.
Annie Oakley joined the William F. Cody "Buffalo Bill" Wild West Show.
The Washington Monument was dedicated on February 21.
Texans and the nation were reading Mark Twain's classic, *The Adventures of Huckleberry Finn*.
Scott Joplin, the black Texarkana artist, was playing ragtime piano in St. Louis.
The cost of Texas state government was a trifle over $3,872,000.

11

An affluent young Texan born into a Houston and Galveston banking, shipping and plantation family, Edward Mandell House, had moved to Austin, where he carefully observed and mastered the workings of state government and used leisure time to parlay his keen but quiet leadership into a major political force which later had much to do with the administration of President Woodrow Wilson and the Federal Reserve System.

John Ireland, an Irish immigrant's son, was governor.

Fashions, described by *Harper's Bazaar*, were upbeat. "Scarfs, handkerchiefs, wide ribbons and the fabrics are emblazoned to imitate medieval banners. Vieux rouge is showing two tones while the new blue is called vieille blouse usee, the color of workmen's shirts. Much beige and cream color and bright gold is being shown. Flowers and scarfs are replacing feathers on hats. Combinations of two materials with long drapery and plain lawn skirts are being used in both suits and blouses."

Telephone service between New York and Chicago had started, and the telephone was in service on a growing basis in Texas.

Texans were still talking of the founding of The University of Texas at Austin and the first class graduated a year earlier by the new institution.

The first appendectomy was performed.

The first gasoline pump was manufactured, but the era of the horseless carriage was yet to come.

It seemed appropriate to Texas, the land of cotton production, that a horse named Joe Cotton won the Kentucky Derby and earned $4,630 for the run.

A man who was to play a prominent role in the Texas Bankers Association for 51 years, William Albert Philpott, Jr., was born in St. Jo, Montague County.

Chester W. Nimitz, future Fleet Admiral, was born in Fredericksburg. And in Austin the eight-ton cornerstone of the new Texas capitol was laid in appropriate ceremonies on March 2, 1885, the 49th anniversary of Texas independence. The impressive project produced the largest capitol building in the United States, seven feet taller than the nation's capitol, at a cost of $1,500,000, not directly taken out of the taxpayers' pockets. This was achieved by trading 3,000,000 acres of public lands in the Panhandle to a contractor for a turnkey job, land appraised at no more than 50 cents per acre and described in 1882 as a "desert waste."

The Bankers Directory of July 1885 listed the basic legal interest rate in Texas as 8 percent with the conventional or contract rate at 12 percent. In case of usury, all interest was forfeited, but usury was not indictable.

Texans of 1885 were moving on a track of bigness. Pride and optimism were united with a free spirit. They recalled the traditions of sacrifice at the Alamo and other shrines, survival from drought and calamity, outlaws and a host of other harsh conditions. These traditions of heroism and sacrifice in the struggle for political independence were alive and green. The traditional brand of rugged individualism was giving way to cooperation. Confidence was as great as the land.

The back country in 1885 was beginning to see the good results of having banks. More were needed.

A vivid account of the way money was handled in Lampasas before the coming of

12

banking in 1884 is recounted by Jonnie Ross Elzner in *Relighting Lamplights of Lampasas County, Texas*. Money was entrusted to merchants for safekeeping. The nearest railroad was in Austin. Mail was received at the post office only twice weekly. No checking system being available, the little cash transferred was simply mailed in an envelope. Merchants were supplied by wagons, often pulled by oxen, over the wagon road which often required days to make the trip from Lampasas to Austin. Freight and passenger lines were almost always the same, and the stage fare was steep—$10. Money carried on a person or in transport was constantly in jeopardy, so novel schemes of concealment were developed. "The place for hiding money in the house was sometimes between mattresses or back of the canned goods," Elzner wrote.

It was the beginning of the age of associations. Texas bankers moved early, the pacesetter among the states to organize a bankers association. The wisdom of the founders put Texas first, and its association has remained at the front in size and service.

A study of the first century of the Texas Bankers Association provides glimpses of the parade of men and women, issues, challenges, solutions. Together they sustain an anecdotal history which tells of the people as bankers and leaders in the development of the social and economic life of Texas and the nation. Texas bankers as business people have always lived and worked on the cutting edge of change in good and bad times. But they have prevailed, and these men and women, these free-spirited Texans and their organization, the Texas Bankers Association, have provided an extra margin for balanced progress.

By 1885 the buffalo herds that had ranged from Texas north to the Indian Territory, through Kansas and beyond, grazing the verdant grass, had been diminished to near extinction.

Invention of the barbed wire fence in the early 1870s resulted in efficient pasturage by homesteaders, and as historian Samuel Eliot Morrison points out in *The Oxford History of the American People*, the range was being "criss-crossed by railroad," and by 1885 these conditions doomed the long cattle drives across unhampered open areas. Cattle and sheep ranches sprang up to replace the open rangeland. The legendary mounted cowboy of the long drive became confined to the less demanding routine of a ranch hand. Many of these early Texas cowboys had been at home in the saddle from their youth and had honed their experiences in the Civil War. According to Morrison, they and the Mexican vaqueros "were the first and best cowboys."

The bankers of 1885 felt comfortable with this new beef cattle industry. Texas caught the ranch ownership fever, a fever that the passage of a century has not cured. Words such as maverick and dogie entered the Texas and American lexicon. The cowboy, originating in Texas, was portrayed in story and song as the gallant horseman, riding to high adventure and a fair lady, defending honor and morality. He was at peace with his purple world at sunset around a thousand campfires. Nothing before had so captivated the imagination of blasé Easterners as did the opportunity for excitement and success in the open spaces of Texas. The vivid imagery was effective in creating a population increase of dramatic proportions.

Gone to Texas!

From the old states that was the cry. Evidence of this is an editorial lament in the Statesville, North Carolina, *Landmark*, January 19, 1883: "A craze for going to Texas seems to have lately taken possession of the people of this section of the State. Many have gone from Rowan, Cabarrus, Mecklenburg, Iredell and Catawba (counties). Young, middle-aged and old people have turned their backs upon their ancestral homes and set their faces toward the State where wealth is to be had without labor and life is a perpetual picnic. Ah! well. The most of them will wish they hadn't," was the viewpoint of the editor.

Many people did believe that in Texas "life was a perpetual picnic." To gaze upon the rich agricultural land after cultivating worn-out hilly fields was a frontiersman's dream.

Gone to Texas!

5
SHAPING an INSTITUTION—
THE FIRST STATE BANKERS ASSOCIATION

The banding together of so much capital and enterprise in one body, and the united influence thereof rightly directed would bring forth good fruit to the Lone Star State.
F. R. MALONE, May 26, 1885

THE INTRICACY OF THE FOUNDING of the Texas Bankers Association unfolds as a slow and programmed process.

A hundred years ago there were no software programs or printouts of models of organization. Potential leadership was essentially parochial. Communications were limited. But there was an abundance of time for thought and reason.

Details of the launching of the Texas Bankers Association, as is true of any new organization, usually focus on the founders, the first meeting and the historic events surrounding it.

How was the Big Idea developed that set the wheels in motion for the three-day organizational meeting in Lampasas?

Publicity in the right place was the first public step.

Frank R. Malone and E. M. Longcope thought about the organization frequently, often returning to the bank in the evening to ponder thoroughly the rationale and process.

Assured of the value of the idea, the plan evolved. It rested on a simple and effective way of spreading the word.

Writing about the development in later publications of the TBA, William A. Philpott, Jr., said:

"They returned one evening—to be exact, the evening of May 26, 1885,— drew the bank's front window shades, wrinkled their eager brows, dipped and re-dipped their pen in the ink-well (happily it was before the day of the so-called fountain pen),

14

and rather laboriously composed a letter to the *Galveston News*. In those days this paper was looked upon as the only public print in Texas worthy of the notice of business men of parts and fashion; and when gentlemen found their fingers itching, a simple remedy was available because of the liberal space assigned by the *News* to 'special' letters from all interior departments."

The letter, later described by Longcope as not being up to the high requirements of his superior, was nevertheless mailed.

Appearing in the *Galveston News*, Thursday, May 28, 1885, the letter gave "verbal raiment" to the Big Idea. It follows:

Texas Banks
Proposal for an Organization—A Conference at Lampasas.
[To the News.]

Lampasas, Tex., May 26, 1885.—It has been suggested that, in view of the good resulting from the organization into state associations of tradesmen, professional men and members of other special interests, and of the eminently practical services offered by the American Bankers association, the banks and bankers of this State should meet together and organize permanently the Texas Bankers association. Why not this summer? It is almost idle to discuss the benefits to be derived. Every bank man in the State will admit the good to be accomplished.

The influence of such an association would be wide-extending, not only toward the development of the material resources of the State, but in the enlargement and expansion of the banking mind. The discussion of practical questions arising from the meetings of the associations would be most profitable; and no less useful in the outcome than profitable.

That the other varied interests of the country are greatly benefited by their state associations no one will deny; then surely the permanent organization of a Texas Bankers association, while of much interest to the banks themselves, could not but accomplish much good to the State and people at large.

The banding together of so much capital and enterprise in one body, and the united influence thereof rightly directed would bring forth good fruit to the Lone Star State.

If we may be permitted to suggest the time, July 9, 10 and 11; and the place, Lampasas Springs.

The meetings of the American Bankers association have generally been held at some great watering-place, free from the cares of business.

We offer our little city with pardonable pride, as eminently suited to such a purpose. The hotel facilities are excellent, the bathing unexcelled, and the beautiful scenery is sure to inspire grand thoughts and purposes. Our handsome, newly-furnished and well-ventilated Opera-house can be obtained for its meetings.

We shall immediately address a circular letter to each banker throughout the State, and earnestly request the cordial co-operation and attendance of all. In union there is strength.

F.N.B.

The communication was signed "F.N.B." in order to avoid "personally selfish entanglements because of the author's own initials" and perhaps to obscure, according to Longcope, himself from the literary shortfall.

Malone was a promoter, an idea man. Later, writing about Malone, Longcope gave this appraisal of the man he called "one of the dearest and best friends I ever had." Said he, "A man is what he thinks, not what he thinks he is. . . . F. R. Malone was a man of great big ideas. Upon one occasion he secured from some of the owners of the Chemical National Bank of New York City their subscriptions to the increased capital stock of the First National Bank of Lampasas, Texas. Nothing approaching this had ever been done in Texas."

In further praise of Malone his colleague mentioned his promotion work for banking and railroads. He noted his training in architecture and accounting, and that he "had received a good theoretical business education at a business college. He was a thorough accountant. He wrote 'ads' as good as the best. He wrote charters of corporations with more ease, dexterity and correctness than any lawyer I knew. He wrote prospectuses of corporations with striking sentences, and glowing paragraphs, all in order—'A place for everything and everything in its place.' That seemed to be his every day motto. Malone was never known to travel around the block to get to the nearest corner."

The "F.N.B." letter brought instant results.

Three days later, after the appearance of the first Lampasas letter, the *News* published a letter from Houston, dated May 29, signed "Ibex." (In those days correspondents were prone to use pen names, and newspapers did not frown upon this hidden identity technique.)

Ibex wrote: "The letter of F.N.B. of Lampasas Springs . . . is timely and is certainly a move in the right direction. The advantages likely to accrue from such a meeting as suggested are too varied and far reaching to enumerate in a newspaper article. . . . I trust your able Lampasas correspondent may succeed in organizing the Texas Bankers Association. Also, I take the liberty of nominating N. B. Sligh, Esq., of Galveston, as the organization's first president."

Who was Ibex?

N. B. Sligh, cashier, Texas Banking and Insurance Company, Galveston, mentioned in the letter, "a thoroughly conservative, retiring and high minded gentleman," it later developed was not "Ibex" and under no circumstances did he toot his own horn.

The mystery was solved. "Ibex" was disclosed as being E. Raphael, cashier, Houston Savings Bank.

No mention of the association proposal appeared in the press for a week.

Then, in a letter to the *News*, dated June 6 and published the next day, Sligh picked up the momentum. He wrote: "I see no reason why the banking fraternity of Texas should not come together once a year, at such time and place as might be agreed upon, but I see a number of reasons why bankers should."

Stating the case positively: "Many of the banking correspondents I do not know in person . . . I would like to meet them . . . know them personally . . . talk with them . . . the successful banker is one who is working not against his fellow bankers, but with them; their interests are the same; they should understand each other. They should combine to help the legitimate interests and defeat the illegitimate. Some will say: Too much of the mutual admiration; a meeting will partake of anything else but

I see no reason why the banking fraternity of Texas should not come together once a year, at such time and place as might be agreed upon, but I see a number of reasons why they should.

16

TEXAS BANKS.

Proposal for an Organization—A Conference at Lampasas.

[To the News.]

LAMPASAS, Tex., May 26, 1885.—It has been suggested that, in view of the good resulting from the organization into state associations of tradesmen, professional men and members of other special interests, and of the eminently practical services offered by the American Bankers association, the banks and bankers of this State should meet together and organize permanently the Texas Bankers association. Why not this summer? It is almost idle to discuss the benefits to be derived. Every bank man in the State will admit the good to be accomplished.

The influence of such an association would be wide-extending, not only toward the development of the material resources of the State, but in the enlargement and expansion of the banking mind. The discussion of practical questions arising from the meetings of the association would be most profitable; and no less useful in the outcome than profitable.

That the other varied interests of the country are greatly benefited by their state associations no one will deny; then surely the permanent organization of a Texas Bankers association, while of much interest to the banks themselves, could not but accomplish much good to the State and people at large.

The banding together of so much capital and enterprise in one body, and the united influence thereof rightly directed would bring forth good fruit to the Lone Star State.

If we may be permitted to suggest the time, July 9, 10 and 11; and the place, Lampasas Springs.

The meetings of the American Bankers association have generally been held at some great watering-place, free from the cares of business.

We offer our little city with pardonable pride, as eminently suited to such a purpose. The hotel facilities are excellent, the bathing unexcelled, and the beautiful scenery is sure to inspire grand thoughts and purposes. Our handsome, newly-furnished and well-ventilated Opera-house can be obtained for its meetings.

We shall immediately address a circular letter to each banker throughout the State, and earnestly request the cordial co-operation and attendance of all. In union there is strength.

F. N. B.

Letter in the *Galveston News*, May 28, 1885, suggesting the idea of a state bankers' association.

business. I do not think so, but as a class do not these men need some rest and recreation. They wear out as well as other men."

Sligh expressed his appreciation of the suggestion of "Ibex," but said "first let us decide on a meeting . . . then someone more suitable than myself could be selected to preside . . . say Col. John Withers of San Antonio.

"There are two hundred banks and banking firms in Texas . . . let those who favor the project say so in a letter to F. R. Malone of Lampasas. If seventy to one hundred respond . . . naming a desirable date . . . take the days with the most votes . . . authorize Cashier Malone to publish results in the *News*," Sligh concluded.

The response to Malone was good, but he was not wholly pleased with the number, according to Longcope.

The ball was rolling. A call for the meeting was issued.

Starting on June 23, 1885, a one-column, five-inch display advertisement appeared in the *News* daily for one month. The ad:

To the Bankers of Texas.

You are most respectfully requested to convene at LAMPASAS, Texas, on July 23, 24 and 25, 1885, for the purpose of organizing a PERMANENT STATE ASSOCIATION OF BANKERS.

It is earnestly hoped that every bank in the State will be represented. Yours fraternally,

C. C. BINKLEY,
President Merchants and Planters National Bank,
Sherman, Tex.

B. F. WEEMS,
Cashier City Bank of Houston, Tex.

N. E. SLIGH,
Cashier Texas Banking and Insurance Company,
Galveston.

J. F. O'CONNOR,
Cashier City National Bank,
Dallas, Tex.

G. R. NEWTON,
Cashier City National Bank,
Fort Worth.

J. K. ROSE,
Cashier Waco National Bank,
Waco.

H. C. DENNY & CO.,
Belton, Tex.

E. RAPHAEL,
Cashier Houston Savings Bank,
Houston.

J. N. BROWN,
Cashier First National Bank,
Brenham.

W. A. KELSEY,
Cashier First National Bank,
Texarkana, Tex.

F. R. MALONE,
Cashier First National Bank,
Lampasas, Tex.

BALL, HUTCHINGS & CO.,
Galveston, Tex.

News items appeared in the press in the interim, referring to the bankers' response to Cashier Malone. On one occasion, optimism having held sway, he suggested that as many as 250 bankers might convene in Lampasas on July 23. Articles defined the elaborate planning under way and the high quality of the entertainment to be expected.

In the July 12 issue of the *News*, Malone stated the purpose and object of the meeting: "A closer personal acquaintance and relationship, the exchange of personal experiences and suggestions, mutual protection against confidence men and other swindlers, attention to the law-making of the State. To demand changes and suggest new laws until money shall become as safe and abundant as in New England; and to urge that the water powers of Texas shall be utilized by manufacturers."

The delegates began arriving in Lampasas on July 22, but attendance did not meet the optimistic forecast. Thirty-one banker-delegates were seated on July 23, and a total attendance of 66, including the wives of four delegates and local Lampasas dignitaries, was reported.

Other details mentioned included the fact that "the better part of two days was spent in business, including organization details and speech making; one day and three nights were consumed in merry-making and frolic as guests of the good people of Lampasas Springs."

Of the 12 banks which promoted the attendance by advertising in the *News*, only six were represented.

Sessions went from 10 o'clock until 12 noon and from 4 o'clock to 6 o'clock, with a four-hour luncheon siesta period "for public frolic in Hanna and Hancock Springs."

After his welcoming remarks Colonel Exall's request for the nomination of Congressman James Francis Miller as temporary chairman was quickly approved.

The work of perfecting the organization began.

Miller presided, reviewed and explained the objects of the meeting. He turned to the business at hand.

Lampasas's Frank R. Malone was named temporary secretary.

A credentials committee was named, consisting of J. K. Rose of Waco, Ed J. L. Green of San Marcos and F. D. Ball of Galveston.

Congressman Miller recognized N. B. Sligh of Galveston for a motion to approve the appointment of a committee on permanent organization. The chair appointed J. N. Rushing of Baird, W. A. Kelsey of Texarkana, C. B. Collins of Luling and F. E. Sanford of Temple.

The meeting was recessed for 15 minutes with instructions to the committee to meet and to report back promptly. That done, Chairman Rose reported: "To the Chairman: Your Committee on Credentials beg leave to report. We find the following representatives, present, from different banks in Texas, and entitled to seats at this convention:

N. B. Sligh, cashier, Texas Banking & Insurance Co., Galveston.
Nicholas Weeks, cashier, Island City Savings Bank, Galveston.
C. B. Collins, cashier, W. R. Johnson & Co., Luling.
W. A. Kelsey, cashier, First National Bank, Texarkana.
F. E. Sanford, cashier, First National Bank, Temple.

J. N. Rushing, president, Callahan Co. Bank, Baird.
Carey Shaw, cashier, Jas. H. Simpson Bank, Columbus.
E. J. Sandmeyer, cashier, R. E. Stafford & Co., Columbus.
J. C. Russell, president, Russell, Galbraith & Son, Lampasas.
Jas. F. Miller, president, Miller & Sayers, Gonzales.
E. F. Baxter, Banker, Navasota.
T. T. Emerson, vice president, First National Bank, McKinney.
J. Lobit of Adoue & Lobit, Galveston.
Guy M. Bryan, Jr., of Clark, Bryan & Howell, Bryan.
J. S. Fowlkes of J. S. Fowlkes & Co., Bryan.
E. A. Armin of Harris & Armin, Flatonia.
F. D. Ball of Ball, Hutchings & Co., Galveston.
F. R. Malone, cashier, First National Bank, Lampasas.
J. K. Rose, cashier, Waco National Bank, Waco.
Ed J. L. Green, president, First National Bank, San Marcos.
I. Dyer, National Bank of Texas, Galveston.
William E. Ellis, cashier, San Angelo National Bank, San Angelo.
C. W. Mertz, president, First National Bank, Cleburne.
W. A. McCutcheon, Panhandle National Bank, Wichita Falls.
E. Raphael, cashier, Houston Savings Bank, Houston.
J. S. Alexander, president, Texas National Bank, San Antonio.
D. W. Cheatham, cashier, Red River Co. Bank, Clarksville.
William Cameron, president, Citizens National Bank, Waco.
Chas. S. House of T. W. House, Houston.
C. W. Phillips, cashier, Hill County National Bank, Hillsboro.
J. E. Longmoor, manager, Rockdale Bank, Rockdale."

The report was adopted, giving formal and legal voting status to the delegates.

A committee was appointed to frame a constitution and bylaws, following the report by Chairman Sligh of the committee on permanent organization. Named were J. K. Rose, W. A. Kelsey, F. D. Ball, E. F. Baxter and Miller.

A committee on program was appointed, consisting of J. N. Rushing, Ed J. L. Green, E. J. Sandmeyer, J. Lobit and F. R. Malone.

Another recess ensued.

Upon reconvening Chairman Miller called on the committee on constitution and bylaws for a report which was adopted.

The "Declaration" portion of the constitution and bylaws stated the purposes of the association: "In order to promote the general welfare and usefulness of banks and banking institutions, and to secure uniformity of action, together with the practical benefits to be derived from personal acquaintance, and from the discussion of subjects of importance to the banking, commercial and industrial interests of the State of Texas, and especially in order to secure the proper consideration of questions regarding the financial and commercial usages, customs and laws which affect the banking interests of the State of Texas, and for protection against loss by crime, we have to submit the following Constitution and Bylaws for 'The Texas Bankers' Association.'"

This declaratory statement coincided with the purposes of the American Bankers Association, and it was used widely by later bankers' associations in the various states as a model.

The Texas Bankers Association was officially founded.

There was time for discussion, all regular business before the convention having been completed. It was suggested that E. Raphael read a paper on "Texas Manufactures," the first formal address made at a convention of the association.

He reminded the delegates of their reliance upon the products of the soil of Texas "for subsistence and the ordinary accumulations of wealth." Noting that the state was producing a million and a half bales of cotton, he cited the importance of manufacturing and use of the raw material. He argued for more beef-slaughtering and packing establishments.

The Texas Bankers Association was officially founded.

With a dash of local pride Raphael reported that Houston "stands first in importance in Texas" as a manufacturing city. "I could dilate at great length on themes germane to this subject, but having taxed your patience sufficiently, will come to a close. . . . I would request my confreres to weigh well the few crude hints here out . . . and when in the course of a few years we will meet again, as an assembly of bankers, let it be in some Texas City where the hum of machinery, mingled with the shriek of a factory whistle, makes music to the tread of a thousand operatives wending their early way to the mill or the foundry; whilst the towering chimneys belching forth the smoke and fire of a hundred furnaces illumines the country for miles around, saying to the approaching stranger: 'This is the Manchester of Texas.'"

That was the spirit of Houston—and of Texas. The masterful oration so stirred the delegates that they requested publication of the speech.

At this point the convention recessed until Saturday morning, giving the bankers and guests a full day to relax and enjoy the comforts of Lampasas and to reflect on their accomplishments—conversation in many cases being aided by a good cigar and a stout refreshment.

Friday's day of relaxation included the bankers' dress ball that evening as guests of the Park Hotel, a gala and "the grandest hop of the season." The bankers enjoyed the hospitality of Lampasas and the hotel. It was a time for "merry-making and frolic" in pleasant surroundings.

After enjoying a hearty breakfast the delegates assembled for important business on Saturday morning, July 25, 1885. Judge Miller called the session to order and announced that the first order of business was the election of officers of the Texas Bankers Association. No disagreements snarled the proceedings of that day.

The following officers were "duly elected" for the ensuing year:

President, James F. Miller of Gonzales; first vice president, N. B. Sligh of Galveston; second vice president, J. N. Rushing of Baird; third vice president, J. K. Rose of Waco; secretary, F. R. Malone of Lampasas; treasurer, W. A. Kelsey of Texarkana; assistant secretary, Carey Shaw of Columbus; assistant secretary, F. D. Ball of Galveston.

The executive committee elected was Miller, Sligh, Rushing, Rose, officers, with William Cameron of Waco, Ed J. L. Green of San Marcos, D. W. Cheatham of Clarksville, T. T. Emerson of McKinney and J. S. Alexander of San Antonio.

James F. Miller, Gonzales banker, attorney and member of the U.S. House of Representa- tives, the first president of the Texas Bankers Association.

Resolutions were offered. A controversial one was presented by Nicholas Weeks of Galveston. It touched on the heated issue of the day—gold-silver:

"WHEREAS, The coinage of silver dollars by this government of the intrinsic value of only 82½ cents, with the artificial valuation of 100 cents, is in reality the creation of fiat currency of 17½ cents on the dollar to the extent of the silver circulation; and

"WHEREAS, This is in direct conflict with the first principles of sound finance, that the coinage of money should be actually worth what its face value indicates; and

"WHEREAS, The gold dollar of the United States is worth all its stamp implies the world over; and

"WHEREAS, This disparity of values of the two coins tends to the withdrawal of gold from circulation in this country, and because of its enhanced value by comparison with silver, will cause gold to become an article of traffic of export abroad, leav-

TEXAS BANKERS ASSOCIATION.

Second Day's Session
[To The News.]

LAMPASAS, July 24, 1885.—The convention adopted a constitution and by-laws and elected the following officers for the ensuing year:

Hon. J. F. Miller, of Gonzales, president; N. B. Sligh, Galveston, first vice president; J. N. Rushing, Baird, second vice president; J. K. Rose, Waco, third vice president; F. R. Malone, Lampasas, secretary; W. A. Kelsey, Texarkana, treasurer.

Executive Committee—Wm. Cameron, Waco; Ed. J. L. Green, San Marcos; D. W. Cheatham, Clarksville; J. S. Alexander, San Antonio; T. T. Emerson, McKinney.

The president and three vice-presidents are also members of the executive committee.

The following resolution was offered by Mr. N. Weekes, of Galveston:

Wheras the coinage of silver dollars by this government, of the intrinsic value of only 82½ cents, with the artificial valuation of 100 cents, is in reality the creation of fiat currency of 17½ cents on the dollar to the

The *Galveston News* carried detailed reports of the first convention. This story documents the action of delegates in adopting a constitution and bylaws and election of officers.

ing in its stead the silver only as our currency, subject to fluctuations, disturbing thereby the current of conservative business; and

"WHEREAS, embarrassments are already felt by the general government in consequence of its 82½ cents silver policy, and as the indications point to still greater and a possible repetition of the panic of '73, by reason of speculation so temptingly invited at the cost of the country at large.

"*Therefore, be it resolved,* by this body, that the true policy of finance is equal justice to all would be to cease the further coinage of the present silver dollar, and that there should exist no disparity in the intrinsic values of the coinage of this Government;

that a dollar should be a dollar alike in silver and gold, and that our honorable representatives in Congress be respectfully and earnestly requested to give aid to such measures as will stop the further coinage of silver dollars of the present inferior value."

The motion brought the convention to life. There was division. The gold standard fellows defended their ground against the onslaughts of the free silver delegates on the motion to adopt the Weeks resolution. A motion to lay the resolution on the table failed.

Cooler heads prevailed before a split developed that might have seriously damaged the newly formed Texas Bankers Association.

The national debate on gold and silver money would soon erupt into a major issue that would torment legislators, presidents, bankers—the people at large. The gold standard advocates, called "gold bugs," would eventually win the battle with the defeat of William Jennings Bryan of Nebraska, the three-time unsuccessful nominee of the Democrats for president and an articulate spokesman of free silver coinage at a ratio of 16 to 1.

The bankers in Lampasas in 1885 finally agreed to let the pending motion for gold "go over for discussion and action to the next annual meeting of the association."

The postponing action calmed the agitated delegates.

President Miller recognized W. A. Kelsey of Texarkana to present a popular resolution which encompassed the grievance of bankers against constitutional prohibition of state banks in Texas.

Delegates listened carefully as Kelsey read: "*Resolved*, that this association memorialize the legislature of the State of Texas to submit to the people an amendment to the constitution providing for the incorporation of banks, and that safeguards be thrown around them similar to that of the National Banking System; the examination of these corporations by a special examiner, and a limit of their lines of discount for any one person or firm to one-tenth of their capital paid in, and a requirement of a sufficient cash reserve in proportion to their deposits."

Although the resolution was "referred to the executive committee with instructions to report at the next annual session of the association," the delegates left no doubt that this issue would receive the unswerving attention of the TBA until the voters of Texas amended the constitution to remove the prohibition against banks and banking corporations chartered by the state.

The battle for constitutional equity was protracted. It did not succeed until 1904, and in 1905 was followed by legislative action to put Texas in step with the other states to charter banks. The state bank charter story will be developed later in this volume.

As the first convention was drawing to a close that warm day in Lampasas, J. S. Alexander of San Antonio was recognized for a motion:

"*Resolved*, that Mr. N. B. Sligh be requested to prepare and bring before the next meeting of the association, a paper on the subject of 'Collections and Exchange'; and that all other members be requested to prepare addresses on any subject pertaining to banking, or the development of the resources of the State of Texas." The resolution was adopted.

Former President Ulysses S. Grant had died July 23, the day of the formal creation of the TBA. Although many of the bankers of the day had served in the Confederacy, ridden and marched hard and long to defeat the Union forces under Grant, they had come to mellow in attitude toward their one-time foe and to appreciate his fundamental compassion and especially his gentlemanly manner in dealing with General Robert E. Lee at Appomattox. They also recalled Grant's impression of Texas when he soldiered there as a young brevet first lieutenant and regimental quartermaster en route to the Mexican War.

The *Galveston News* carried a detailed account of Grant's death and his last days of suffering with throat cancer. So the final formal action of the TBA's first convention was unanimously to pass "Resolutions of deep sympathy, in the loss of the great soldier and statesman, General U. S. Grant."

Quietly the delegates concluded their meeting with the announcement by President Miller that the executive committee would meet upon adjournment of the convention. They were pleased to hear Miller's statement that the second convention of the TBA would meet "at Lampasas Springs, Texas, on the third Tuesday in July, A.D., 1886."

The first convention, the organizational meeting, of the TBA was adjourned. Strong leadership had assumed command of the fledgling organization. The 31 delegates at Lampasas returned home convinced that the proper beginning had been achieved, but that more participation was needed. So the cry for bringing other bankers into the membership was heard across the Lone Star State.

When President Miller convened the first meeting of the executive committee, he was pleased that all members were present.

The following business was transacted: "N. B. Sligh was authorized to audit the bill of the *Galveston News* for printing. James F. Miller was authorized to audit other bills occasioned by the formation of the organization.

"Instructed the secretary to invite each banker to prepare and submit an address on some important topic.

"Respectfully request that Mr. C. B. Collins of Luling prepare a paper, to be read at the next annual convention, on the relations of banking to agriculture.

"Authorized secretary to procure necessary supplies for his office, and instructed treasurer to pay bills for same.

"Appointed a meeting of the executive committee in the city of Galveston, on the last Wednesday in October, 1885."

The executive committee did meet in Galveston on October 28 and took up routine matters, stressing the campaign of Secretary Malone to enroll all Texas banks as members of the association. The membership cost was $5.00 per bank.

And 1885, the benchmark year for the TBA, ended on a note of triumph for the association, the first and largest of all state associations for bankers.

The American Bankers Association had been organized in the Town Hall at Saratoga Springs, New York, in the summer of 1875. The idea was conceived by two young St. Louis bankers, James T. Howenstein and Edward C. Breck, on a frosty January day that year. On the way home from the bank they saw a sign announcing, "Women's Suffrage Mass Meeting."

Big Idea!

And 1885, the benchmark year for the TBA, ended on a note of triumph for the association, the first and largest of all state associations for bankers.

Howenstein commented, "If women can get together to heal their sorrows and woes, why cannot bankers get together to shoo their sorrows?"

Seven months later 350 bankers from 32 states and territories met in the New York spa and elected an executive committee to perfect plans for a permanent organization. Charles B. Hall, cashier, Boston National Bank, Boston, Massachusetts, became the ABA's first president.

Two young bankers in Lampasas—Malone and Longcope—had the TBA idea.

6

THE GENTLEMAN from GONZALES

In this day and age we have a class of men known as politicians, men who are professional politicians, men who have no principle that they will not sacrifice for the sake of office, and who will advocate any theory, will pander to any prejudice, will assent to anything as a fact that they believe will make them popular with the people and secure votes.

JAMES FRANCIS MILLER

W E HAVE MET JAMES FRANCIS MILLER at the time of his election as the first president of the TBA in Lampasas, July 23–25, 1885.

His biography includes the fact that he was born in Winnsboro, South Carolina, August 1, 1830, moved to Texas with his parents in 1842, and attended the public schools and Reutersville College. He studied law and was admitted to the bar in 1857, then opened a law office in Gonzales. With the advent of the Civil War he entered the Confederate service in 1861 as a private in Company I, Eighth Texas Cavalry, "Terry's Texas Rangers," and served throughout the war. Resuming the practice of law under the shingle of Miller and Sayers in Gonzales, he became a local judge and was involved in banking and stock raising as well. In 1868 his law firm opened the private banking and discounting house, Miller and Sayers.

In addition to being the first president of the TBA, he was the first president of the Texas Livestock Association, the forerunner of the Texas and Southwestern Cattle Raisers' Association.

Miller went to Washington in 1883 as a Democratic member of the 49th Congress and was reelected two years later. When his term expired March 3, 1887, he did not seek reelection. After returning to Gonzales he devoted much time to the activities of the Presbyterian Church and the Masonic Order, serving as Grand Master of the Grand Lodge of Texas. He maintained an active interest in the TBA until his death on March 3, 1902, in Gonzales.

26

Frank R. Malone, credited with the leading role in organizing the TBA, died at his home in Dallas, February 22, 1922. A native of Tennessee, he did his first banking work with the old banking house of Mitchell and Glover in San Marcos. Next, he moved to San Antonio and managed the private bank of T. C. Frost (later Frost National). Lampasas Springs attracted Malone, and he became cashier of the First National Bank. In 1887 he moved to Dallas and was interested in the old North Texas National Bank, the first Texas bank to have a capital stock of $1,000,000. During the later portion of his life Malone was identified with investment banking in Dallas.

7
GOING FIRST CLASS
at the PARK HOTEL and SPA
IN 1885

The Saratoga Springs of the Southwest.
DESCRIPTION OF LAMPASAS AND THE PARK HOTEL, 1885

WHY LAMPASAS, TEXAS, FOR THE FOUNDING of the Texas Bankers Association? What was it like in 1885?

History notes that "The artesian springs . . . had a great deal to do with the settling of Lampasas County. The Spaniards heard of the springs from the Indians many years before the white man came to this part of Texas."

The name Lampazos was given to the river by the Spanish Aguayo Expedition in about 1721, "because of the many cockleburs and water lilies in the region."

The town of Burleson, named for an early settler family, was later changed to Lampasas Springs and then shortened to Lampasas.

Says Gordon Chapin, manager of the Chamber of Commerce, "The 1870–1895 era was a very active time for Lampasas and its people. The Santa Fe Railroad was completed to Lampasas in 1882. The courthouse was completed the same year, several spas were in operation, our first bank was opened in 1884, and, of course, the Texas Bankers Association was formed here in 1885."

The coming of the Santa Fe produced a business boom, and the town's population grew to 10,000. A syndicate of wealthy Galveston railroad men developed the town into the "Saratoga Springs of the Southwest." They purchased an interest in 1,476 acres of land for the "purpose of constructing a large hotel and resort near the Hancock Springs." The Park Hotel, with its 200 rooms and "a great dining room, parlors and ballrooms," became the focal point of the spa.

27

Impressive was the word for the new hotel.

Built as a palatial pleasure and health resort on 200 acres on a hill through the east and west portion of the 700 block of South Springs Street and West 6th, it was described as the largest frame hotel in Texas at the time. Its facilities also included quite a number of separate summer cottages, "completely equipped, for families, couples or bachelors." Many of the young bankers lodged in the bachelors' quarters at the 1885 convention.

The hotel was 331 feet long and two stories tall, with broad galleries on each floor extending the length of the building; its large rooms were well ventilated and lavishly furnished.

The builders had not skimped anywhere. The spacious halls were carpeted, and the parlors were remarkable for the high quality of design and furnishings. The ballroom or dancing hall would accommodate hundreds of guests. Concerts and lectures, provided by the Park's management, were frequent, and the banker delegates were entertained royally by the hotel at a reception and ball on the second day of the 1885 meeting.

Although the use of electricity was fairly new, the hotel lighted every nook and corner, "and there were electric bells in each room."

Offering the finest cuisine, the dining hall was 60x80 feet in size, "well lighted and a beautiful scenery of nature was presented from its windows."

A further touch of elegance was provided by a house orchestra, "in attendance all through the year," to provide guests with music indoors or out as the weather and mood indicated.

The manager paid a lot of attention to the hotel's guests; they liked the pampering and wanted to return. The bankers shared the general enthusiasm for the place; it seemed appropriate that the TBA was organized by satisfied men in impressive surroundings, both natural and man-made.

Adding to the hotel's fine attractions was a promenade which ran from the main building to the sulphur spring. There was no close communion between ladies and gentlemen in the bathhouse—separate compartments were provided, each compartment with 20 bathrooms, as well as magnificent pools, described as 40x60 feet and from three to six feet deep.

For the children and the aging and infirm, additional shallow baths were provided near the main building by ten tubs which could be filled to varying depths up to four feet. Pipes were placed from the springs to the hotel, and four hydraulic rams forced the water, heated by a steam boiler, for use in the tubs. There was no water shortage—enough flowed from the springs to propel a gristmill.

To enhance the interesting landscape, there were "shady nooks, quiet retreats, and rustic seats." Lovely drives and walks beckoned. The family cottages were to the north of the hotel, shaded by live oaks. Beyond these, at a distance of 100 yards, were the ten cottages that formed "Bachelors' Row." And in front of the hotel were tennis and croquet courts.

The railroad promoted special rates from Texas cities to Lampasas for hotel guests. Upon arriving at the station, they were transported by a mule-drawn streetcar which

The Park Hotel in Lampasas Springs, a luxury
facility in 1885. In the concert room of this
building, first floor, near wing, Colonel Henry
Exall welcomed the delegates to the founding
convention of the Texas Bankers Association.

Bachelor's Row, Hancock Park, Lampasas
Springs, the facility for bachelors in 1885,
which took care of the overflow from the hotel.

29

ran from the depot east of town, through the business district and westward to the Park Hotel; the fare, 5 cents.

Duly impressed with the whole setup, the TBA delegates voted to return to Lampasas for their second convention in 1886.

Unfortunately, the hotel's preeminence lasted only a few years, doomed by the extension of the railroad beyond Lampasas and by the concurrent decline of the community. One historian writes that "by 1891 the business of the hotel had decreased to the extent that the upkeep equalled or surpassed the income."

The once-glamorous facility was used by the Keely Institute, an institution to cure alcoholics. General use of the sulphur baths, and strict abstention from spirits, did wonders for persons addicted to alcohol. But even that phase of the hotel's life did not endure. In 1894 Centenary College moved to the facility. Ten years after the TBA was organized, the building and contents were destroyed by fire.

Texas bankers were in the vanguard of an army of bankers which picked up the enthusiasm for forming associations. They saw in the infant TBA many positive factors, not the least of which was the chance to get together in a desirable situation, a convention, where a community of interest prevailed. They also knew that controversial issues faced Texas, the country and banking. The best of leadership was required. It was available from the beginning with James Francis Miller, bolstered by other capable officers and members.

PART TWO

Banking in Texas—
Merchant Princes
To National Charters

1

A TEXAN WILL TRADE ANYTHING

*Trading and bartering are more common in Texas than in any other part
of the United States.*
FERDINAND ROEMER OF GERMANY, visiting Texas in 1846

COMMERCIAL BANKING HAS ITS ROOTS IN ANTIQUITY.
History reveals banking activity in ancient times, albeit in a simple form, by the
Babylonians, Assyrians and Athenians. Its development advanced with Rome and
medieval Europe. In banking's genealogical tree there are such institutions as the Bank
of Venice in the year 1171; the Bank of Genoa, 1320; and the Bank of Amster-
dam, 1609.

Goldsmiths developed England's first banking business. Sir Thomas Gresham
(Gresham's Law) was a goldsmith. The oldest banking business in England continuing to operate in its original location is now Martin's Bank, established by Gresham
in 1563 "at the Sign of the Grasshopper."

Barter, the direct exchange of one commodity for another, has been practiced for
ages. All manner of things have been used by developing cultures as mediums of exchange. In the early days of this country commodities were given a value and served
as "money" in the absence of specie. In the temperate regions of Europe, Asia and
Africa, the cow, for example, became a standard barter unit. The wampum of the
North American Indians is another example of a barter item. Even Aristotle affirmed
the use of the cow for barter employed by Dionysius in levying taxes upon the people

of Syracuse. Up to fairly recent times the standard price of a wife among the Zulu tribesmen was ten cows. The word pecuniary is from the Latin *pecunia* (money), derived from *pecus*, or cattle.

Precious metals go back a long way as a medium of exchange. Gold and copper are said to have been the first metals used by man. The Egyptians, at least 3,000 years before Christ, knew gold, copper and silver. The first known coins, according to experts, were struck about 700 B.C. in Lydia.

In the early days of Texas barter was a major form of exchange, and the art of swapping or bartering became a keenly developed practice.

William Ransom Hogan, in his book, *The Texas Republic*, described the hard times in Texas. As late as 1850, he points out, the state had only five towns with populations in excess of a thousand people, "and none with more than five thousand. . . ."

William Bollaert, visiting Texas in 1843, documented that the barter system was widely used. He wrote of the trade in his notes: "Cotton for sugar and Coffee—Bacon for boots—Corn for Calomel and quinine & Whiskey— Beef for Brandy." As noted by Hogan, "The system whereby commission merchants in Galveston, Houston, San Augustine . . . advanced supplies to planters before selling their cotton amounted to a combination of barter and credit."

The German geologist, Ferdinand Roemer, stopping at a farm between Gonzales and New Braunfels in 1846, made this observation:

"During our extended stay, the young people in the home of Mr. King made us all manner of offers for bartering. One wanted to trade or sell a horse; the other who was soon to be married, wanted to trade a good cow and calf for a black frock coat; a third wanted my saddle with which he had fallen in love, and offered me a much better one in trade, according to his opinion. Boys from eight to ten years participated in the bartering with articles of small value and showed a shrewdness seldom found in boys of the same age in Germany. Trading and bartering are more common in Texas than in any other part of the United States. A Texan is ready at any moment, even while traveling, to trade or sell anything he wears, whether it be his coat or shirt, if he can make an advantageous trade. He expects this from anyone else. He has no conception of becoming attached to an article. . . ."

Hogan concludes that the practice of barter is understandable because of the currency dilemma and the confusion engendered by its variety. He notes the uncertainty of paper money that brought forth this observation in 1837 by a Brazoria merchant to one of his business associates: "There is such a medley of Paper money on ma[r]ket that one does not know what is good and the only safety is to pass it on as you get it."

The need for a banking system was obvious.

The traditional basis for banking has been the lending of money. Money-lenders, in one form or another, have been around for a long time.

An early American writer observed, "The business of banking, in its widest sense, is to collect in banks the capital of a community, that which is either money or can readily be turned into money, and upon the capital so collected to build up, by proper management and machinery, a credit which will expand and enlarge its usefulness to the community."

The dramatic change in banking and financial institutions which began in the

The traditional basis for banking has been the lending of money. Moneylenders, in one form or another, have been around for a long time.

1970s, increased by action of Congress and the regulators in the 1980s, has brought about a mix of financial institutions in Texas and the nation, with broadened and highly competitive powers. Still, the basic definition and mission of commercial banking holds true. Money and credit are the basis of a modern economic system. Banking in its present form—and its rapid evolution sometimes startles bankers who remember the former years—is geared to meet the demands of a changing economy and the expectations of an informed consumer.

Although young in history's panorama, banking development in Texas is worth telling about. That story reaches back to Texas under Mexico, 1821–1836, parallel with the period of immigration of the Anglo-Americans and the colonization by Stephen F. Austin on the fertile lands between the Brazos and the Colorado rivers. Moreover, it coincides with the beginning of efforts to establish Texas as separate from Mexico.

The years 1821–1836 embraced the period of the major issues of "hard money" and the Second Bank of the United States. President Andrew Jackson destroyed the bank with his famous veto in 1832 of legislation which renewed its charter. While this was a major issue back East, it had no application to Mexican Texas, except to strengthen the view of anti-bank followers of Jackson, such as Sam Houston, who were emerging as the political leadership and molders of policy in the Republic of Texas in 1836.

2
THE MEXICAN PERIOD—
FIRST BANK CHARTER

There is hereby granted the establishment of a Bank in the Department of the Brazos, which shall be styled the Commercial and Agricultural Bank—Citizen Samuel M. Williams as Empresario, shall take the necessary measures to carry it into operation.
DECREE OF THE SUPREME GOVERNMENT OF THE STATE OF COAHUILA AND TEXAS,
April 30, 1835

MEXICO FREED ITSELF FROM SPAIN by revolution in 1821. In establishing the Mexican empire Augustin de Iturbide, leader of the independence movement, declared himself emperor. Texas became a province of Mexico the same year.

As is normal in political practice, Iturbide appointed one of his trusted activists in the revolutionary cause, José Felix Trespalacios, as the political chief of Texas. Trespalacios had followed a somewhat nomadic life, pursued by the Spanish Mexican government, and had sought asylum in Havana and New Orleans. Life abroad widened his acquaintance with the simplest forms of banking and the use of paper notes. His interest was piqued—Mexico had no paper money.

At the end of the revolution Trespalacios returned to Mexico to reap the rewards of victory. He was appointed governor of the province of Texas and assumed office at the provincial capital in San Antonio. One of his major problems was the difficulty of receiving gold and silver money on a regular basis to pay the troops and government officials stationed there. Shipments traveled the precarious route from the Mexican subtreasury in San Luis Potosí to San Antonio. Regular paydays were uncertain. The troops and their families grumbled when the money did not come through; they, along with the government officials, had to scrounge for credit with the merchants.

Trespalacios remembered the benefits of banking and bank notes he had seen in New Orleans: paper money redeemable in specie seemed to be the answer.

As pointed out in an article by C. E. Castaneda, published in the *Bulletin of the Business Historical Society* of The University of Texas (1954), Governor Trespalacios ordered a national bank to be established in San Antonio, Banco Nacional de Texas, "the first chartered bank west of the Mississippi."

This colonel of Mexico's imperial army and political head of Texas had taken the action subject to the approval of his government, but he did not wait for the approval. A bank was established October 21, 1822. Castaneda described the action as "the magna carta . . . of chartered banks in Texas." It established a simple form of banking, note issue and circulation, 14 years before Texas's independence.

A truly innovative idea, it had the cooperation of the local council, but the flaw in the plan was that it had not been cleared with his superiors in Saltillo, headquarters of Nuevo Leon, Tamaulipas and Texas, for presentation to Mexico City. Notes circulated widely around San Antonio, and Trespalacios made a strong request for ratification of his action by Emperor Iturbide. Unfortunately, the home government did not view the action as a simple matter. It failed to receive bureaucratic approval by the dictatorship, but the government announced that Mexico would launch a universal note as national currency. The rub was that the notes were not redeemable in specie at face value. This undermined the faith in the system and put the Banco Nacional de Texas in difficulty with the national currency. Iturbide decided that the bank's notes would be replaced by the national issue. The bank came to a sudden halt.

The brash action of Trespalacios moved Mexico to issue paper currency, and the short life of the bank is a milestone in Texas banking history, as was noted by Joseph M. Grant and Lawrence Crum in the important volume, *The Development of State-Chartered Banking in Texas*. The action, they pointed out, was important "not only because it was the first bank in the state, albeit in a very limited sense, but also because of the general distrust of bank note issues that it helped to engender." They also observed, "This distrust was manifest in the failure of lawmakers of Texas to provide for a state banking system until the enactment of a Texas State Bank Law in 1905."

The idea behind the Trespalacios bank stirred the imaginations of the people of San Antonio and of the sparsely settled province by filling a need and demonstrating the value of sound bank notes backed by specie.

The Anglo-Americans in Texas used barter and circulating coin.

Stephen F. Austin made no effort to establish a bank in his colony, however. He knew banking well, having been a banker with his father in St. Louis; he also knew the heavy toll the banks suffered in financial panics. The Anglo-Americans in Texas used barter and circulating coins.

The need for banking was growing. Part of this need was filled by mercantile houses which performed limited sideline banking functions without charters or regulation for their customers and friends. These mercantile-banking houses first developed in the Gulf Coast centers.

A remarkable young man, Samuel May Williams, migrated to San Felipe de Austin in 1821. A native of Providence, Rhode Island, born October 4, 1795, he lived as a youth in Baltimore, learned the mercantile business, moved to New Orleans, worked as a bookkeeper and as a private secretary to General Andrew Jackson. With his excellent credentials Williams landed a position with Austin, who had met him in New Orleans and urged him to join the Austin colony. Austin did not tolerate floaters and undesirables in his colony; he apparently trusted Williams implicitly because the latter held the position until 1835. Fluent in Spanish and French, Williams had beautiful penmanship and kept impeccable records.

In his work with Austin, Williams had frequent contact in business matters with Thomas F. McKinney, one of the "Old Three Hundred" in the Austin colony. A community of interest, based on their equally astute business capabilities, developed. McKinney and Williams formed a commission-mercantile business in 1834 at Quintana at the mouth of the Brazos River. The business prospered, grew and moved gradually to include a banking function. In 1837 they expanded to Galveston, where they owned steamers and were dominant in the cotton trade in that city and in Houston.

This early private banking house began at a time when there were no banks in Texas. Gold and silver were scarce. The enterprising firm discounted promissory notes, extended credit to their far-flung customers and accepted drafts. The Samuel May Williams Collection in the Rosenberg Library, Galveston, has preserved an important record of the firm's significant activities.

As a responsible citizen of Texas and a friend and employee of Austin, Williams had good standing in Mexican circles. With this favorable status—and the desire of the Mexican authorities to placate the rumblings among the Anglos—Williams was given a charter from the Coahuila-Texas congress for a bank to be established in the Department of the Brazos. This affirmative act was taken April 30, 1835, and was the first official bank charter issued in Texas. The 20-year charter was for the Banco de Commercia y Agricultura.

Stringent controls were attached to the charter, including capital paid in before the bank could open. Bank notes would be permitted; interest rates were stipulated at 8 percent annually for a loan not exceeding six months; the rate for more than six months was 10 percent. The Williams charter also provided for statewide branches, a provision that never gained a foothold in Texas. And the governor was to name a commissioner to examine the bank annually.

Raising $100,000 in specie paid in was no easy task. Finally in 1847 the requirements were met, the Banco de Commercia y Agricultura became the first chartered bank in Texas. Meanwhile, McKinney and Williams had a lead role in financing the

Texas Revolution. They were to Texas what Robert Morris was to the American Revolution.

The Williams charter, as printed in English, follows:

**SUPREME GOVERNMENT OF
THE STATE OF COAHUILA AND TEXAS.**

The Constitutional Governor of the State of Coahuila and Texas to all its inhabitants, know ye: that the Congress of the same State has decreed the following:

The Constitutional Congress of the free, independent, and sovereign state of Coahuila and Texas, has thought proper to decree:

Art. 1. There is hereby granted the establishment of a Bank in the Department of Brazos, which shall be styled the Commercial and Agricultural Bank—Citizen Samuel M. Williams as Empresario, shall take the necessary measures to carry it into operation.

Art. 2. The capital of said Bank shall not exceed one million of dollars, divided into ten thousand shares of one hundred dollars each.

Art. 3. Subscribers to the amount of at least three thousand shares, having been obtained, the Empresario shall call a meeting of them, and proceed to the election of eight Directors, who shall appoint a President from among themselves, and shall discharge the duties of their office for one year.

Art. 4. To obtain the office of Director, it is required to be a citizen of the State, and the owner of at least five shares.

Art. 5. The votes shall be given at the rate of one for each share, but no one subscriber shall have more than fifty suffrages, whatever may be the number of shares he may own. Absent Stockholders may vote by proxy.

Art. 6. The Direction shall be renewed annually, and the convocation for this purpose shall be made forty-five days previous to the expiration of their term of office, and the election for the Directors shall be held eight days before the close of the current year.

Art. 7. By-laws shall be formed by the Directory for the government of the general and special affairs of the Bank.

Art. 8. The notes which may be issued by the Bank shall be signed by the President and Cashier, in the name of the Company, and the Capital of the Bank shall be responsible for the payment of their values. The Bank can sue and be sued.

Art. 9. For the encouragement of Commerce, the Arts, and Industry, the Bank can make loans, charging at the rate of eight per cent. per annum, when the term of the loan does not exceed six months, and up to ten per cent. when it passes that period, requiring of the borrower the necessary security.

Art. 10. The Stockholders shall give security in real estate in the Republic, for the value of their shares, and as soon as one hundred thousand dollars at least shall be paid into the vaults of the Bank, it may commence operations, under a previous examination made by a Commissioner, to be appointed by the Government, who shall likewise annually take cognisance of the affairs of the Bank.

Art. 11. This Bank shall exist for twenty years, and can establish branches in any part of the State.

The Constitutional Governor of the State will understand it for its compliance, causing it to be printed, published, and circulated.

JOSE MARIA MIER, PRESIDENT.

DIEGO GRANT, *Member and Secretary.*

JOSE M. J. CARBAJAL, *Member and Secretary.*

Therefore I order it to be printed, published, and circulated, and that due compliance be given to it. Done at the city of Monclova, this 30th day of April, 1835.

AGUSTIN VIESCA.

J. MARIANO IRALA, SECRETARY.

(Courtesy Rosenberg Library, Galveston, Texas)

Prior to the revolution Texans had met in 1833 to prepare a constitution to be presented to Mexico. Anti-bank feeling had surfaced by that time. A proposal to provide for banking, although generally supported by delegates, was negated by Sam Houston's strong feeling against banks. Instead, a provision prohibiting banks was adopted. It read: "No bank or banking institution nor office of discount and deposit nor any other moneyed corporation nor bank establishment shall ever exist during the continuation of the present constitution." Although the Mexican government never approved it, the document clearly established the power and feeling of Houston and other leaders.

3
THE REPUBLIC of TEXAS—
BANKING OVERLOOKED

. . . that as the geese saved Rome, so Mr. Bullock's pigs saved Texas.
QUOTE IN THE BANKING HISTORY BY JOHN JAY KNOX

RELATIONS WITH MEXICO continued to disintegrate, resulting in Texan action at Washington-on-the-Brazos, March 2, 1836. The stunning defeat of Santa Anna by General Houston at San Jacinto established the Republic of Texas, virtually without funds and no chartered banks. (The Williams charter had not been activated at that time.) A bountiful land in resources and enthusiasm, however, was a valuable asset, even without public funds.

The constitution of the Republic of Texas, ratified September 5, 1836, was silent on banking.

One of the first actions of the republic was the naming of McKinney and Williams as commissioners to go to the United States and attempt to borrow a million dollars, using public lands and public revenues as security—another example of the key roles the merchant-bankers played as the forerunners of banking and private bankers in a critical time.

Although President Houston was criticized for allegedly favoring his friend Williams in banking actions, he denied it. The new government ratified the previous action of the Mexican government in giving a banking charter to Williams, but the panic of 1837 and generally poor economic conditions again made it impossible to raise the $100,000 capital needed.

An unexpected action in many respects was taken by the congress of the republic on December 16, 1836, when it authorized the Texas Railroad, Navigation and Banking Company. Houston favored the bill, but changed his mind when substantial opposition developed. The bank did not come into being.

One of the amusing proposals of this period was the unsuccessful attempt to establish a hotel and bathhouse with banking privileges at Velasco.

A staunch opponent of banking was Dr. Anson Jones of Brazoria County, the last president of the Republic of Texas before statehood. He was proud of his effective opposition to banking proposals.

Meanwhile, McKinney and Williams continued to serve informally as bankers to the new government. In appreciation of their generosity to the government they were permitted in 1841 to issue $30,000 of their promissory notes to circulate as money. Again, this practice met strong opposition. Congress repealed the authority in 1844, striking down any vestige of authority for the note issue, and Texas marched to statehood without any authority for bank notes. The dominant political forces in Texas carried forward their anti-bank prejudices to revive them in statehood, beginning December 29, 1845. They would be spelled out in the new constitution—this time not to be overlooked.

In the period of the republic the financial bind was an enormous problem. But the leadership did not develop a procedure for banks and for securing financing. For example, President Mirabeau B. Lamar faced the continuing and deepening dilemma of an empty treasury, no commercial treaties and recognition only by the United States when he assumed office in 1838. He recognized the need and proposed a national bank, but the congress rejected the proposal. Instead the legislators authorized paper money in the form of "Red Backs." The Lamar proposal envisioned the bank as the government's fiscal agent; an exchange regulator; a bank of deposit, loan and discount, with branches "established at every convenient and suitable part of the Republic." The vote against the bank was 16 to 14.

In 1840, the financial situation at a crisis point, attempts were made to float a $7,000,000 bond issue in France, and the advocates of a national bank for Texas felt that the funds could be used to start a bank.

The entire concept came to a halt over an incident which has an appropriate place in the colorful history of Texas.

The negotiations with France were upset, it is said, by a herd of swine owned by a hotelkeeper in Austin, a Mr. Bullock. Austin had been recommended by Lamar as the seat of government and was occupied in 1839 when the Austin area on the Colorado River was still an Indian frontier.

Back to the pig story.

It seems that the French minister, one M. de Saligny, had a fine horse which was housed and fed corn in a stable where the hotelkeeper's swine wandered to eat the corn dropped from the feed trough. The minister's servant, resisting the incursion by the hogs, drove them out of the stable and killed one. Mr. Bullock, so the tale goes, thrashed the servant, whereupon M. de Saligny filed a strong complaint with the government of the Republic of Texas. Bullock was arrested. Pending trial, his bond was signed by the secretary of the treasury.

The minister sauntered into Bullock's hotel later, and the hotelkeeper threw him out. Another complaint; another arrest; and another release signed by the treasurer as bondsman.

By this time, word of the incident had spread around the small capital city and

environs, reported in the press, and the incident had grown from a small fracas to an international incident. The public took sides with Bullock and his pigs, forcing the Texas government to protest and ask for the Frenchman's recall. The trouble with this was that M. de Saligny was a close friend of the minister of finance of France with whom the Texas bonds were being negotiated. The outcome was predictable— negotiations were broken off. Texas lost its $7,000,000 bail out, and along with it went the proposed national bank and funds to alleviate the miserable financial mess in the new nation.

Observed one writer, "What the results would have been had the loan been made, one can only conjecture; but a well-posted writer of the day says that as 'the geese saved Rome, so Mr. Bullock's pigs saved Texas.'"

On the eve of annexation to the United States, Texans looked back on a turbulent history in many respects, including the many financial problems and great need for a banking system and a stable currency.

Mexican Texas used as its currency gold and silver, along with a few bank notes brought in from the United States. The population was sparse, currency scarce. Nearly everything was done on a barter system; very few transactions were for cash. The "hammered dollar" was used by Mexico, which had retained a substantial amount of silver when freed from Spain. The Spanish dollars were "hammered" or altered to remove the royal effigy; the defacing was a slap at Spain and was designed to keep the money at home. The coins continued to circulate until the Texas Revolution, augmented by United States bank notes. Texan treasury notes never circulated at face value, the "Red Backs" dropping to as low as 2 cents on the dollar in 1842.

No bank operated in Texas during the republic period. Filling some of the financial gap was the prosperous merchandising house of two brothers, Robert and David G. Mills, first founded at Brazoria and in 1849 moved to Galveston. The firm operated as R. & D. G. Mills and had phenomenal success in merchandising, plantation operations and private banking, which made it one of the wealthiest in the state. The business affairs of the firm were vast; its steamers moved cotton and sugar from Texas to all parts of the world.

This type of early Texas success attracted a lot of attention and customers. From the outset R. & D. G. Mills advanced credit to their customers and dealt in exchange. As an example of their high standing, Texans used "Mills Money" issued by the company. No banks being available, along with the governmental prohibition against bank notes, the Mills firm acquired a large supply of bank notes from a defunct Mississippi bank. In a shrewd and effective way the law banning bank notes in Texas was evaded when the notes (some say up to $300,000) were countersigned by R. & D. G. Mills and circulated. This action—the creation of "Mills Money"—was a substantial help to Texans by providing a reliable and recognized medium which substituted for gold and silver and was not depreciated. Notes with the signature of the two brothers became Texas money in every sense of the word, and were as "good as gold, or even better."

No bank operated
in Texas during the
republic period.

4

SAM HOUSTON—
JACKSON'S PROTÉGÉ

The Bank is trying to kill me, but I will kill it.
ANDREW JACKSON, veto message of the act to renew the charter of the Second Bank of the United States, 1832

AT THE TIME DETAILS FOR ANNEXATION between the United States and Texas were approved, delegates to the first constitutional convention turned their attention to the writing of the important document. The issue of banking was high on the agenda when delegates assembled in Austin on July 4, 1845.

Although Sam Houston, a delegate, was absent, his powerful influence was there. As a protégé and political disciple of Andrew Jackson, Houston had gone to the Hermitage in Nashville, Tennessee, to see the dying Jackson. One of "Old Hickory's" last letters to Houston and to the citizens of Texas was to urge a provision against banks to be included in the new Texas constitution, a letter that was widely used by the anti-bank delegates. They won, 47—7.

By his election to the presidency in 1828, Jackson had broken the political power

Sam Houston opposed chartered banks for Texas, but he was a close friend of Samuel May Williams, and many felt that his anti-bank attitude was from his training as a follower of Andrew Jackson. (Courtesy Institute of Texan Cultures)

of the eastern dynasty. The Jacksonian Era brought many changes in style and substance, including his veto of the charter renewal by Congress of the Second Bank of the United States, a central bank that was generally well operated and one that had brought discipline to the state banks in limiting their currency issues. Jackson favored local banking, viewed the national bank as a "monster" and felt that it should be destroyed.

41

Congress, in a bitter period of controversy, approved the extension of the bank's charter which was to expire in 1836. That set the stage for Jackson to veto the act. "The Bank is trying to kill me, but I will kill it," Jackson said. The veto death of the bank was July 10, 1832. Although the U.S. Supreme Court had held the bank constitutional, the president made the veto stick. It was a severe blow against banking stability. The veto ended the concept of a central national bank for years, resulted in increased power of the states over banking and gave Jackson the opportunity to put the funds of the United States in so-called "pet banks" around the country.

Houston, a native of Virginia and son of a Revolutionary War officer, moved to Tennessee, served in the military, won fame with Jackson in the Creek War, served two terms in the U. S. Congress and rose to the governorship of Tennessee. After a period of disillusionment he moved to Arkansas and in 1827 arrived in Nacogdoches, Texas. He was well prepared for the role of frontier hero and quickly plunged into the struggle for independence from Mexico. His place in history was assured when he defeated Santa Anna while in command of the Texas forces. He became the first president of the republic, served another term in 1841, helped ensure the annexation and then served 13 years in the U. S. Senate. In 1859 he became governor of Texas. Opposing secession, he refused to acknowledge the authority of the government of the Confederate States. Failing in health, he resigned in 1861 and died two years later, July 26, 1863, at his home near Huntsville. Interestingly, Houston had led the successful Texas Revolution, following in the footsteps of his father in Virginia who had fought for the American Revolution.

Houston's loyalty to Jackson never wavered. With his young son he arrived at the Hermitage on the day his mentor died, June 8, 1845. Leading his son to the bedroom where the wasted body of Jackson lay, with tears in his eyes Houston is quoted as saying, "My boy, try to remember that you have looked on the face of Andrew Jackson." Jackson had convinced Houston of the importance of Texas annexation, an action engineered by President John Tyler and approved in March 1845, formally adopted that first year of the James K. Polk administration.

In the 1844 campaign, with running mate George M. Dallas of Philadelphia, the campaign slogan was "Polk, Dallas, and Texas!" Texans remembered the Dallas name by designating it for a new county and town.

5

PRIVATE BANKS EXPAND—
BANKERS, DRY GOODS
and SCISSORS

It provides a humorous slant on the life of those days . . . .
JESSE A. ZIEGLER of Houston on Ball, Hutchings and Company's early times

THE PROGENITORS OF A LATER PERIOD of private banks prior to the Civil War such as R. & D. G. Mills, included H. Runge & Company, Cuero and Indianola, in 1845; D. Yturri, Brownsville, 1848; Ball, Hutchings and Company, Galveston, 1854; B. A. Shepherd, Exchange and Collection Office, Houston, 1854. The present Groos National Bank, San Antonio, emerged from a general mercantile business and dates its beginning back to 1854. The firm of D. & A. Oppenheimer was established in San Antonio in 1858. It continues as a private bank. First Hutchings-Sealy National Bank, Galveston, claims its beginnings as the oldest bank, through mergers over the years, back to 1847 when John Sealy and John Henry Hutchings formed Hutchings, Sealy and Company, a dry goods firm in Sabine Pass, and in 1854 the banking house of Ball, Hutchings and Company.

Writing in the *Texas Bankers Record* (*TBR*) in March 1936, Jesse A. Ziegler of Houston discussed banking history in Texas in 1836. He noted that John H. Hutchings, father of Sealy Hutchings, was a bookkeeper and chief clerk for Mills. Tracing the development of the business from a general merchandise and commission house business, Ziegler wrote that Hutchings and Sealy later became associated with George Ball, beginning the firm of Ball, Hutchings and Company in the 1840s. Their advertisements in the *Galveston News* hailed their business: "Bankers, Commission Merchants, General Wholesalers, Dealers in Dry Goods, Boots and Shoes—Hardware, specializing in scissors."

"It provides a humorous slant on the life of those days when we contemplate a gigantic firm of the nature mentioned advertising scissors as their speciality, while on the other hand they carried the sugar barons and the cotton kings on the coastal regions of Texas for literally hundreds of thousands of dollars," Ziegler wrote. He recalled his boyhood in the 1860s and the activities of Ball, Hutchings and Company, remembering Williams' Wharf, "where their individually owned steamboats unloaded huge casks of sugar, and countless rows of hogsheads of pure golden syrup and molasses. In the springtime the warmer weather would cause fermentation and the bung-stoppers would fly out with an explosive noise somewhat akin to a small cannon.

"Today, I can look back with the clear vision of that early childhood and see those eminent and outstanding men, George Ball, J. H. Hutchings and John Sealy, seated in their swivel chairs, watching the gold and silver roll into them in kegs and sacks . . . . It was often said that a visit to the offices of their firm was like walking into the

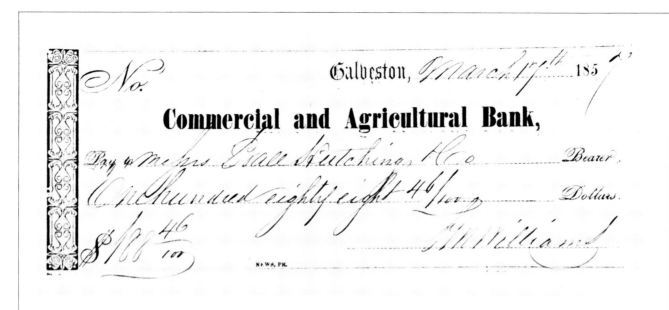

This check on the Commercial and Agricultural Bank, Galveston, March 17, 1857, was payable to Ball, Hutchings and Company. It is signed by Samuel May Williams. (Courtesy Rosenberg Library, Galveston, Texas)

House of Rothschild, Baring Bros., or Brown, Shipley & Co., of London. Particularly was this true when they were receiving the cotton kings and sugar barons from the great coastal or bottom plantations of the state."

Upon the death of Samuel May Williams, the good will and deposits of his bank were taken over by Ball, Hutchings and Company. "Later, during the course of their early existence," Ziegler said, "the firm . . . and its successors, Hutchings, Sealy & Co., unquestionably financed and assisted in establishing more bankers, flour mills, gins, oil mills and compresses, than any banking firm in Texas during the same period."

Heavily invested in railroad development, the company sold its Gulf, Colorado and Santa Fe Railway to Atchison, Topeka and Santa Fe "at a price reported from twenty to twenty-five million dollars," Ziegler reported. Hutchings, Sealy and Company merged with the South Texas National Bank in 1930, to become Hutchings-Sealy National Bank, and in 1958, with the First National Bank of Galveston, the first of the national banks chartered in Texas in 1865, to become First Hutchings-Sealy National Bank.

6
TEXAS
and the CONFEDERACY

And a Texan sorely tried by the failure of Bragg's commissariat during the Chattanooga campaign said that if he ever got back to his father's house he "intended to take a hundred biscuits and two large hams call it three days rations, then go down on Goat Island and eat it all at ONE MEAL."

QUOTE IN *The Life of Johnny Reb* BY BELL IRVIN WILEY

B Y A VOTE of 168 to 8, on February 1, 1861, the Texas Secession Convention adopted an ordinance to take the state from the Union. Sam Houston opposed the action. The move, however, was ratified by overwhelming vote of the people. So Texas joined the government of the Confederate States in Montgomery, Alabama. Governor Houston, refusing to take the oath of allegiance to the Confederacy, caused the office of governor to be declared vacant, and Lieutenant Governor Edward Clark became governor.

Texans responded to military service in large numbers, and some continued to fight until the last day, June 2, 1865, when the final surrender was described as "a mere formality." Texas was the last state to be readmitted to the Union.

During the Civil War private bankers continued to function, but there were no chartered banks of issue. The losses of war caused serious disturbances, ultimately bringing the destruction of the fortunes of some of the merchant-bankers. Showing a population of around 605,000, Texas had taxable wealth of around $295,000,000. The people faced monetary inflation, depreciating Confederate money, wild speculation, profiteering, rising prices and the eventual repudiation with the fall of the Confederacy.

In his carefully documented book, *A Monetary and Banking History of Texas (1821–1929)*, published by the Fort Worth National Bank in 1930, Professor Avery Luvere Carlson of Texas Christian University, wrote: "In Texas as in other States of the South, Confederate treasury notes and bonds, notes of Southern banks, obligations of Southern States and cities, as well as corporation and individual paper, commonly known as 'shinplasters,' flooded the State. Moreover, Texas contributed to the financial debacle through the issue of city, county and State warrants, which added to the volume of currency in circulation."

The immediate outcome was that the Constitution of 1866 reaffirmed the prohibition against banks which was also in the Constitution of 1861.

A new force had entered the nation, a national banking system, established by Congress and the Lincoln administration in 1863 as a way to help finance the depleted treasury of the Union during the Civil War. The action immediately gave states

A new force had entered the nation, a national banking system, established by Congress and the Lincoln administration in 1863 as a way to help finance the depleted treasury of the Union during the Civil War.

a competitor in the business of chartering banks, a power that had resided exclusively
in the states since Jackson's destruction of the Second Bank of the United States with
its 27 branches managed from Philadelphia.

7
UNION and the NEW SYSTEM—
NATIONAL BANKS

*He had said that no duty of the federal government was more imperative "than the duty it
owes the people of furnishing them a sound and uniform currency."*
BRAY HAMMOND, *Sovereignty and an Empty Purse*, referring to ABRAHAM LINCOLN.

T HE RECONSTRUCTION GOVERNMENT OF TEXAS changed the prohibition against
banks in the Constitution of 1869. This action resulted in the chartering of 48 state
banks, but that privilege was repealed by the Constitution of 1876.

By the National Bank Act of 1863, which narrowly passed Congress, the comptroller of the currency was authorized to issue national bank charters, to be strictly
regulated and examined, with a requirement of $50,000 capital, a large amount to
subscribe in postwar Texas. Since Galveston was the financial center of the state at
the time, it was appropriate that the first charter for a national bank was issued to the
First National Bank of Galveston, September 22, 1865. Headed by T. H. McMahan
of the private banking firm, the new bank's capital was $200,000. Its deposits ex-
ceeded $385,000 by October 1, 1866.

Three other national banks were chartered in 1865 and 1866. The National Bank
of Galveston was given the second charter March 9, 1866, and was later voluntarily
liquidated, its assets being acquired by W. L. Moody and Company. The First National Bank of Houston was chartered March 22, 1866. It was granted a new charter
May 3, 1933, when its name was changed to the First National Bank in Houston. By
merger with the City National Bank it became the First City National Bank of Houston. The San Antonio National Bank was the fourth national bank chartered in
Texas, July 30, 1866. Chartered banking had come to Texas.

8

RECONSTRUCTION, BANK EXPANSION
and the
REIGN of PRIVATE BANKING

. . . the private bank proved to be the outlet for the development of a financial system.
AVERY LUVERE CARLSON, historian

THE HEAVY CAPITAL REQUIREMENTS for a national bank charter prevented the rapid development of the national system in Texas. With this impediment and the constitutional prohibition against state-chartered banks, the end of the Civil War brought a sudden spurt in banking. The moneylenders and the mercantile bank operations of antebellum times were succeeded by the increasing numbers of private bankers. As Professor Carlson described it, " . . . the private bank proved to be the outlet for the development of a financial system. The period from the panic of 1873 to the panic of 1893 may well be designated as the 'Reign of the Private Banker in Texas.'"

The omission in the 1869 constitution of the prohibition against state banks was a kind of escape hatch. The constitution did not specifically approve banking; it was simply silent on the subject. Some historians feel that the change of heart represented a more pragmatic approach because of the advent of national banks and expansion of private banks.

The legislature acted by authorizing a limited number of banks through special acts. Thirty banks were authorized in the years 1870 and 1871; additional charters were granted during the next two years, but only eight banks actually opened for business. According to Grant and Crum, the first bank to receive a state charter was the Texas Banking and Insurance Company, Galveston, approved July 1, 1870, with capital of $150,000.

First to open under a state charter was the Island City Savings Bank, Galveston, which closed in 1885. Reorganized, it became the Texas Bank and Trust Company, later the United States National Bank. Some other banks authorized by the legislature at the time were: City Bank of Houston, July 21, 1870; The State Central Bank of Waco, August 8, 1870; Citizens Bank of Navasota, March 31, 1871; Galveston Bank & Trust, December 2, 1871; City Bank of Sherman, April 11, 1873; City Bank of Dallas, May 31, 1873.

The Galveston Bank & Trust Company was the first state bank in Texas to be given trust powers. Henry Rosenberg was its first president and the prime mover in its establishment; others were Isador Dyer, Albert Fall and J. H. Hutchings.

The development of private banks tracked with national bank activity, beginning in 1865. Prior to that year there were no regular banks in the interior of Texas. According to Carlson, a "few merchants in Austin, Dallas, San Antonio and Waco carried on exchange business as a convenience for their customers in the drygoods, grocery and general merchandise trade." By 1868 there were 15 private banks in Austin, Belton, Brenham, Galveston, Houston, San Antonio and Waco, and of the 15, seven were in Galveston, two each in Houston and San Antonio. Since they were not required to file reports, there is no way that a full listing of these institutions can be made. It is obvious, however, that the vast cotton trade necessitated merchant houses to do at least a limited banking business; the unincorporated private bank was the immediate answer to the need.

The Reconstruction years produced a large number of private banks. In 1869, for example, 20 additional institutions were opened in the state. By the end of the year there were 35 or more. As described by Carlson, "A number of interesting developments in banking have occurred in this State. For instance in December 1869, Charles Schreiner of the village of Kerrville and August Faltin of Comfort opened a mercantile concern at Kerrville, in a small building 16 x 18 feet in size. Since there were no banks in that section of the State, Faltin and Schreiner were frequently called upon to perform numerous banking functions in connection with their store. The cattlemen in the community usually received gold and silver for their stock. Some of these coins were Spanish doubloons, gold coins varying in value from $5.00 to $16.00. Many of the cattlemen . . . turned their coins over to the store for safekeeping, and simply wrote an order to Faltin and Schreiner to pay their bills about the village. As the firm had no safe, the coins were deposited in a box placed underneath some loose boards in the floor. A barrel of salt and some boxes were placed over the plank. Other boxes of specie were secreted in the homes of the partners and in other unsuspected places. Although the store was robbed frequently, no money was ever secured; yet Faltin and Schreiner paid specie on demand. Thus originated a unique business which survives to this day as the Charles Schreiner Bank at Kerrville." Carlson's descriptive analysis of the private bank could easily have been the source of the phrase, "salt your money away."

By 1870 there were at least 43 private banks, and they continued to spring up, mostly as small operations only incidental to mercantile businesses. Comparing the number of private banks with the national charters shows the result of the difficulty of acquiring a national bank—there were only five in operation. The $50,000 capital was the major detriment to a national charter.

Another story Carlson related was the banking partnership in Fort Worth of Tidball, Van Zandt & Company in 1873. With one bookkeeper and capital of $10,000, they formed a private bank in a small building 25 x 30 feet in the town of about 1,000 inhabitants, located at the junction of the Baxter Springs and Chisholm trails. Drovers brought cattle through the town en route to Abilene, Kansas, the rail terminal, and the bank helped meet their credit needs.

Major Khleber Miller Van Zandt, a Civil War veteran, recalled the private bank and an incident that Carlson described: " . . . an outfit of cattle drovers camped one night southwest of the city, purchased a liberal supply of provisions at a store, and paid for the articles with a glistening $20 gold piece. The overjoyed storekeeper rode to town and paid his family physician. The physician rushed across the street and paid his overdue grocery bill. The valuable coin chased about the village during the

By 1870 there were at least 43 private banks . . . mostly as small operations only incidental to mercantile businesses.

48

Drawing of the First National Bank of Fort
Worth, located at Second and Throckmorton.
Founded in 1877, it was built in the style of a
frame cottage. (Courtesy Institute of Texan
Cultures)

day, paid over $200 in debts, and in the evening came back to the original store-
keeper in payment of some hay he had previously sold. Then, it was deposited in the
bank for safekeeping, where it served as gold reserve for several days. This experi-
ment convinced the pioneer of the value of sound money and safe banks."

Speaking at a Newcomen Society dinner in Fort Worth in 1977, Paul Mason, chairman of the First National Bank, related the story of the oldest national bank in Fort
Worth. A Confederate officer, Captain M. B. Loyd, along with Clyde P. Markley,
opened the former California and Texas Bank of Loyd, Markley and Company in
Fort Worth in 1873. A private bank, it was domiciled in an "unpretentious two-room
cottage." Properly situated, it served the California Gold Rush and the expanding
cattle business. The private bank provided needed exchange for the travelers.

The year 1873 was one of panic in financial circles, identified with the failure of

49

the large investment house of Jay Cooke and Company. The depression caused the failure of 5,000 businesses. Mason, reviewing the situation, noted that in Fort Worth "desolation set in. The population dropped to less than 1,000 and once again, empty houses lined the streets of Fort Worth."

The new stabilized currency of national banks convinced the prudent person that the days of the need for exchange in specie would soon cease. National bank notes were seldom redeemed. So Captain Loyd withdrew in 1876 from his former bank and in 1877 formed the First National Bank in Fort Worth, the ninth national banking charter in Texas. Loyd, with his son-in-law Samuel Burk Burnett, helped develop the large cattle empire with the brand 6666 (Four Sixes). Texas was the source of a growing cattle industry to feed people back East, and the new industry rebounded quickly after the 1873 depression.

While the population of Texas grew 35.5 percent in the decade from 1860–1870, from 604,215 to 818,579—from 23rd to 19th in rank among the states—it was nowhere near the 184 percent growth rate of the previous decade. The latter period was at a time of turbulence, the Civil War and Reconstruction, a period of political stresses, great poverty, economic upheaval following the devastation of war. The Old South had traditionally been the source of immigration to Texas. States of the Confederacy, including Texas, had little money. The miracle of the decade of Reconstruction is that it provided an expanded opportunity for bank charters and temporarily removed the prohibition against banks in Texas. It required guts and confidence to launch a bank; Texans seemed to have both in abundance but very little money.

As in other areas, Texas's economy was largely based on agriculture, with 70 percent of the state's people in that economic segment. Value of farmland increased during the period; manufacturing took a giant leap forward, helping keep the population "in reasonable comfort."

Although railroad development had reached a total trackage of 711 miles in 1870, this was insufficient for the area to be served. The back country needed economic organization, transportation and credit. The Reconstruction Convention of 1869 took note of the problems to the extent that in finance the delegates authorized the chartering of a limited number of state banks, beginning in 1870—a period that inaugurated feverish activity for these special charters.

Attempts to establish branch banks as well were made in this period. The Bank of Texas, founded in 1871, was to be established in Austin with "authority to place an agency in any town in the State, or in any other locality." In the same year the Merchants and Planters Savings Bank, Austin, was authorized "to establish such and as many branch offices in this State or in other States, as its directors shall provide." This authority, before the days of the McFadden Act, was a forerunner of recent discussions about interstate banking. Additionally, the Banking, Insurance and Mutual Aid Association of Texas, along with the Home Insurance and Trust Company, in Austin and Galveston respectively, had permission to establish branches. None took the plunge to branch banking, however.

The legislature in 1871 passed enabling legislation for the chartering of savings banks, but, for constitutional reasons, the law did not become effective until it was amended in 1874, the year the legislature turned over the chartering of state banks to the secretary of state.

Texas's history in Reconstruction marks a period of bitter upheavals in politics, including military rule under General Philip Sheridan. Carpetbag rule ended in 1873 with the election of Governor Richard Coke. On January 17, 1874, President U. S. Grant announced that it would "be prudent as well as right" to go along with the vote of Texans who selected Coke and turned down E. J. Davis, the candidate favored by Sheridan. After nine long and troublesome years Reconstruction in Texas was over.

Although the Constitution of 1869 was a product of Reconstruction rule, its provision for state banks was hailed as a break for Texas development. However, the Constitution of 1876 reinstated the old anti-bank provision. Banks chartered under the previous constitutional provision were permitted to continue under a grandfather clause. The door to state banking slammed shut, Texas returned to the previous condition of banking: national banks and private banks.

Writers have shown the burgeoning of private banks during the period from 1876 to 1905, the date the constitution was amended to permit state banks. Private bankers felt that their business was just that—private. Not incorporated, not chartered, no reports were required. They generally resisted the growing feeling by Texas authorities that private banks should be regulated. Private banks avoided regulation until April 23, 1923, the date from which establishment of any new private banks was prohibited. Existing private banks had the right to continue. Most of them switched to either national or state charters, but a few have remained to remind us of the reign of private banking in Texas.

Reconstruction in Texas produced a number of national banks, including the new charters for institutions in Galveston, Houston, San Antonio, Jefferson, Denison and Austin. Total resources were almost $2,870,000, a substantial growth in the six-year period prior to 1873, reflecting the overall growth of Texas.

A classic example of an evolving institution from private bank to state charter and national bank began in 1871 when W. H. Gaston and A. C. Camp started a banking and brokerage business in Dallas, using "a dry goods box for a counter and their pockets for safes." The bank became City Bank of Dallas in 1873; City National Bank in 1880, later merging with American Exchange National Bank to become the First National Bank of Dallas.

Although the Constitution of 1869 was a product of Reconstruction rule, its provision for state banks was hailed as a break for Texas development.

Texas Bankers Association Convention in
1887. (Courtesy Rosenberg Library, Galveston, Texas)

PART THREE

The TBA Crusade
For Equity Through
Constitutional Reform

1
BANK ISSUE JOINED—
TBA PROVIDES a FORUM for ACTION

There are persons who . . . cry out loudly against all banks and corporations . . . . They would choke the fountain of industry and dry up all streams.
SENATOR DANIEL WEBSTER, March 12, 1838

B Y 1880 TEXAS RANKED 11th among the states in population. The people were there, but the system to serve them was inadequate because of restrictions against state banks.

National banks continued to be chartered. By 1900, according to Carlson, the "national banks had become so numerous that they virtually dominated banking affairs in Texas." And the number increased dramatically after 1900 when the capital requirement was reduced from $50,000 to $25,000.

No easy task, it required 20 years of effort by the bankers through the TBA, along with visionary political leadership, to effect a change to provide a balance between national and state banks. The period 1885 to 1905 is a story of gradual success.

The organization of the TBA in 1885 provided a forum for discussion of issues and for action to develop banking, and through organization to protect it from political and criminal attacks.

It was difficult to overcome the legacy of Jackson's opposition to national banks, the sordid story of "wildcat" banks and excessive use of paper currency, lack of proper regulation and a general feeling against corporate power. Anti-bank feelings were deep in Texas, and they lingered long.

Anti-bank feelings were deep in Texas, and they lingered long.

53

Speaking in the U.S. Senate, March 12, 1832, Daniel Webster, a banking supporter, said: "There are persons who constantly clamor. They complain of oppression, speculation, and pernicious influence of wealth. They cry out loudly against all banks and corporations, and a means by which small capitalists become united in order to produce important and beneficial results. They carry out mad hostility against all established institutions. They would choke the fountain of industry and dry all streams."

In 1885 the spokesman for this philosophy of Webster was Congressman James F. Miller, the first president of the TBA.

Efforts were launched early to ensure increased attendance at the second convention in Lampasas, July 20–24, 1886. Secretary Malone actively publicized the meeting on the front pages of the Galveston and Dallas newspapers. He urged every bank in Texas to send a representative.

Although no copy of the proceedings of the second convention has been located—and diligent efforts were made over the years—reports of the convention show that President Miller could not attend. He was involved in pressing duties in Washington. N. B. Sligh of Galveston, first vice president, presided. The big issue of the convention, in addition to routine association business and election of officers, was the issue of silver coinage.

Sligh struck a positive note: "We meet under the most favorable circumstances. Our broad fields, rich with golden grain, assure us that our millions of people will have ample breadstuffs. Our cotton fields are beginning to whiten with the promise that we may have the largest crop Texas has yet produced, while on our broad plains thousands of cattle show that we not only have enough to provide this great State, but enough for the millions beyond. Our banks and bankers have been fairly successful this year, the usual dividends, with some surplus, being the rule."

The gold-silver issue, advanced by resolution at the first convention and postponed until the second meeting, was taken up. Nicholas Weeks of Galveston, the proponent of the resolution for temporary suspension of silver coinage, convinced the delegates to support the resolution. It was adopted and forwarded to the American Bankers Association (ABA). Delegates and guests had time for leisure activities at the Park Hotel, along with an outing on the Lampasas River.

Sligh, a talented orator, read a paper on exchange and discounts. He was elected president to succeed Miller. The influence of the prominent Galveston bankers was coming to the forefront. They succeeded in having the third convention in that city in 1887, even though Lampasas again had its strong supporters.

Although the 1885 convention had asked the executive committee to study a resolution by W. A. Kelsey for the incorporation of banks through amendment to the constitution, no action was taken. The issue would be taken up in 1887.

With its fish chowder, seawater and boat rides, described by William A. Philpott, Jr., in the *TBR*, Galveston "found it easy to gain consent of the bankers to act the host to the Association."

Galveston had much to offer the bankers. The 49 accredited members and 32 guests gathered in the prosperous and enchanting city, August 9–11, 1887, for the third convention. Discussions no doubt covered the unusual experience Galveston had,

A record-breaking freeze and snowstorm struck Galveston in 1896 as seen in this dramatic photo of George Sealy's mansion! (Courtesy Rosenberg Library, Galveston, Texas)

along with all of Texas, in the rough winter of 1886–1887. Even the oldest inhabitants could not recall a more severe blast from the weather. The *TBR* reported: "The bay was frozen over, the snow hampered all outdoor activities; ice and the low temperatures that continued for a week disrupted shipping; icicles split sails; snow delighted the hearts of youth, affording opportunity for sledding and sleighing. . . . Then, to quote an old newspaper, 'that was the year the bankers came in hordes to wrangle over free coinage of silver, and bathe their befogged brains in the cool surf.'"

President Sligh convened the first session August 9, 1887, "in the airy parlors of the Beach Hotel." After his address, which included the welcome to Galveston, Colonel Exall of Lampasas was asked to respond, "which he did most gracefully in a speech well fitted for the occasion." His brief but cordial remarks showed that moving the convention to Galveston had not miffed the Lampasas people. Sligh observed: "As bankers and business men we meet in convention to compare notes, to talk over our methods, to try to improve some practices, and to impress upon ourselves the importance of holding fast to others."

Noting the old saying "Wharever the hen scratch dar be de bug," he said, "Wherever money is, man's ingenuity, the world over, is at work to get it. The art of protecting it and investing it safely, that the 'talent' may increase is our key note. At the same time the interests of our State are identical with ours. We then have not only in view the interests of capital and labor wherever banded together in the legitimate enterprise for the good of our State."

The anti-bank issue surfaced. Sligh asked, "Is the prohibitionary clause in our State Constitution respecting the establishment of State Banks a wise one? If you think not, agitate the matter," he admonished the delegates.

After the session adjourned the delegates and guests took an excursion on the Gulf "aboard two sailing vessels and one steam yacht . . . a majority of the visitors, especially the ladies, preferred the steam yacht. . . ." And to end a perfect day the bankers partook of a fish chowder supper and enjoyed a concert by a military band.

A major debate erupted on the second day about collections. The question arose over a par collection system adopted by the Dallas banks which had the result of making that city a clearinghouse. The Galveston banks rejected the idea. One suggestion was for a charge of 25 cents on all items, whether collected or not. Several experiences of collections were recited. One banker vowed that "half the sight drafts sent to his house for collection had to be returned unpaid, leaving the bank to realize nothing whatever for attempting the collection." He asked what to do. Baird's J. N. Rushing broke the tension of the debate. Said he, "The best thing the gentleman can do under such a circumstance is to move away from such a town."

And to end a perfect day the bankers partook of a fish chowder and enjoyed a concert by a military band.

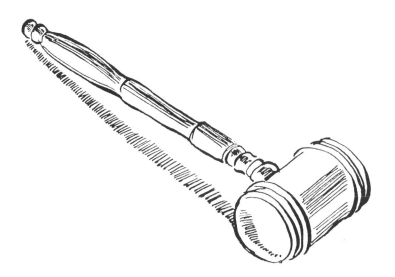

56

2
DEVELOPMENT of TBA
CONVENTION ISSUES
and TRADITIONS

What can measure the resources of Texas? The hand of God alone
can hold the balances. . . .
COLONEL W. B. DENSON, Galveston greeter, 1887

EARLY CONVENTION DEBATES established the traditions of the TBA for mature thought in convention proceedings and demonstrated the debate maturity of the delegates.

On the par collection issue, for example, it was decided in 1887 that the TBA couldn't effectively bind the banks of Texas to any agreement on fixed rates because only "about 25 percent of the banks are represented, and that those who are not members of this association would not be bound by any rule adopted by the association."

Ed J. L. Green of San Marcos, one of the TBA founders, was elected president. Galveston won over Houston for the 1888 convention.

After a discussion of the anti-bank issue and the lack of voter understanding and support of constitutional amendments, J. H. Labatt of Galveston stirred the convention with his call for action to amend the constitution, Section 16, Article XVI, with "a section liberal to capital to be engaged in banking, without the right to issue paper money, under careful supervising laws of the State. . . ."

Remembering President Sligh's suggestion to those who favored constitutional change for banking to "agitate the matter," the delegates liked Labatt's ringing address and suggestions.

Ending on a positive note, the third TBA convention delegates had taken firm stands on issues of the day, flexed their forensic powers and furthered the TBA's crusade for equity through constitutional reform.

Bankers in other states saw the advisability of emulating the TBA; the movement to form state associations was now spreading across the country.

The convention habit was well established by 1888 as delegates and guests in greater number than ever before assembled in Galveston for the fourth annual convention of the TBA. The sessions were held in Harmony Hall, beginning on Tuesday, June 19. Fifty-one delegates answered the roll call.

Colonel W. B. Denson turned on the hospitality spigot at the outset to welcome the bankers "to our island home; to the warm hearts of a proud people . . . who

The trust committed
to Texas is great, and
who can measure the
capabilities?

delight today to honor you." He described Galveston as the "Venice of the golden fields of Texas."

At a time when rhetoric was a jewel, Colonel Denson had many a gem, and it is a shame that the tape recorder had not been invented to capture his superb address. Here's a sample: "Here, where this planet pulsates in the waves of the old ocean that break upon our shore, and these same waves beat back in turn upon other continents, and break at the feet of our people, we see and recognize the brotherhood of man, nations linked to us by a great highway, paved and ballasted by the hands of God, leading up to our very doors. . . . What can measure the resources of Texas? The hand of God alone can hold the balances—the ships ride at anchor at our doors to bear our bread and beef and cotton to the millions of our fellows beyond the sea. The trust committed to Texas is great, and who can measure the capabilities?"

President Green spoke on the tariff situation and hoped for reform. He opted for support of port and deep-water development for Texas's coast as paramount to all other questions. "We are entitled to such liberal appropriations from the general government as will insure one port, if not more, where the largest seagoing vessel may find safe roadway," he suggested.

Noting the "prejudice against organized capital for banking purposes," he urged the bankers to help dispel this prejudice "by honest methods," and he held out the olive branch "to the great agricultural association" and the spreading agrarian revolt in Texas.

Crime against banks was in the news. Green recommended that the TBA's constitution and bylaws be amended "to authorize the executive committee to offer suitable rewards for the arrest of bank robbers and forgers, and to provide a fund for that purpose." This was the first time a TBA president had advocated a program against bank crime. Delegates voted to levy an assessment of 1/20th of 1 percent upon capital stock and surplus of member banks to provide a fund to fight crime.

In the earliest days of the TBA convention, the program was not developed in detail until the delegates arrived. A committee was usually named to "map out a programme for the ensuing business of the convention."

Delegates at the fourth convention approved a resolution for a sub-treasury for Galveston. A. B. Smith of Fort Worth suggested that the banks of Texas require compensating balances of the regular borrowers "to maintain credit balances equal to a fair percentage of the accommodations." Said he, "A banker need not be a poet or a philosopher, a man of science or of literature, an orator or a statesman. He need not possess any one remarkable quality by which he may be distinguished from the rest of mankind. It is only necessary that he possess a large portion of that quality which is called common sense." And he suggested that common sense called for the banking interests to insist upon credit balances.

The versatile N. B. Sligh discussed the future of national banks. He was the first Texas banker on record to advance the idea of "banks taxing themselves voluntarily for the purpose of raising a fund for the protection of depositors."

Treasurer John Caro Russell reported that the financial records of the TBA showed a cash balance of $423.12 on hand August 12, 1887. Dues from 105 banks in 1888 totaled $525. Total expenses amounted to $215.10. In urging increased memberships, he said the "objects [of the TBA] are profit and pleasure."

Texans of 1888 were proud of their state. "Texas was born of Tital mold, and she can't help being better than other states," W. Goodrich Jones of Temple told the convention.

Houston's J. E. McAshan, speaking on "Bank vs. Depositors," traced the development of banking, using colorful examples to humorously ridicule the uninformed depositor for lack of understanding of the institution. Said he, "When the inquisitors were informing Galileo in polite but emphatic and unmistakable language that his notions about the earth's movements were entirely wrong, and tenderly exhibited to him a pair of thumb-screws as an inducement for him to retract, I have no doubt that some rural customer was in a bank asking the teller if he should endorse the check on the front side or the back side." Then he turned his barbs to the tellers. "The bank teller we all know to be a most unapproachable and magnificent personage, more dogmatic and dictatorial than the president, and, compared with whose authority, that of the cashier is merely fictitious and nominal. He occupies a magnificent pedestal and is one of the great unadulterated, unmitigated unwashed wonders of the nineteenth century."

McAshan, one of the leading banking orators of his day, said: "Banks are the most powerful friends that have ever been devised for the great masses of the people." The world, he said, is made up of two elements—bankers and depositors—and that "The monstrous chaff of the demagogue that legislation favorable to banks is class legislation and opposed to the interests of the people, is the most absurd and glaring sophistry."

Now residing in Dallas, Colonel Henry Exall invited the delegates to meet in that city in 1889, assuring them that the people of Dallas "would meet them at the gate with honest hospitality, and welcome them to their hearts and homes." Dallas was selected.

The founding members of the TBA were moving the organization forward. J. Z. Miller, Sr., of Belton, was elected President. The traditions they established—such as the rotation of meeting cities for the annual convention—remain a century later. So does the debate and consensus on issues.

Although the TBA was growing, it lacked the financial support for a paid professional staff, a step that would be taken many years later. The early founders and leaders were volunteers in every respect, often serving at considerable sacrifice, but this did not hamper the quality of their service. They set the pattern for voluntary service that has guided the TBA for a century.

The conventions for the first few years are significant to the history of banking and the TBA, for they detailed the mold and thrust of banking and the association.

When the 68 banker delegates arrived in Dallas for the fifth annual convention on May 8, 1889, they received a royal welcome to the county seat city of 38,000, grown from a tiny village since 1850. The city had a new skyscraper, and electric cars replaced the mule-pulled cars on the street railways.

Texas pride was everywhere. Dallas was a good place to show it.

The early founders and leaders were volunteers in every respect, often serving at considerable sacrifice, but this did not hamper the quality of their service.

President J. Z. Miller urged the legislature to "enact the most stringent laws compatible with the constitution for the safety of monied loans, and to make such loans of a higher character than ordinary debts."

He appointed a committee to compile a secret "cipher code for the sole use of this association." The committee favored a code, and it was adopted.

Not at all timid about pursuing anti-crime measures, he urged the legislature of Texas "to enact laws punishing robberies by force of arms with death—naming such crimes as shall come within purview of the law."

For the first time the TBA treasury had a cash balance of more than $1,000, Treasurer Carey Shaw reported. The association now had 97 dues-paying members, at $5 per member.

Having approved a cipher code, the TBA members wondered how the secret procedure would work:

It would be this way: A special committee was to designate banks eligible for membership, "giving each bank a number on such list and submit to this association during this session with closed doors, a plan for the use of signals or signal words in telegraphing for the ensuing year, which shall only be used in conjunction with the code. . . ." The doors were closed and the code numbers assigned.

3
THE INNOVATOR POINTS the WAY

*The future of banks must depend in a large measure upon the guarantees of
safety afforded the people.*
E. M. LONGCOPE

ONE OF THE STIRRING MOMENTS of the fifth convention was an address by E. M. Longcope of Lampasas, known for his important efforts in founding the TBA, because it put on the record the argument by an intelligent banker for state banks.

Longcope argued: "It is impossible not to observe at present a well defined expression of good will in the public mind toward the banks of Texas. On the part of the banks, I may say this feeling is reciprocated. Bankers do not fear open-handed discussions of their measures and policies. Inviting confidence, it is idle to suppose they would promote plans to prejudice the interests of the people. The business welfare of a community is the midnight thought of a true banker. How best to promote that interest, to develop a spirit of progress and to aid in the accumulation of the wealth of the people, this is the aim of legitimate banking," the young cashier said.

Turning to the prohibition of banks by the constitution, Longcope observed that the restraint "was born in a so-called spirit of revenge. . . . It breathed antagonism. It fostered prejudice. It struck a blow at the vital interests of Texas, a recovery from which it has taken years to effect, and this recovery is not wholly effected yet.

"Following this step of our constitution makers, indeed preceding and accompanying it, a fear of prejudice was engendered, in the public mind against the National Banking System. Orators, with the tongue of an Alcibiades, but with no more knowledge of finance than babbling babes, fed the flames of passion in the people's breast with diatribic shavings. In a small way, I was one of them, and hurled my feeble thunderbolts at the iniquitous measure," he admitted.

"Gentlemen, I was mistaken. A more wonderful system of finance was never conceived by the thought of man," he told the delegates.

He praised the good record of private banks and then turned to the need for state-chartered banks.

"But what I wish to impress upon you is that an incorporated bank, paying all its taxes, of whatever character and description, to the state government, amenable only to the laws of our own people, can be made as great a tower of strength, under Texas laws, as well as under Federal. Why then can we not go to work in a systematic way to influence the public mind for chartered banks?"

It was a pithy question. Longcope laid out the course of action for an amendment to the state constitution: First, "we must in advance offer the public some guarantees of good faith. We should not go before the people unless we are prepared to offer them every measure of safety consonant with good banking." Other points he suggested were shareholder responsibility, the value of savings to the poorer classes, provisions that would permit small towns in Texas to have banking facilities "which cannot now be enjoyed by them." He suggested the creation of a banking department, loan restrictions, reserves and a capital requirement of $25,000. He also called for stern and severe punishment for bank directors who violated their oaths, stockholder liability and establishment of a fund to guarantee bank deposits. He noted that only two national banks had failed in Texas in the period of 1865–1889, with depositors losing $48,000 in one and nothing in the other.

Longcope concluded his noteworthy address: "The future of banks must depend in a large measure upon the guarantees of safety afforded the people. When these are completed to the highest point of perfection known to banking science, a degree of prosperity unheard of in the history of the world will be the heritage of our people and the bonds of amity and good will be forever strengthened."

The Dallas convention was aroused to action. A committee was appointed to consider the recommendations made and appropriate action to be taken.

4
THE TBA'S FIRST
MAJOR ASSIGNMENT—
AMEND the CONSTITUTION

The history of banking in Texas is an epitomized history of hostility to the institution.
J. E. MCASHAN, Houston banker

THE STRATEGY WAS NOW CLEAR. The TBA had found a consensus in its battle for an amendment to the constitution. Able leaders—national, private and state banks—joined the crusade. The cause was just; the TBA was solidly placed to carry out its first major assignment.

J. E. McAshan of Houston spoke on the history of banking in Texas. "Banking, while dependent upon public confidence, is not a confidence game. The honest banker, handling in a few years enough money to pay the public debt of the United States, on a salary sometimes small, and always modest, free from the taint of corruption, preferring the afflictions of honest competency, to luxury secured through the malversations of trust, is to me a grand moral spectacle. . . . Fidelity to trust! It alone is the impress which gives to human dross its currency. Without it gold has no value, birth no distinction, station no dignity, beauty no charm, age no reverence.

"The history of banking in Texas is an epitomized history of hostility to the institution," the popular banker-orator said in reciting the anti-bank constitutional conventions and prohibitory clauses to chartering banks. "These things sufficiently evince the animus of our people to our profession. It is not so much these statutes and the laws which we condemn and deplore. It is the hostility, and crudity of the public opinion which gives them birth, that causes the banking fraternity of the world at large to regard them in amazement. . . . in Texas they impede the roll of the car of progress. . . . The growth of banking in Texas demonstrates fully and completely the absurdity and unreasonable nature of the opposition to proper, honest and legitimate banking."

He paid tribute to the early bankers of Texas who founded their "houses upon the impregnable rock of commercial honor and integrity."

McAshan's address glowed with such lines as, "Sparkling over historical plains where the mockingbird sits in the magnolia and, facing the coming morn, pours forth an exultant anthem to the grandeur of our native state, there placidly, proudly shining is the Lone Star of Texas."

Delegates set a precedent on the final day of the meeting by allowing the future secretary $100 per annum for his services.

After electing Nicholas Weeks of Galveston president, formal invitations for the next convention were extended by Weatherford, Houston and Gainesville. Houston was selected.

62

Before the convention adjourned former TBA head, James F. Miller of Gonzales, discussed the history of usury in a major address. Tracing it from Mosaic law, he said, "In truth and in fact, usury laws seem to be based on no sound reason, or enlightened statesmanship; but upon the prejudices and jealousies of the poor, or borrowing class in the several states." The old Roman rate of interest was 12 percent, Miller said. England, while not prescribing any rate, prohibited excessive rates such as 40 percent, and in 1571, in the reign of Queen Elizabeth, the rate was set at 10 percent. James I reduced the rate to 8 percent in 1624, and Charles II dropped it to 6 percent in 1660. In Anne's reign the rate was reduced to 5 percent, and in 1834 the defense of usury as to negotiable securities was abolished. Queen Victoria's reign brought the repeal in 1854 of all laws against usury.

"The rate of money, like the price of other commodities when too high, soon regulates itself," he said.

While the traditions of England appeared in the usury laws of the original thirteen states, Massachusetts was the first American state to follow the English example by abolishing usury laws on July 1, 1867. Miller cited 13 states and territories that had no usury laws in 1889, and in most states only the forfeiture of interest charged was the penalty for usury.

He reviewed the usury situation in Texas, citing the constitutional provision that prohibited a rate of interest in excess of 8 percent. By contract the rate was limited to 12 percent with the legislature to "provide appropriate pains and penalties to prevent and punish usury." The statutory penalty was the forfeiture of the entire interest, "but it expressly provides that the principal sum shall always be recoverable," Miller pointed out.

The advocates for legislative change to lower the usury ceiling were organizing. Miller resisted the change. He noted the business or contract rate was on the decline, dropping to 8 percent as the influx of capital came in from other states, sustaining his argument that money as a commodity sets its rate in the marketplace.

(The battle over interest rates is never-ending. The TBA, as other state bankers associations, finds it necessary to seek legislative relief from antiquated usury laws on many occasions.)

The first five years of the TBA firmly established its usefulness, produced strong leadership, developed a consensus and forum, and identified problems that needed attention. Chief among these was constitutional reform, crimes against banks, interest rates, collections, currency reform and silver coinage, resistance to anti-bank and anti-business legislative and regulatory measures. The association also aided Texas development on a broad base, including agriculture, manufacturing and deep-water port development.

W. Goodrich Jones, TBA secretary, bemoaned the paucity of association records relating to its history. "The facts surrounding the first conception and origination of the association seem to be shrouded in as much doubt as is the birthplace of Homer," he wrote. "Some of our members have been transient; like the asteroids they have darted into our atmosphere, flaring up in our assemblies with an auspicious brilliancy and light, then only to be gone again," he said.

His tabulation of attendance was: 1885, 31 members; 1886, no record; 1887, 48

The rate of money, like the price of other commodities when too high, soon regulates itself.

W. Goodrich Jones, Texas Bankers Association secretary, was a crusader for history and records. He presented this impressive register to the TBA in 1891.

members; 1888, 51 members; 1889, 68 attending; and 1890, 58 members present.
Although records are limited, the deliberations of the first five conventions have been
fairly well documented in this history. While the ensuing conventions will be cited,
along with any unusual questions and actions, the story of banking and the TBA
henceforth will be related to issues and events, bankers and the TBA, and interesting
anecdotes and stories.

5

CRITICAL DECADE of the 1890s— GAINING POLITICAL CLOUT

*When you all get as old as I am you will sometimes be unable to call the name of your
nearest neighbor. I don't know why it is every old man has that same trouble.*
COLONEL J. Z. MILLER of Belton, proposing a permanent badge for members

THE CRITICAL DECADE of the 1890s for banking and the TBA was launched
May 6, 1890. The association met again in Galveston. President Weeks proudly announced that many banks had been created in Texas during the year with no failures
reported; growth was broadly based. Population figures were impressive as 1890 began: Dallas had grown from 10,358 to 65,855 since 1880; Galveston, to 55,413, from
22,248; San Antonio, 55,000, from 20,350; Fort Worth, 33,000, from 6,563; Austin, 27,248, from 11,013; Waco, 28,000, from 7,295; Houston, 42,710, from
16,513. The new census figures of dramatic growth gave all of Texas a strong base for
a vibrant decade. Now bankers, through the TBA, were seeking to change political
attitudes by demonstrating to the people the need for change.

At the May 1891 convention in Austin, the first held in the capital city, G. A.
Levi of Victoria was the TBA president. With a record attendance of 106 present, he
got down to business immediately, noting that most of the early hours of a convention were spent in "personal pleasures and idle discussions." A man of vision, Levi
asked Austin's A. P. Woolridge to submit "suggestions on a course of reading and
study to be recommended to the regents and faculties for such students. . . ." The
organization became intensely interested in education, a tradition which continues to
this day.

On a negative note, the number one issue of the TBA—the constitutional
amendment proposal—had been adopted as a joint resolution by the legislative committee, but it had been killed after it got beyond the committee, the delegates were
informed. This did not dampen the resolve to continue the battle.

"Should banks pay interest on deposits" was the intriguing subject of a paper by
James A. Patton of Houston. He thought "that from the 12th century down to the

present time we have one and all been under the mesmeric influence of interest-paying banks."

As was customary at almost all meetings, Judge James F. Miller was called to the podium. He lambasted the Farmers' Alliance "which has recently come to be a political power, and is without reason hostile to banks and banking systems." Suggesting that some of their leaders are "not men of ability, are not men who have been successful in any line of life and yet this class of men formulate the political theories of this state, they formulate its financial policies," the former congressman averred.

Moved by the old warhorse's rhetoric and logic, one delegate jumped up and shouted, "Hurrah for Miller!"

Resuming his address, the venerable gentleman from Gonzales said: "There is another trouble, the last evil that I shall allude to, and it is a vicious one. In this day and age we have a class of men known as politicians, men who are professional politicians, men who have no principle that they will not sacrifice for the sake of office, and who will advocate any theory, will pander to any prejudice, will assent to anything as a fact they believe will make them popular with the people and secure votes," he charged.

For the TBA, 1892 was a watershed year.

James Stephen Hogg, the first native-born Texas governor, had been elected in 1890, moving up from attorney general, an office in which he had been publicly acclaimed for his reform measures. The Democrats controlled Texas. At the party convention in 1892 a platform was adopted that contained a plank for a constitutional amendment "permitting the incorporation of state banks under proper restrictions and control for the protection of the depositors and the people."

The long-awaited break appeared to be at hand.

In his strong reelection campaign Governor Hogg, now with heavy statewide support for his progressive program, endorsed the idea, promising to recommend it to the 1893 legislature for action. George Clark, his opponent, opposed state banks. The issue was joined. Hogg was reelected in a bitter campaign. As promised, Hogg presented it to the legislature, but it was 10 years before anything happened.

When the eighth convention met in Waco on May 10, 1892, President J. W. Blake of Mexia and 87 other bankers were present. One of the significant features of the convention was the departure from the previous way of selecting officers "from the recommendation of a special committee" to officers "elected from the floor of the house."

As a result of this change, Colonel A. P. Woolridge of Austin was elected president, passing over other officers who were in the chairs of succession. E. M. Longcope survived the change by being reelected secretary.

While bankers believed the decade would be a dramatic one, nobody anticipated the critical depression of 1893. When President Woolridge called the convention to order in San Antonio on May 16 of that year, it was at the beginning of a long-term economic panic that crippled finance. Although Texas bore the panic less painfully than other states, the depression was a matter for bankers to fear.

As was often the case, outlaws were the subject of one issue before the TBA convention. The association had requested member banks to "contribute to a fund for

The Democrats controlled Texas. At the party convention in 1892 a platform was adopted that contained a plank for a constitutional amendment permitting the incorporation of state banks.

Early TBA conventions were held in Harmony
Hall, Galveston. Photo c. 1894. (Courtesy
Rosenberg Library, Galveston, Texas)

the relief of the families of the brave men who recently lost their lives in a conflict
with the notorious Dalton gang, who had almost succeeded in robbing two banks in
Coffeyville, Kansas."

Woolridge set a specific course for the TBA: "It is our duty and privilege to regard

ourselves as charged with responsibility and vested with the right to speak our ma-
tured convictions upon matters affecting the economical and financial welfare of
Texas. No important financial question should arise but this association should have
some opinion upon it, and that opinion it should modestly but bravely declare," he
said.

Following his own admonition, he spoke out strongly against the free issue of silver. "I think it is impossible by a mere arbitrary act of government, great as may be its
influence and power, to make equal what is not by nature so."

One of the policy decisions of the TBA was made when a request was presented for
membership in the association by the West Texas Bankers Association. The delegates
took the position that "it is the purpose of this association to have single bodies for
membership, not concrete bodies. . . ." No strong feeling emerged to show substantial support for amending the TBA constitution to permit a change, and so the
matter was dropped.

Colonel J. Z. Miller proposed the creation of a permanent badge with the member's institution and name on it because "when you all get as old as I am you will
sometimes be unable to call the name of your nearest neighbor. I don't know why it is
every old man has that same trouble." Idea approved, the minutes reported.

The harsh recession continued in 1894. President T. J. Grose of Galveston hoped
that the austerity would strengthen the resolves for "a broader conservatism and more
intelligent comprehension of our obligations," he told the convention in Fort Worth
in May. There were political stresses and unrest "and the antagonism of labor towards
capital." He mentioned the farmer-labor warfare "towards the character of capital
represented by banks; and later, fury seems to have succeeded enthusiasm for the
overzealous, and self-constituted leaders, teaching behind closed doors and in secret
conclave, have at last educated the people to believe us little less than criminals,
denouncing us as robbers when we insist upon our just dues, as Shylocks when we
practice a becoming caution, as impertinent if we venture an opinion as to the financial policies of the country, and marking us for utter annihilation should we aspire to
political office."

The delegates commended "most heartily the action of Grover Cleveland . . . for
his wise, statesmanlike and patriotic course in endeavoring, under the most trying
circumstances, to uphold the honor, integrity and stability of our currency."

By convention time, May 1895, prosperity was raising its welcome head. President
A. S. Reed of Fort Worth told the delegates in Galveston that the nation "seems to
be upon a wave of returning prosperity. . . ." The TBA, now with a membership of
187, rounded out its first decade. Reed concluded that "its record is high, and the
interest preserved in its workings and meetings is much above the average in other
states. Still, it must be remembered that this is the pioneer state bankers association."

Reed had suggested at the Waco convention that the TBA establish a district system. He cited the New York Bankers Association and its system, called a group system, where each division in the state had its local organization deriving its authority
from the state association. He figured that the district system would help dampen
some of the excessive competition which was causing some bank failures.

A survey by the association indicated considerable interest for a reciprocal draft system. The delegates approved it.

Legislative needs included a public warehouse bill, repeal of the anti-bank constitutional provision and taxation. Considerable focus was put on the issue of currency reform and the Baltimore Plan for a flexible currency, a plan that had been endorsed by the ABA. The debates turned on the issue of one kind of currency, a "national currency."

The TBA constitution was amended to drop the offices of second and third vice presidents and second assistant secretary, and created five new appointive offices— "chairmen of the districts." The district system began in Texas with the action of the 1895 convention.

A San Antonio banker, J. N. Brown, was at the helm of the TBA when the cotton crisis of October 1895 struck Texas. He told the association convention in Dallas in 1896 that speculators, including some bankers, "placed an unreal value" upon the commodity. Brown opposed, as did his predecessors, free and unlimited coinage of silver. "Such a course would in my opinion be as foolish as jumping off a precipice in order to test the law of gravitation," he said.

Delegates figured they had made a mistake in eliminating the office of TBA second vice president; they restored it.

Statistical reports indicated bank capital, January 1, 1896, in Texas was $37,000,000; surplus, $6,500,000; undivided profits, $2,987,295; individual deposits, $36,848,395; loans and discounts, $49,525,000. Total number of banks was 410, of which 213 held national charters with a capital of over $21,000,000.

A generous Western Union Telegraph Company "will send free the family and social messages for members of the Texas Bankers Association, while in session in Dallas," an announcement reported.

Changes to redistrict the state for the association were approved, upping the total to 13, each being numbered.

Socially, the delegates and guests were invited to attend the bicycle races, to be guests for a luncheon at the brewery and a grand reception at the Oriental Hotel. The concluding event was a glittering reception at the Dallas Club.

Persistence paid off for Colonel J. Z. "Jozack" Miller of Belton. For a long time he had wanted the association to hold its convention in the "little town" of Belton, and he made one last passionate plea for the 1897 convention. The delegates gave "Jozack" his wish. The old colonel, former TBA president and highly regarded banker, was overjoyed.

Gainesville's C. C. Hemming came to the presidency of the 195-member TBA. The association noted the tragic death of Frank Dorsey, cashier of the City National Bank of Wichita Falls, in February, while defending the bank's property against a robber. "His death was speedily avenged. By what means it is hardly necessary to state, but we believe the manner in which justice was so speedily dealt met the hearty approval of all good citizens," the report said.

Belton, the smallest town in which a convention of the association had been held, rolled out the red carpet for the 13th convention in 1897, following the May meeting custom. Delegates were housed in the Belton House, a small but hospitable place, and the people of the town cooperated fully to make the convention a long-remembered one.

J. E. Longmoor of Rockdale began his administration as TBA head, and J. W. Butler of Clifton was elected secretary. Butler's service to the TBA was long and competent, and he became somewhat of a legend for the depth and quality of his service.

The association had a district system when the bankers met in Austin in 1898. President Longmoor reproved the delegates for not making the system work better; only a few meetings had been held. He plugged for state-chartered banks and a state clearinghouse system, and touched upon the war with Spain. "Let those who will, condemn the government for its course. I shall not be one of them," he declared.

Texas bankers were warned that efforts were being made in Washington to create a government Postal Savings Bank, viewed as "but another step toward a paternalistic form of government. The fertile brain of the wily politician is ever busy hatching out scheme after scheme, by means of which our government is to step into the shoes of her own people, and snatch from their hands, as it were, that which is rightfully theirs," the report said.

Fort Worth's M. B. Loyd was elected and installed in the presidency.

A Panhandle private banker, D. J. Young, cashier of the Canadian Valley Bank, prepared a paper on the problem of private banks. He advocated state chartering of banks. "Under the existing conditions, anyone having enough money to buy a safe and rent an office, can open a bank and place his capital at any figure he wishes to have it, although he may be entirely irresponsible, and not have a dollar of his capital paid in. There are hundreds of small towns in this state where it is impossible to have national banks, and the people have to depend on the honesty and integrity of the private bankers for the safety of their money," he suggested in calling for regulation and examination of the private institutions.

A lot of flag-waving oratory was heard at the 1899 San Antonio convention—the TBA's 15th. The Spanish-American War was fresh in everybody's mind. President Loyd welcomed ten ladies in attendance—the era of substantial attendance by by women was yet to come. San Angelo's George E. Webb was elected president.

At the end of the 19th century many of the members who were at Lampasas in 1885 were still active in banking, but the roll of passing years would soon remove many of the colorful Civil War colonels and silence their unique rhetoric.

To the founding fathers banking in Texas and the association owe a substantial debt. Just as any group inherits the rewards of sacrifices of pioneers, today's banking system in the state should, on occasion, glance back at these remarkable people, view them as performers in their day and times—often with pronounced human frailties—who molded a good organization into an instrument of service to banking and to Texas.

Marion State Bank, Marion, c. 1910—Building occupied by the bank and Waldorf Club Saloon.

Panhandle National Bank, Wichita Falls, prior to 1886.

Early street scene in Brady—Buildings opposite west side of the public square, including the bank-saloon and Len Lewis Hotel.

First National Bank, Canyon, in 1901—Note
the young tree protected by barbed wire.

The Muenster State Bank, Muenster—The
old and the new, 1940.

Frost National Bank, San Antonio—Exterior of Col. T. C. Frost's store, Texas Stockman and Farmer. Second floor is the Frost National Bank.

The teller area at the National Bank of Commerce of Dallas, located at the corner of Elm and Poydras in downtown Dallas, c. 1899.

The First National Bank of San Antonio is an architectural gem.

Delta National Bank, Cooper—Opened in August 1900 in temporary headquarters in the City Drug Store. Customers were given apples as a friendly gesture.

6
TEXAS BANKERS on the GO—
AND a TBA YELL!

Longhorn, shorthorn, cotton, wheat
Texas products can't be beat!
Texas, Texas, every day,
Texas, Texas, TBA!
TBA YELL USED IN 1905

THE BEGINNING of TBA post-convention travel started with a special excursion after the San Antonio meeting in 1893. Fifty-seven people boarded the train for Laredo and then on to Monterrey. One banker described the trip: "By the light of the early dawn we opened our eyes with delight and wonderment upon a beautiful valley, circled by grand mountains, wherein lies the beautiful city of Monterrey. We were soon on the alert, that nothing might escape our eager sight, smell or taste. Now, as our tastes differed, some repaired to the little shops where mescal, wine, beer and other soothing liquids were dispensed for the great comfort of the weary traveler." They visited other exotic places, shopping as they went, buying everything. "I really believe if a Mexican had come along with a saw mill and said it was hand made that some of our party would have purchased it," he wrote in his journal. Perhaps gaudy evidence of that first TBA excursion could still be found in many grand homes of descendants of these banker tourists.

Texas bankers enjoy travel. There have been excursions to Havana, beginning as early as 1902. The first boat trip to the ABA convention was in 1922 when 225 Texas bankers went to New York City via the Cuban city, taking an extra week for the trip and splendid cruise. The same type of boat excursion was taken in 1928 at the peak of economic prosperity before the collapse of 1929.

Texas bankers have traveled together by train to all sorts of places. And in recent years the group tours of the TBA have included many foreign lands.

A group of Texas bankers went by special train to the Lewis and Clark Centennial Exposition in Portland, Oregon, in 1905. They toured the Pacific Northwest area, including Yellowstone, Spokane and Seattle. Each excursionist wore a "duster and white cap—labeled TBA." It was a preppy group for 1905.

No, they didn't sing the "Eyes of Texas" as that song was yet to be written. But whether asked or not, according to the report, the group, upon the slightest provocation, gave its Texas yell, the first of any state bankers association. It was Texas, Texas, TBA! all the way.

On another occasion the bankers would pile out of the train at its various stops with railroad crew hats, properly identified.

Yes, history is made up of many things—especially in Texas.

7
THE TBA and the
TURN of the CENTURY

*The time has passed when a Texan's chief pride lay in knowing it was
the largest state in the Union.*
H. P. HILLIARD, TBA president, 1902

THE NEW CENTURY ushered in a new generation of leaders. The 20th provided a new beginning for Texas and its bankers.

A remarkable growth in population placed the state sixth in the United States with a count of 3,048,710.

Signs were emerging that the public and its representatives in Austin were now taking a different view of banking and business.

At the Fort Worth convention in 1900 President Webb rejoiced "over the generally prosperous conditions for which our citizens are justly proud." He was exuberant that memberships in the association had increased to 246.

The TBA's momentum for concerted action on many issues carried forward to the 17th convention in Houston in 1901. President F. F. Downs of Temple urged the delegates to go on the excursion to the "recently discovered Beaumont oil fields,

Signs were emerging that the public and its representatives in Austin were now taking a different view of banking and business.

The gushing oil stirred the imagination of all.

Spindletop. . . ." Five coaches carried 125 delegates on the special train from the Southern Pacific station. Bankers gawked at the spectacle! They saw "100 oil derricks at Gladys City. The Star and Crescent well was released for the benefit of the visitors and obligingly 'gushed oil to a height of 75 feet' to the amazement and wonder of the visitors." Beaumont bankers entertained the guests.

Money!

The gushing oil stirred the imagination of all. The front runner of the great oil industry of Texas was witnessed by the people who handled money. They were enthralled with the potential for economic development.

The violent hurricane of 1900 sneaked up on the island city of Galveston on Saturday morning, September 8, after being "lost" at sea for several days as a tropical disturbance. The horror of the next 24 hours was indescribably severe—the lowest estimate of loss of life at 5,000, 3,600 buildings destroyed, with water sweeping across the island in areas "leaving nothing but death and desolation in its path." When Sunday morning dawned on the stricken Galveston, 20 percent of the population had been lost in the 12-hour span of terror. Word spread through Texas and the world; aid began to pour in as the city counted and buried its dead, but it was not until a full survey of the damage had been made that the severity of the situation became known. In all of this citizens maintained an indomitable will—"no suggestion that Galveston should be abandoned and the years of effort wasted." No part of the city escaped damage; banks, public buildings, homes—one half of the base for taxes destroyed— all suffered. Bankers joined in the work of rebuilding a stricken city from its ruins.

When Texas bankers returned to Galveston in March 1902—only 18 months after the storm—they marveled at the progress the city had made, rising to virtual restoration. On the day the bankers arrived, the citizens of the city voted for a massive seawall to be built as protection against future storms.

Local bankers and citizens showed the delegates the toll of the storm and the recovery. Photographs showed the damage, including the serious wreckage of Moody's Bank downtown at 22nd and Strand.

President Hilliard of Austin addressed the delegates. His remarks typified the change of TBA emphasis and its new crop of leaders. The association had established a bank money order system for its members—a first—offsetting some of the express business and post offices. Convention speakers included persons not engaged in banking. The association took up the cudgel in behalf of a member bank, Citizens National in Tyler, in a suit over a bill of lading and retained counsel to represent the bank.

Bankers were urged to participate in the 1903 St. Louis World's Fair, the Louisiana Purchase Exposition, "to get Texas before the world."

Hilliard urged reestablishment of the Bureau of Statistics and History, and ample funds to support its activities, observing that the children of Texas need to be taught "the resources and capabilities of the several sections of the state." Said he, "The time has passed when a Texan's chief pride lay in knowing it was the largest state in the Union. . . . The day of the 'longhorn' in Texas has passed. The time is gone when the credit of the cowman is measured by the coarseness of his oath or the efficiency of the cowboy by the height of his boot heels or the diameter of his spur rowels.

"I have seen in my 22 years in Texas the prairie schooner, drawn by 36 mules, give

The Great Galveston Storm in 1900 damaged many of the city's banking houses. Moody's Bank, for example, was hard hit. (Courtesy Rosenberg Library, Galveston, Texas)

way to the 10-wheel Mogul and the train of 60-ton cars. The covered wagon by the Pullman car for long distances; while for local transportation, the electric car, the rubber-tired buggy and the automobile now do the work formerly left to the horse, the mule or the ox. I have seen the tent of the buffalo hunter give way to the box house of the squatter, and this, in turn to the substantial home of the modern farmer. Where many of you now live in your palatial homes in the prosperous cities of the Panhandle, or of Western Texas, surrounded by all that 'civilizes and embellishes mankind,' but a few short years ago the rank thistle nodded in the wind and the wild fox dug his hole unscared.

"The Indian whoop is heard no more. The buffalo are gone. The man with the hoe has taken the place of the one, while the shorthorn and Jersey have supplanted the other. I have seen interest rates drop from 5 percent per month to the same rate per annum," the TBA president reported.

His masterful address contained considerable humor: "Some years ago a Kentuckian, filled to overflow with the boast of 'pretty women, fast horses and good whisky,' visited one of the European countries, and, when introduced to the prime minister, said: 'I am from Kentucky, sir.' 'Kentucky, Kentucky. O, yes, that is where the gentlemen sit in chairs, put their feet on the mantel and spit in the fire. O, yes, I am glad to meet you, sir.'

"I would see Texans imbued with an esprit . . . which would make every man feel it is his duty to his state to cherish those sentiments and practice those virtues which would make her citizenship recognized and respected as exemplars and patrons of education and liberality. We should be liberal and not prone to criticise," he concluded.

The association continued to grow, reaching 400 and giving it a rank of fifth in the country among banking associations, led only by New York, Pennsylvania, Illinois and Missouri. The membership entitled the TBA to eight representatives in the ABA convention.

Another statistic catching the attention of the delegates was the report that Texas had achieved first rank among the states in the number of new national banks established since the change in capital requirements in 1900. In the previous 14 months 94 national banks and 44 private banks had been established.

The report proclaimed: "Texas has astonished the world with her oil discovery."

J. E. McAshan, the Houston banker-orator, became TBA president. Secretary J. W. Butler happily announced that 325 people were attending the convention, the largest to date.

After the convention 150 of the delegates, including many ladies, left by train for New Orleans, and on to Havana, Cuba, for four days of vacation on the island, stopping at Key West going and coming.

The political climate for banking legislation appeared to be improving, and the delegates again endorsed the idea of state banks and urged Governor Joseph Sayers to include it in his call for a special session of the legislature.

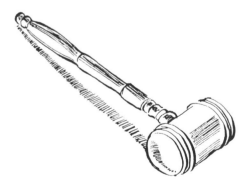

8

INCHING ALONG—
MOMENTUM for STATE BANKING
and the ROLE of the TBA

*We favor the submission of a constitutional amendment authorizing
the charter of state banks. . . .*

PLATFORM PLANK OF THE DEMOCRATIC PARTY OF TEXAS, 1902

THE BIG BREAK for the establishment of state-chartered banks came in 1902. The Democratic party, meeting in Galveston, adopted a platform plank in its campaign document to put the issue to a vote of the people.

The plank stated: "We favor the submission of a constitutional amendment authorizing the charter of state banks of discount and deposit under restrictions and regulations for the protection of stockholders and depositors, similar to those governing national banks." Word of the favorable action was widely circulated.

TBA Secretary Butler of Clifton, who had just established *The Texas Banker*, published the first issue in July 1902. Butler, an innovator in many respects, promoted the journal as previously authorized without expense to the TBA "to keep the members advised of the work of the association." The journal was put to good use in spreading the word to bankers.

In compliance with the party's platform, Governor Lanham, the last of the Civil War veterans to serve as chief executive, submitted the issue to the legislature.

The proposed amendment authorized the incorporation of corporate bodies with banking and discount privileges and provided for a system of state supervision, regulation and control; stockholder liability was included; branching was prohibited. The latter provision created some opposition and controversy.

Nevertheless, with the strong support of the TBA and its legislative committee headed by Colonel A. P. Woolridge, the general assembly passed the bill in both houses by resounding majorities.

But it was not until 1904 that the people of Texas had the opportunity to vote on the proposed amendment. Much work was left to be done; the TBA was geared to do the job.

Meanwhile, the entire banking community of Texas was saddened by the death of James F. Miller in Gonzales, July 3, 1902, at age 69. The first president of the TBA, he had participated in its activities from the beginning and was a powerful advocate of banking development. The former congressman was dead on the eve of the association's long-sought victory for a dual banking system in Texas.

The colorful J. E. McAshan, TBA president, held the office in a critical year. He began his banking experience as an errand boy in T. W. House's Houston bank, Sep-

The colorful emblem of office of the president
of the TBA was worn as a badge of honor,
beginning in 1903, when a gold pin for past
presidents was also approved.

tember 9, 1872. He knew how to use his ability and influence to bring about positive
action by the legislature. He had distinguished himself by leading the effort against
legislation in Congress to permit branch banks and the issuance of asset currency. His
advocacy of opposition led to concerted action by Texas in opposition to the bill. *The
Houston Post* gave McAshan high marks and suggested that he would make a good
governor; "the Houston gentleman . . . is not only a scholar and a gentleman, but
also a man of unlimited tact and rare executive ability, just such a man as Texas de-
lights in honoring," the newspaper said editorially.

Presiding at the 1903 convention in May, at Wood Lake between Sherman and
Denison, McAshan demonstrated his tact: He paid tribute to the 1902 legislature as
"a wise, intelligent, honorable body of men. They were always pleased to extend to
the members of this association every proper courtesy in the way of hearings and
assistance," he observed. He then gave accolades to Colonel Woolridge and the legislative committee for their good works. "Any members who attended the meeting
[executive committee session in Austin] . . . must have been impressed with the immense importance that the work of this association is, and always has been, to the
banks of Texas, and everyone must have been impressed with the necessity and value
of cooperation. Few people realize the vast political power of small banks. It is an
influence of an absolutely irreproachable character and for this reason, must be enormous," the president asserted.

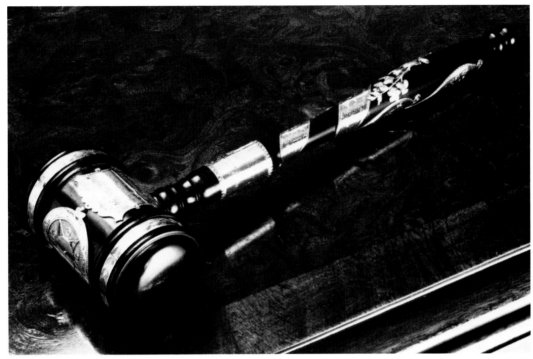

Since 1903 the TBA president has used this handsome gavel at each annual meeting. Made of solid ebony, it is embellished with enameled bluebonnets and gold plates. It has been used vigorously on occasion to preserve decorum at conventions when issues under discussion evoked heated debate.

Membership gains were reported by the association, now at 470, but the $5 dues had not been increased since 1885. Even so, the secretary was voted a salary of $400, with an additional $300 as special compensation.

A suitable gold badge for past presidents was approved.

Colonel Woolridge explained the proposed constitutional amendment, tracing the development of the anti-bank feeling in Texas since 1845. He attributed it to "the evils of bad banking in the old states" brought to Texas by the pioneers, and urged support and action for the amendment.

At each convention since 1903 the association's president has used the handsome gavel made of solid ebony, embellished with enamel bluebonnets and gold plates. Engraved on the gold trimmings is the name of each president from 1902 to 1926. Since 1926 there has been no space for more names.

At the conclusion of each convention the gavel is carefully returned to its place of safety to await another annual convention.

Who provided the gavel?

In 1902 the convention was presided over by H. P. Hilliard who was cashier of Austin's American National Bank. A short time later he moved to St. Louis to head a new bank. But he remembered the TBA, returned to the 1903 convention and presented the gavel to the association. It bears this engraved label: "To the Texas Bankers Association with grateful recollections of H. P. Hilliard, ex-president, St.

Louis, May, 1903." In presenting the gavel Hilliard told the delegates, "I am desirous that you should have some tangible proof and evidence of my affection for you."

In 1903 there were two commemorative Louisiana Purchase Exposition gold dollars at the top of the gavel head and end of the handle, but evidently through the wear and tear imposed on a gavel when conventions are spirited, the gold dollars disappeared long ago.

The story is told that at a hotly-contested session in San Antonio the TBA president rapped with the gavel so hard that it lost its head—for the moment—during the parliamentary tangle. With the violent whack by the presiding officer to restore order, the head flew off and landed in the vacant front rows; fortunately no delegate or guest was wounded by the flying hunk of ebony!

As has been said many times of the gavel: "If this piece of gold- encrusted ebony had the power of speech, what convention tales it could tell!"

The presidency of A. V. Lane of Dallas further confirmed the new type of TBA leader. A native of New Orleans, he had received a Ph.D from Vanderbilt University in 1882 and had taught mathematics at The University of Texas before entering banking in 1888.

For the first time delegates voted to hold the 1904 convention in El Paso—the most important city between Fort Worth and Los Angeles, the invitation noted. A rapidly growing place, El Paso had a population of 35,000 and was described as a city that "can give visitors any kind of a time they are looking for, regular or short order, at any hour of the day and night."

9

BOLL WEEVIL BLUES—
BUGS on the SQUARE

The first time I saw the boll weevil, he was settin' on the Square. . . .
"THE BOLL WEEVIL SONG," folk tune in the Cotton Belt

THE COTTON BOLL WEEVIL HAD INVADED Texas and was a major subject of discussion at the 1903 convention. One speaker, deploring the spread of the harmful insect, avowed: "You who have not contended with that bug, little know the disaster that awaits you in case he gets full away here. An old, gray-headed boll weevil, with his wife, can start out in April, and show you up a family of over 12 million grandchildren and great-grandchildren in October. That is fact. . . . A gentleman who is well informed about them told me he had immersed one of them in water for over 12 hours and he could not drown him. He put him in whisky for 15 minutes, and when he got over his jag he was just as well as he ever was. There are but two ways to kill a boll weevil. One way is to catch him with a hammer, like you would a hickory nut. The other is to put him in a fire and burn him up. We are in a dilemma."

Indeed! Many bankers and business people knew the value of cotton as well as the farmers. In spite of other serious matters before the convention and the need for funding the program of the TBA, delegates appropriated $500 to be used to fight the invader. After all, Texas's cotton empire provided an economic base of major proportions. Whatever happened to it happened to 70 percent of the population who depended upon it one way or another.

An alarming development took place in 1892 when the boll weevil was found near Brownsville. The pesky insect, moving across the Rio Grande with the development of cotton in the Brownsville area, began its triumphant march across Texas and the Cotton Belt to the Atlantic, normally advancing about 50 miles per year. By the early 1900s most of the cotton-growing region of Texas had been infested. In some areas of east Texas the losses ran as high as 90 percent. By 1911 the battle against the weevil was producing results, and the TBA was a major factor in the fight. Meanwhile Texans and other cotton belt states were singing the "Boll Weevil Song," a folk tune that had many versions. Obscure in its origin, it had pathos in its many verses:

OH, THE BOLL WEEVIL IS A LITTLE BLACK BUG,
COME FROM MEXICO THEY SAY,
COME ALL THE WAY TO TEXAS JUST A LOOKIN' FOR A HOME.
THE FIRST TIME I SAW THE BOLL WEEVIL,
HE WAS SETTIN' ON THE SQUARE.
THE NEXT TIME I SAW THE BOLL WEEVIL, HE HAD ALL HIS FAMILY THERE.
JUST LOOKIN' FOR A HOME, JUST LOOKIN' FOR A HOME.

Other verses told of the devastation to the farmer, merchant and banker by the seemingly indestructible insect.

Texas Bankers Association Tour, New York City, 1907, at the ABA Convention—Members and spouses wear bibs at the banquet. Inscription on back of the photo: ". . . believe this was at Del Monicos or Shanleys. Banquet given by Samuel Morse, steamship owner." (Courtesy Institute of Texan Cultures)

PART FOUR

Watershed Years for Banking and the TBA

1
VICTORY at the POLLS—
TBA WINS its MAJOR GOAL

*If all members would cooperate when a united front is desirable, this association would
indeed be a power.*
J. W. BUTLER, TBA secretary

THE EPOCHAL YEAR FOR BANKING in Texas was 1904, for it was on November 4
that the voters ratified the constitutional amendment to permit the State of Texas to
charter banks. The favorable vote was substantial.

At the El Paso convention in May 1904, delegates, led by President Lane, gave a
strong push to the idea. After electing W. H. Rivers of Elgin as president, delegates
felt the membership, now at nearly 600 of the 684 banks in Texas, should go home
and push for favorable action at the polls. They did exactly that.

The Democrats at their state convention had endorsed the proposed amendment
to charter state banks. The issue became a partisan matter when the Republicans
opposed it. *The Dallas News* published the Republican platform which described the
bank issue as an attempt to "saddle a wild cat currency upon our people." Earlier the
same newspaper had reported the favorable action by the Democrats. Also, the Texas
Bar Association gave its support to the proposed amendment. *The Houston Chronicle*
endorsed the amendment editorially, commenting that "it . . . will have the support
of the wide-awake and far-seeing business men of Texas." Bankers were urged to clip
the editorial and ask their local newspapers to print it.

When the joint resolution had been adopted by both houses of the Texas legislature in 1903, its Section 2 required the governor to give notice for submission of the
resolution to the vote of the people at the next regular election.

Texas voters in the November 1904 general election gave the TBA a major vic-

Texas voters in the
1904 general election
gave the TBA a major
victory.

tory—one that had been its principal goal since the formation of the association. Henceforth, Texas would have a provision for state-chartered banks in its constitution. The next important hurdle was to get the legislature to enact appropriate legislation under the new amendment.

Telling the good news to all the bankers, *The Texas Banker* in its December 1904 edition hailed the accomplishment. TBA secretary and journal editor, J. W. Butler, summarized the favorable vote this way: "Much credit for the success of the measure is due to the metropolitan press of the State, who gave much space in timely editorials for 10 days preceding the election, enlightening the public mind. . . . If all members would cooperate when a united effort is desirable, this association would indeed be a power." He concluded by congratulating the bankers for their unity and work.

2
STRUCTURING a
STATE BANKING SYSTEM

Let them be undisturbed!
CRY OF THE "OLD BULLS" AGAINST PRIVATE BANK REGULATION, 1905

COLONEL SAM WEBB, TBA treasurer, member of the Texas House of Representatives and Albany banker, prepared a bill to provide for carrying out the amendment. Some felt the statute should be framed after the Missouri law and considerable controversy developed as to the specifics. Serious objection was raised to the suggestion that private banks be regulated.

It was hoped and believed that the legislature convening in Austin in January 1905 would quickly enact a banking bill. The TBA anxiously awaited the introduction of the bills. Governor Lanham urged the legislators to move with caution. Webb's bill was widely discussed, because it provided for private bank regulation. At some of the district meetings the "old bulls" of the TBA rose to urge the association to avoid taking part in efforts to regulate private banks, noting that the TBA had always preserved harmony among its membership. "Let them be undisturbed," was the cry. Some said the constitutional amendment had been silent on private banks, and that had been taken in good faith to get private-banker support for the state-chartered banks.

As the furor heightened Representative Webb stood his ground that all banks should be incorporated to protect the interest of the depositor and the public. The process halted in the House; the Senate moved next. Senator Thomas B. Love of Dallas put together the bill that finally became law. His bill, as did the Webb proposal, called for the regulation of private banks as well as state banks. It created trust companies. But the private bankers refused to budge on regulation. Their strong battle against the proposal resulted in its elimination from the bill as finally passed. It did, however, require the private banks to use the word unincorporated in parentheses with their name.

Anxious moments prevailed among the TBA leadership as the banking bill languished in the legislature. The membership was urged to make their views known, no effort was spared, and action finally came. The legislature approved the bill before adjourning *sine die* and made it effective August 14, 1905.

The new statute provided for banks of deposit and discount, savings banks and trust companies. Certificates were to be issued by the secretary of state. Five or more people, three of whom had to be residents of Texas, with a minimum capital of $10,000 in towns of 2,500 or more, could be granted a charter. Double liability on stock was provided. The new law specifically denied bank branches. Instead of creating a banking department, the legislators economized by giving the task of bank supervision to the commissioner of agriculture, insurance, statistics and history, with instructions that each bank under his jurisdiction be examined at least annually, for which he was allowed an extra $500. Four bank examiners were to be employed at $2,000 each, plus travel expenses.

The voters and legislators restored state-chartered banking in Texas after a period of 30 years. Writing of the events, Dr. Carlton said: "The principle of publicly regulated banks had become thoroughly established in America, and in Texas."

3

CHARTER PROLIFERATION—
THE LINE FORMED EARLY

The growth of the state banking system in Texas during its first five years was spectacular.
JOSEPH M. GRANT and LAWRENCE L. CRUM, in their history

T HE NEW LAW ushered in a period of feverish bank chartering activity, for the pent-up demand for state banks throughout Texas was now ready to be accommodated, and the line for bank charters began to form early.

In their important book, *The Development of State-Chartered Banking in Texas*, Joseph M. Grant and Lawrence L. Crum give a vivid description of this activity; many sought to be issued the first charter. "August 13 fell on Sunday. The secretary of state announced that the department would not be open on that day but that charters could be filed after 8:30 a.m. on the next day, Monday, August 14. The secretary also stated that any charter filed under the name of the First State Bank of Texas would not be accepted, since the First State Bank of Texas, Hillsboro, had been chartered before the adoption of the Constitution of 1876. Although the bank had been chartered, the authors found no evidence that the bank ever opened for business."

Records indicate the first state bank in Texas chartered under the act of 1905 was the Union Bank and Trust Company of Houston, which opened August 21, 1905; it began with capital of $500,000. The second charter went to American Bank and Trust Company, also of Houston; third, American Bank and Trust Company, San Antonio; the Bank of Somerville got charter number four. All four filed on the first day, August 14, 1905.

W. J. Clay, the superintendent of banking, made the first official call for a statement of condition on September 30, 1905. There were 22 banks and seven trust companies with resources of $4,341,000 reported. One year after the law became effective, there were 115 banks and 21 trust companies in the state banking fold in operation in Texas. Trust companies were chiefly banking houses with minor trust business at first. There was one savings bank organized in the first activity.

Now Texas had three banking systems: national, state and private.

The TBA executive committee met at the Driskill in Austin on February 8, 1905, to structure a convention program for the meeting in Dallas in June. One of the proposals approved provided a separate session at the convention for trust companies and savings banks. R. H. Wester of San Antonio assumed the task of preparing for the trust business.

Another act of the legislature in 1905 was the depository bill, something the TBA had been promoting for years. Commented *The Texas Banker*: "No more will there be a hoarding of the cash in the state treasury, but the far better system of placing it in circulation through the banks under absolute safety, will prevail. . . . Surely the work of the Texas Bankers Association is effective."

When the delegates gathered in Dallas in June 1905, there was victory in the air. Too, the TBA had announced a post convention tour that would take the tourists to Portland, Seattle and Yellowstone Park. "Leave your old blue coat at home; put on your laughing jacket; attend the birthday party (the 21st for the TBA) and have a good time. . . . Pack your grip or trunk; come prepared. . . ." President W. H. Rivers wrote that the excursion was priced at $112, including rail, Pullman, meals, hotels, tours. (This was the tour which trotted out the famous TBA yell.)

Rivers proudly announced that association membership had reached 630, with more than 98 percent of the banks in Texas members. He told the assembly in the Opera House of the successful fight by the TBA for constitutional reform and adoption of the new state law, praising bankers who attended the Democratic convention in Houston to help get that body's endorsement. He praised the newly organized Southern Cotton Growers Association. Colonel Rivers had attended the meeting in New Orleans, and he urged bankers to cooperate to see that farmers received good prices for cotton. He warned that recessions are cyclical and voiced fear that the drive against the trusts in the country might trigger a down-turn in the economy.

Paying tribute to the founders of the TBA at Lampasas 21 years earlier, Rivers said: "These great men of far-seeing minds . . . planted a little shrub; when they had completed their work, they looked at it and said, 'It is not an acacia, neither is it a cedar plucked from the mountains of Lebanon; let us name it the Texas Bankers Association.' This little shrub stood there for a number of years apparently making slow progress in growth, yet these great men digged about it and nurtured it. All this time, however, it was sending out its roots and fastening itself so firmly that no financial storm could wreck it. After a while it began to grow and bloom. Today it stands an immense tree in full bloom, spreading its great fragrance all over the state of Texas, and every banker in every town and city can worship under its branches."

Wednesday, June 14, 1905, was another significant day for the TBA. Delegates in Dallas authorized its incorporation. Signers of the charter of incorporation were J. L. White, McKinney; C. A. Beasley, Houston; J. W. Butler, Clifton; Sam Webb, Albany; and W. H. Rivers, Elgin. At the time total assets were $1,783.84 in money.

Secretary Butler detailed the unique character of the TBA among state bankers' associations: Largest percentage of membership; first to inaugurate a bank money order; first to undertake protective work; first and only association publishing a monthly magazine (not owned by the TBA); first to hold a memorial service every convention; first to exhibit bank advertising collected from its members; first to make a feature of its annual reunion a tour or excursion for the pleasure of its members. He said the association was "pressing into the forest of new ideas," all the while increasing the usefulness of the organization and its practical benefits.

The association met for its 22nd convention in San Antonio in May 1906, with J. L. White of McKinney as president. Now the largest city in the state, San Antonio had a population of 93,000. Said White: "Near where we now stand the earth drank the blood of Texas martyrs, and this baptism of blood made Texas an independent republic, and was the stepping stone that made her one of the great states of the Union. Texas, now being the fifth state in the confederation of states, and it will be but a few years more until she will in population and wealth rival New York, the now empire state." He touched upon the San Francisco earthquake, "the calamity that came and for a moment caused our blood to congeal and our hearts to cease to pulsate, by its blackness and horror. . . ."

Speaking on the new banking law, the TBA leader admonished: "We see but one trouble, and that is the great multiplicity of small banks; that, I think, hangs as a menace over the future banking business of this state."

The TBA had pursued two innovative services. One was to have a detective to run down and convict forgers and swindlers "depredating upon members of this association." The other was an arrangement with a time lock expert to "clean and inspect and guarantee time locks for its members."

General William R. Hamby of Austin, who had succeeded his fellow-townsman, Colonel Woolridge, as chairman of the legislative committee, reviewed the workings of the new banking law. Said he, "Under the present law a state bank can do almost anything a national bank can do except issue money, and can do many things a national bank is prohibited from doing." Although the law had flaws, it was altogether desirable. Of the 89 banks chartered to that date, 39 were in the $10,000 capital range.

Although the association's structure was providing an effective service, there was not a full-time professional staff. The secretary, a banker, had to work many tedious hours to overcome the mountains of detail. J. W. Butler provided numerous innovations in the TBA programs, including preplanned conventions with topical subjects,

91

membership promotion and retention, publications and liaison with the now seven TBA districts. How he did all this and served as a bank cashier, later president, was an amazement then and now to anyone who knew the situation. Moreover, attendance at the conventions in recent years had ranged from 350 to 550, a far cry from the 31 delegates in 1885.

The first change was announced by Butler in the August 1906 issue of his privately owned and edited magazine. "With this issue," he wrote, "Mr. W. W. Windom, assistant secretary of the Texas Bankers Association, (of Farmersville), assumed the position of editor. . . . I desire that the monthly be continued, and I shall do all in my power to foster it." For five years he had prepared copy and other details necessary. Butler was overworked and tired; he had founded the magazine, *The Texas Banker*, without cost to the TBA as a personal project, not intended for personal profit. He spent "oft times weary hours at night preparing this magazine," he said. In assuming the editorship, Windom wrote that Butler's health was being threatened by his many responsibilities.

Currency control became a subject of major national discussion for the next six years, culminating in the establishment of the Federal Reserve by Congress in the Woodrow Wilson administration. Bankers in Texas and elsewhere had discussed the necessity for currency control. The issue took on major status when the ABA through its legislative committee recommended at its 1906 convention in St. Louis: "That a currency commission of seven members be appointed by the president and confirmed by the Senate, this commission to be non-partisan, the comptroller of the currency to be a member . . . and the other six members to be appointed."

The New York Bankers Association, along with others, feared the St. Louis convention might take a position contrary to theirs. They scheduled a special meeting prior to the ABA convention; each state association was invited to send one representative. TBA President C. A. Beasley of Houston appointed Edwin Chamberlain of San Antonio to represent Texas. There was concern that the New York bankers wished to concentrate more banking power in their domain, and the issue became a regional as well as a national concern. Many theories of currency control were advanced; the issue occupied the proceedings of nearly every banking meeting, including the TBA.

As a sideline of sorts *The Texas Banker* published a list of the world's richest people, headed by J. D. Rockefeller, who was listed at $600,000,000. Two South African gold and diamond moguls came in second and third, $500,000,000 and $400,000,000, respectively. Banker J. P. Morgan was down the list at $150,000,000; journalist Joseph Pulitzer, $20,000,000; and the last of the long list of multimillionaires was Queen Wilhelmina of Holland, $20,000,000, inherited. Observed the editor in Texas, "These stupendous figures. . . . Every great fortune in America can easily be traced to its beginnings of small savings."

Several changes were made at the May 1907 convention in Corpus Christi. President Beasley, with many others, acclaimed the services of Secretary Butler who announced that he must step down as elected secretary because of health and business demands. He was succeeded by Austin banker J. W. Hoopes, who was to make an everlasting imprint upon the TBA and banking.

There was concern that the New York bankers wished to concentrate more banking power in their domain, and the issue became a regional as well as a national concern.

Issues before the convention were the invasion of banking by express companies, insured bank deposits, railroad development, legal points in banking, safeguards for bills of lading, waterway improvements, legislative matters and labor-saving devices.

4
PROSPERITY and PANIC

The banks of Texas are in unusually good condition.
COMMISSIONER THOMAS B. LOVE, October 23, 1907

TEXAS BANKERS HAD BEEN REMINDED by Colonel Rivers in 1905 that a recession might be in the offing. The events of October 1907 proved the point that prosperity, generally prevalent since 1896, was not enduring. The Panic of 1907 hit like a prairie storm, striking a major trust company in New York City and the corporate giants, causing bank runs and stock market collapse. Near-total economic disaster was averted when the federal government deposited funds in the New York banks, and other banks came to the aid of the troubled institutions.

In Texas Thomas B. Love, state senator from Dallas credited with being the progenitor of the 1905 state banking law, had been named commissioner of insurance and banking on August 31, 1907. Sensing the desirability of allaying fears in Texas, he issued a statement October 23 which declared the banks "in unusually good condition." Noting that they had a third more cash on hand than a year previous, he concluded: "There is absolutely nothing in the Texas banking situation, so far as the state banks and trust companies are concerned, which should not inspire the usual degree of confidence in them." He also asserted that none of the Texas banks were involved with the Knickerbocker Trust Company failure in New York.

The short-lived panic abated, and Texans believed that the crisis was passing. But the situation in neighboring Oklahoma was eyed with concern. The governor of that state declared a banking holiday when banks were unable to secure adequate currency. Texas banks limited withdrawals, but many had to resort to money substitutes, such as scrip, during the money crunch in the 1907 cotton-marketing season. Bankers were frank with their customers; apparently the latter understood the money shortage dilemma and accepted good substitutes. The Panic of 1907 was soon over; confidence was restored. Commissioner Love reported that the banking damage in Texas was minimal. Two national banks closed, one temporarily; the other liquidated without loss to its depositors. Five state banks closed, three temporarily; about 12 private banks closed.

Liquidations rose to 23 during 1908. The crisis convinced those considering new charter applications to back off for a time. In 1907—before the panic—there were 147 new banks chartered, but only two charters were issued in the last three months of that year. Business picked up quickly, however; there were 606 state charters issued in 1908, and 584 state banks were in operation. Apparently the new opportunity for bank speculators had caused some banks to be established that were weak and marginal from the outset.

As Grant and Crum point out, "The growth of the state banking system in Texas during the first five years was spectacular." From August 14, 1905, through August 31, 1910, 636 charters were issued, with total resources of $69,497,041. Of the 636, 52 surrendered their charters during the five-year period, 12 never opened, and four became national banks; four merged, and 29 were liquidated. "Remarkably," Grant and Crum said, "only three banks failed, although another five institutions were closed temporarily. As far as can be determined, no depositor or creditor of a liquidated state bank lost any money."

5

DEPOSIT GUARANTY a REALITY: DISSENSION in the TBA RANKS

Why should the strong carry the weak?
ARGUMENT USED BY ANTI-BANK DEPOSIT MEMBERS, 1908

WHEN THE 1908 TBA CONVENTION assembled in Fort Worth in June, President Edwin Chamberlain, San Antonio banker, and the other delegates had the crisis of the previous few months—the Panic of 1907—in mind, and the convention program reflected their concerns. The first problem they had was to get to Fort Worth—high water and railroad washouts had severely limited travel. The southwest Texas crowd was stranded in Hillsboro, and they wired President Chamberlain that they would hold the convention there unless he dispatched a new locomotive and "built a bridge or two." The same lament came from the Panhandle contingent who asked that the convention "pass emergency measure providing aerial transportation for us. . . ."

The issue of insurance of bank deposits brought about a heated discussion as lively and timely as it was controversial.

Commissioner Love advocated guarantee of bank deposits. The issue of insurance of bank deposits brought about a heated discussion "as lively and timely as it was controversial," the report said. Before the delegates was the fact that Oklahoma had just passed its deposit guaranty law, and Kansas had one on the books. Bankers divided on the issue; one side argued that it was fallacious "to force the strong to carry the weak." The other asked, "Why is it communistic to tax banks for the protection of the people?"

Confusion reigned in the convention hall, one fellow demanding order so he could hear the debate. Chamberlain had difficulty in maintaining proper order. The tempest continued until the suggestion was made that, in the absence of a full membership in attendance, the secretary was to poll the entire list to vote yes or no on the question of guaranteeing bank deposits. Secretary J. W. (Fred) Hoopes, attending his first convention, must have considered resigning from his new office, but he held fast and polled the membership. TBA members voted "heavily against the proposal."

The movement was growing, however—and in a little more than a year the state had its deposit guaranty law on the books, a law that was to occupy TBA deliberations for years to come.

The idea first originated in New York in 1829, a statute that was later repealed. Other states tried it at one time or another. Congress had many bills under consideration after the Panic of 1907. Promoted by the Populist movement, the idea was not new. The TBA heard the proposal in 1889 when E. M. Longcope advanced it as a part of his argument for a state banking system. The Texas legislature faced the issue and rejected it, although the banking committee favored the bill. But the issue was so controversial that the bankers knew it would come up again for legislative consideration.

The association, polled in 1908, had a strong division within its membership on the issue. There were 210 who favored it; 282 were opposed. A cleavage between state and national banks surfaced in the poll. Most national banks opposed the deposit insurance idea which was strongly supported by the smaller banks. The larger banks found the idea objectionable because they would be taxed in one way or another to help the smaller ones. The battle became one of heroic proportion. *The Texas Banker* accused Love of using the proposal as political leverage. The Texas Democratic Party resolved in favor of deposit guaranty, and Governor Thomas M. Campbell, running for reelection, endorsed it. When the legislature convened in 1909, the stage was set for enactment of a bill. But the legislature locked over the issue; each house adopted its own version and refused to budge. Governor Campbell was determined to have a bill; he called the assembly into special session, threatening to keep the legislators in session all summer until a deposit guaranty law was enacted. After more furor the legislature produced a sort of compromise, enacting a law which offered the plan of insurance endorsed by the house or the bond plan preferred by the senate. The bill was sent to Governor Campbell on May 11. He affixed his signature on May 12, 1909.

Describing the bill in an article in 1974, Sam O. Kimberlin, Jr., TBA executive vice president, wrote: "The new law was lengthy and complex but, rather briefly, it required all state banks either to become members of the 'Depositors Guaranty Fund,' or to join the 'Depositors Bond Security System.' Under the former, the member banks paid mutual assessments into a central fund to be used to pay depositors their total amount on deposit in any member bank that failed. Under the latter, a surety bond equal in amount to the capital stock of the member bank was posted with the state. The law permitted three individuals, approved by their county judge, to execute the surety bond or to look into the financial strength of the individual sureties. National banks were permitted, but not required, to become members of either of these plans."

Private banks were eliminated from participating in the Depositors' Guaranty Fund but might, provided that they met certain requirements, protect their depositors by the Bond Security System.

The intensity of the controversy is demonstrated by the threatened move by state banks in 1908 to organize a State Bankers Association to promote the law. Commissioner Love favored the idea, but the TBA prevailed—no separate organization was created.

The law provided for bank assessments on average daily deposits at the rate of 1 percent at the beginning, later reduced to ¼ of 1 percent, until the Guaranty Fund reached $2,000,000. The Bond Security System required a bond insurance policy equal to the amount of the capital stock of the bank.

Most Texas banks joined the Guaranty Fund. The first report showed that as of August 10, 1910, a total of 541 banks preferred the Guaranty Fund, and only 43 selected the Bond Security System. As a result, the whole program fell under intense criticism. With the help of the TBA, the Texas legislature passed a repeal act, and Governor Dan Moody signed it February 11, 1927. The Texas experience was used in the next decade to argue against deposits of banks protected by federal insurance.

6

THE TBA THRIVES
as ISSUE-ORIENTED BANKERS
SUPPORT a BROADER INVOLVEMENT

It is our privilege and duty to contribute to the just solutions of these problems. . . .
W. H. FUQUA, TBA president, 1911

WHEN T. C. YANTIS OF BROWNWOOD assumed the TBA presidency in 1908, he took over at a turbulent time in the association's history. But conditions in Texas and the state of the association were good, he told the 1909 convention in Houston. "Texas is an open field for capital, with the assurance that every investment will bring large returns," he said. Texas was doing well in ranching, oil-production, fruit growing, truck farming and cotton. The TBA had 946 members.

There were national issues that loomed in the near distance to test the wisdom and judgment of bankers. Pending in Congress were such legislative matters as the tariff and the income tax. In Austin the lengthy sessions of the legislature had caused the assembly to be dubbed "The Great Political Convention."

The issue of deposit insurance had divided the association; as a consequence, no policy position was taken by the TBA on guaranty insurance. The political situation was uncertain, too. One of the forward steps during the year was the employment of S. W. Fisher of Austin as TBA attorney "to furnish members without cost his opinion on any legal question" and to represent the association. Another positive sign was the report of the TBA's districts; the system was in place and growing, having survived its shaky beginnings.

A spirited contest for president developed; two popular members, Judge O. E. Dunlap of Waxahachie and James W. Butler of Clinton, were in the race. Dunlap won in a close ballot, 143–139, for president in 1909–1910. There was additional discord as evidenced by the election of Tom Slack of Fort Worth for treasurer over Tom Nees of Nacogdoches.

The TBA was working through its currency committee with the ABA on currency studies and keeping up with developments in "matters that we have been asking for, for so many years."

The first decade of the 20th century brought Texas and the nation a mixed bag of opportunities and problems. For banking, the coming of the state banking system, deposit guaranty insurance, rapid expansion of banks and other economic conditions resulting from fast population growth, development of agricultural and industrial bases—and more—had attracted widespread attention. Tracking this progress—and often in the forefront—the association gained increasing respect for its performance. In the 25 years of the TBA's existence, the value of the organization had been clearly demonstrated in many categories, chiefly legislative and regulatory. In the beginning the meetings were largely gatherings of a few prominent bankers, many of them of Civil War vintage, where varied discussions were held with speakers talking of the glories of the past and predicting a great future. The social side of the meeting was stressed.

With the turn of the century a new type of banking leadership had emerged. Issue-oriented leaders, they were better trained for the demands of discount and deposit banking. They supported a broader TBA involvement in issues. The rapid expansion of Texas required its people to change many of their old concepts. There was, however, a strong feeling of camaraderie among the TBA officers, a hallmark of the earlier years.

The association leadership decided about 1908 to travel by rail as a group to the seven district meetings. Thus began the annual train movement each February until rail travel was no longer desirable, the journey later called the "Flying Squadron," a legendary event in TBA history.

Operating banks in Texas had become a fairly profitable enterprise. The Comptroller of the Currency reported that the average dividend on national bank capital in Texas in the decade ending 1905 was 9.09 percent; the U.S. figure was 7.55.

El Paso, the city of the TBA's 1910 convention, symbolized the type of progress that Texas cities and towns were making. Development in the Rio Grande Valley by water storage projects was impressive. There were many social amenities in the historic old city to entice convention delegates. One delegate, in promoting the El Paso convention site, declared that one of "its chief attractions is that it is farther away from home than any other city in the state."

The first decade of the 20th century brought Texas and the nation a mixed bag of opportunities and problems.

As Judge Dunlap opened the meeting in El Paso in May 1910, some of the major issues were currency control and the proposal to create the U. S. Postal Savings; the latter became a reality that year. Before leaving the city, delegates elected W. H. Fuqua of Amarillo as president. Fuqua was the first of the Panhandle area bankers to head the TBA.

He presided over the 1911 convention in Dallas, a meeting of significant import. Delegates established the *Texas Bankers Record*, the official journal of the association to the present time.

Fuqua told an amusing story, an incident he said related to Captain Schreiner of Kerrville, the pioneer banker of that area: "One of his old-time customers called in one day, and in response to a remark by the captain replied: 'Yes, it is nearly thirty years since I first opened an account with you. At that time, there was no bank nearer to me. There are plenty of them now, and they often talk business to me. I say to them, yes, boys, you have plenty of wet weather banks. When grass is good, plenty of rain, stock fat, you can let a fellow have more money than he wants, but what I want is a good dry weather bank—one that sticks right square to the cowman when the grass is short and the water holes dry, and takes chances on having an investment in tannery stock when spring comes."

"Now," said President Fuqua, "we have lots of this spirit of 'dry weather banking' among the bankers of Texas, and this staying with a customer when the hard times come is what has made so many strong banks in Texas today. It is one of the factors that is going to make the Postal Savings Banks in Texas only a small competitor with banks. We have been running 'dry weather' banks in one sense of the word—the literal one—up in the Panhandle for some time, but the rain has been bounteous recently and we are now hoping for better things."

The association leader endorsed the concept of a central banking system as a source of strength in times of stress. Admonishing the delegates, Fuqua said, "We meet here at an hour when the thought of the American people is in a ferment over the problems of the wise regulation of moneyed institutions. It is our privilege and our duty to contribute to the just solution of these problems. . . . I believe with that eminent scholar and profound publicist, Governor Woodrow Wilson of New Jersey, that wealth does not create public distrust or public jealousy; that the masses of men in this country honor in their fellows that large economic power that enables them to acquire wealth in a legitimate way, and use it in the way of large service." He urged the public to take the view that "capitalistic institutions" exist for the purpose of constructive service and were made necessary and "called forth by our unparalleled economic conditions and opportunities. . . ."

Speaking as one of the new generation of banking leaders, Fuqua said: "What we need in public life is a broad constructive statesmanship with larger powers of initiative, capable of grasping the full force of the great dissolution of old conditions and the breaking of the new day. We need now . . . in our public life men who can direct us in the great task before us of bringing forward all that is best and most enduring in our past; past ideals and conditions, and organizing them into the larger ideas and broader principles demanded by the present hour. Thus we shall build together our glorious past and our greater future, and the wealth of our country shall stand with

The "Flying Squadron" was one of the TBA's most popular features and a pleasant way of making the round of district meetings an-nually. The tour group is pictured at the rail-road station in Houston about 1909.

the beneficent rather than selfish ends as the star of its hope and purpose and grandly lead the happy millions of our countrymen to the realization of a worthier and better and larger life in that new and brighter and greater day for ourselves and the world whose dawning even now begins to adorn the eastern horizon."

The association, Fuqua said, was in a "flattering state of prosperity," through increased memberships and participation.

Another TBA milestone was passed when Hoopes, the Austin banker and elected secretary, found the duties of his office so involved with 1,193 members that it was "deemed advisable by me to personally secure and establish a permanent and independent office, which I have done, and I am now maintaining such an office in room 609, Scarborough building."

Although the action did not create a full-time professional staff, it was the first permanent home of the TBA in Austin. He documented the work of the busy office with impressive totals of mailings and other activities.

He paid a memorial tribute to Colonel W. J. B. Patterson, who had worked in the office as assistant and who had edited the *Texas Banking Journal*. Patterson's death was lamented by proper resolution for "his cheerful disposition, kind heart and close companionship." His loss had put a heavier burden on the secretary, and it was obvious that the association was moving toward a staffed headquarters. Hoopes reported that $8,538.15 was the cost of running the office, including his salary of $1,800, protective rewards, stamps, telegraph, printing, etc. What a bargain for the bankers of Texas! The secretary's office expenses were sustained by a cash balance of $12,668.34.

The first civic project sponsored by the TBA was the Corn Club. Each member was asked for $1.00 to support the club. Prizes were awarded to the champion corn growers of Texas, including a trip to Washington and New York or a year in "A&M College with expenses paid." The banker response was less than sensational, with only $360.68 received. The difference was made up, President Fuqua individually paying over $700.

By resolution the delegates approved a currency plan advanced by U. S. Senator Nelson W. Aldrich of Rhode Island, chairman of the National Monetary Commission, identical with the position of the ABA, with such amendments as had been proposed by the Currency Commission. The Aldrich plan envisioned a national currency system and other ideas for a central bank for monetary control. The resolution was not quickly adopted, however; one delegate moved that it be laid upon the table because of the lack of opportunity for opposition to the Aldrich plan to be heard. The delegates insisted that the issue was too important to be put aside. On a viva voce, only the banker who made the motion voted to table. A rising vote then approved the resolution on currency control.

After the controversy had ended President Fuqua thanked the delegates for the opportunity to head the association, an experience he described as the May and June time of his life, "the spring that will ever be green."

In an unusual gesture he placed in nomination the name of his successor, General William R. Hamby of Austin, "a man who has lived a life which is open, and one that no one can say anything derogatory about." Hamby was elected by acclamation and escorted to "the president's seat amid continuous cheering." The new TBA president had come to Texas in 1853 and had served in the Confederate army and cavalry. Having been born in Tennessee, he returned there and became adjutant general, but eventually came back to Texas and was made editor of the Austin *Statesman* in 1882. He also represented Travis County in the legislature. He was one of the organizers of the American National Bank and later was an officer of Citizens Bank and Trust Company. His service to the TBA was immeasurable.

A rising vote then approved the resolution for currency control.

7
TEXAS BANKERS RECORD ESTABLISHED

I believe every one of you should stand behind the proposal that an organization of the magnitude of ours is entitled to publish and own a periodical which shall have dignity, which shall have character, which shall be representative of this eminent association.
WALTER FLAVIUS MCCALEB, author-banker, 1911

THE TEXAS BANKERS RECORD (*TBR*), one of the foremost banking journals, began publication in September 1911 as the official organ of the TBA. How it began was recorded in the convention proceedings and in a special issue observing its 50th anniversary in 1961. Editor William A. Philpott, Jr., having a special flair for writing and history, told of the incidents surrounding its creation.

"On a bright May day in 1911 (the 18th to be exact) the *Texas Bankers Record* came into being," he wrote. "Birthplace was Dallas, during the closing hours (say, about 11:55 a.m.) of the 27th annual convention, Texas Bankers Association. The enabling act was a motion made by W. F. McCaleb, president, West Texas Bank and Trust Company, San Antonio."

With President Fuqua in the chair, "The nearness of the hour to final adjournment of a long convention caused the delegates to be restless and impatient. They were weary and hungry—and, perhaps, thirsty besides. Finally Walter McCaleb gained the attention of President Fuqua and was recognized," Philpott recalled.

Said McCaleb: "For more than a year . . . I have been talking a bankers' journal, which shall be representative of the bankers of this state, which shall be published under the auspices of our association," he began.

"I shall simply put the motion briefly and frankly. I believe every one of you should stand behind the proposal that an organization of the magnitude of ours is entitled to publish and own a periodical which shall have dignity, which shall have character, which shall be representative of this eminent association," McCaleb stated.

"Therefore . . . I desire to move you, sir, to this effect: That a committee of three be appointed, with plenary powers to bring into existence a journal which shall be officially issued under the auspices of the secretary's office. . . . I do not see how anybody can offer objection to the proposition, unless the question of expense be raised . . . ." McCaleb's motion was quickly seconded by Howell E. Smith, cashier, First National Bank, McKinney. Some parliamentary discussion followed, then the question was put formally. The vote was 99 ayes and 8 noes. Selected to serve as a committee to establish the journal were Secretary Hoopes, chairman, with McCaleb and Nathan Adams of Dallas. No time was lost in planning, and the first issue was published in September 1911—and the magazine has appeared each month since then.

From the outset, the *TBR* insisted on even-handed news of banking in Texas, and in issue number one is this significant sentence: "Nothing save what appears as advertising is paid for in this journal."

101

THE Texas BANKERS RECORD

VOLUME ONE   AUSTIN, TEXAS   NUMBER ONE

OFFICIAL PUBLICATION
TEXAS
BANKERS
ASSOCIATION

Official Report of the U. S. Cotton
Crop for the Year Ending
September 1, 1911
By Henry S. Hester, Secretary New Orleans
Cotton Exchange

The Numerical System
As Recommended by the American Bankers
Association

Relations Between Banks and Life
Insurance Companies
By R. C. Burton, State Insurance Actuary

SEPTEMBER, 1911

Cover page of the first issue of the *Texas Bankers Record*, 1911.

102

Mrs. Edgar L. Steck, first editor of the *Texas
Bankers Record*, published since 1911.

TBA secretary Hoopes, as vice president of the Austin National Bank, knew nothing about journalism or the intricacies of a publishing plan; he relied on the counsel of friends in the newspaper field. He did first things first: selection of an editor and a printing house.

Hoopes made the right decision, Philpott affirmed. As editor he selected a person who knew about bankers and banking, besides having experience as a feature story writer for newspapers. She was Miss Lena Riddle, who for several months had been chief clerk in the State Banking Department in Austin under Commissioner Ben L. Gill. She resigned the clerkship and undertook the establishment of the magazine. Her name appears as managing editor of the first issue of the *Record*, and she selected the name. Earlier financial publications had priority on other titles: *The Banker, The Texas Banker* and *The Texas Bankers Journal.*

The Austin printing company, the Firm Publishing House, was selected as printer. In 1912 Edgar L. Steck bought control of the firm, changed the name to E. L. Steck, a publishing, printing, bookbinding and stationery business. The Steck firm printed the magazine until 1915, when the publication was removed to Dallas and printed by the Egan Company.

Miss Riddle, described by Philpott as a "woman fine in mind and heart," edited the *TBR* for the first year. Mr. Steck was "a likely and eligible bachelor—so Lena Riddle became Mrs. Edgar Steck when the *Record* was just 12 months old," Philpott wrote.

Philpott was a young newspaperman and was invited by Miss Riddle to succeed her as editor of the *TBR*. He put it this way: "In the summer of 1912, when Miss Lena . . . said to me, a half-baked, garden-variety newspaper man: 'Phil, Edgar Steck, bless his heart, wants me to marry him this autumn. I want you to accept the editorship of the *Record*. . . .' She said yes to Edgar and I say yes to Miss Lena."

In 1961, after being editor for 49 years, Philpott wrote that the staff was composed of three people: Philpott, Milton Boswell, associate editor since 1939 (later editor when "Mr. Phil" retired), and Mrs. J. O. Tyler ("Miss Lillian"), associate secretary of the TBA.

When Philpott retired from the TBA in 1964, Milton Boswell succeeded him as editor. Boswell retired in 1981 and was succeeded by George Seagert.

"The magazine has survived one print-shop fire, one city flood, one printers' strike, three depressions, and three wars—and has never missed one issue," Philpott wrote.

The father of the idea, Walter Flavius McCaleb, was one of the literary and banking leaders of the period. He had earned degrees at The University of Texas and the University of Chicago, receiving his Ph.D. in 1900 as a member of Phi Beta Kappa. For a time he edited the *Philadelphia Public Ledger.* His first banking position was president of Continental Bank in Cleveland, Ohio. He returned to Texas and held top banking positions; when the Federal Reserve Bank of Dallas opened, he was vice chairman of the board. He was also a prolific writer of Texas history.

The *Record* had a literary and banking giant to push for its creation. Although the delegates were in a hurry to get home from the convention in 1911, they had the good judgment to listen to McCaleb and to follow his leadership, resulting in a magazine that has met the test of time in an impressive way. Beginning with Miss Lena Riddle, each editor—William A. Philpott, Jr., Milton E. Boswell and George H. Seagert—has handled it gently.

She said yes to Edgar and I said yes to Miss Lena.

104

8
CURRENCY CONTROL:
WILSON GETS SUPPORT
from TEXAS

We suffer from crises because of our unscientific system of currency.
WOODROW WILSON, 1912

THE YEAR 1912 WAS A HISTORIC ONE for Texas and the nation—and for banking. Three candidates for the presidency of the United States were on the record for currency reform. William H. Taft, seeking reelection on the Republican ticket, said: "Banking and currency reform is necessary to the interests of the people." Theodore Roosevelt, trying to recapture the presidency as a third-party Bull Moose Republican, said: "There must be a revision of our currency laws, because to leave them as they are means to incur liability of business disaster." And Governor Woodrow Wilson, the nominee of the Democrats, had this view: "The question of currency reform is very near to the prosperity of the country. We suffer from crises because of our unscientific system of currency." Wilson won the election. A new era for banking and currency reform was launched.

Colonel E. M. House of Austin had been one of the early promoters of Wilson. Son of a leading Houston private banker, merchant and plantation owner, Thomas W. House, he was able to use his wealth and political acumen to throw the 40 votes of Texas behind Wilson at the Baltimore convention. A close relationship developed. Wilson scored a heavy victory over Taft in Texas. Colonel House declined any appointive office from Wilson, but the president depended upon his advice, and many of the events of the Wilson presidency were closely related to the role of the powerful Texan. House believed that the new president's commitment to currency reform and a system of central banking was valid; he supported it and worked to keep the idea on track.

A continuing issue with the TBA, currency reform was the major point of discussion when the association met in San Antonio in 1912. President Hamby, ill at the time, was unable to attend the convention; others presided. After recovering, the general prepared his remarks for publication in the *TBR*.

"We are all agreed that our currency and banking laws are defective and that some remedial financial legislation is demanded, but like all God-fearing people we are somewhat divided on the plan of salvation. . . . It is earnestly hoped the discussion of the currency question will give to our country a banking system that is absolutely sound and scientifically elastic; one that will maintain unimpaired the integrity and the independence of the individual bank," he avowed.

The seeds for a central bank for the nation were being sown; Texans were helping to bring the idea to fruition. The battle would soon be decided.

House believed that the new president's commitment to currency reform and a system of central banking was valid; he supported it and worked to keep the idea on track.

105

9
TEXAS WOMEN
BANKERS ASSOCIATION—
ANOTHER FIRST for the TBA

We want it distinctly understood that we are not agitators.
ANNIE L. ALLEN, Texarkana banker, 1913

THE 1912 TBA CONVENTION authorized the formation of a Texas Women Bankers Association, an organization that flourished for six years as the first organization of its type.

Banking in Texas in the early years was strictly a male role. But the situation was changing. In 1912 the *TBR* featured women officers of banks who had established a reputation for good banking in the business world of men. More of these female bankers were taking part in the TBA convention. At the San Antonio convention that year the "idea of a Texas Women Bankers Association, to be an auxiliary to the Texas Bankers Association, was conceived by the progressive women in attendance. . . ." After consulting informally with the TBA officers, the first bankers' association for women was created. Elected as first president was Miss Lena Riddle, the *TBR* editor. Mrs. S. R. Coggin of Brownwood was named vice president; Miss Robbie Cariker, Cushing, second vice president; Miss Kate Mitchell, Franklin, secretary; Miss Minnie Hester, Lexington, treasurer.

After consulting informally with the TBA officers, the first bankers' association for women was created.

A committee to draft the constitution was named. The women bankers voted to meet in May 1913 at the TBA convention in Galveston. Dues for the group were set at $2. General Hamby applauded the organization: "We give the ladies a cordial welcome and shall watch with signal interest the evolution of their usefulness." The purpose of the new organization was to study the banking laws and to learn more about banking. From the outset they gave much attention to the school savings bank plans, the automatic thrift club for working girls to "enable girls to accrue a bank account who would never in the world do so at the rate of ten cents a week."

"In the very beginning we want to correct any erroneous impression that may be abroad that we are seeking more rights. We want it distinctly understood that we are not agitators," Miss Annie L. Allen, Texarkana, secretary in 1913, pointed out.

The Texas Women Bankers Association prospered until World War I, when the difficulties of attending meetings and being away from their banks apparently caused the organization to disband at the TBA convention in Galveston in 1918. The women bankers of Texas stepped forward to fill even more important bank posts while the men were in war service. They enhanced their reputation for competence and loyalty, proving to early supporters that their confidence had been well placed.

Miss Leffler Corbitt, the organization's president and an Austin banker, said: "This is the first war in the history of the world in which women have participated more as a unit than as individuals. . . . There is a solidarity about our patriotism that we have never realized up to this time."

The Texas Women Bankers Association was organized in 1912, under the TBA, as the first of its kind in the nation. It thrived until World War I. The women bankers met at the time and place of the TBA convention.

PART FIVE

Monetary Control and The Federal Reserve System

1

WILSON PREVAILS: CONGRESS APPROVES the FED

The hope of 1913 has been realized—a new monetary system for these United States.
COMMENT, *Texas Bankers Record*, January 1914

HE FIRST IDEA FOR A CENTRAL BANK was advanced by Alexander Hamilton. He disagreed with Thomas Jefferson over the constitutionality of a central bank, Jefferson believing that the national government lacked the authority to establish such a system. Hamilton won; the Bank of the United States was created. Congress saw the need for a bank in the economic disarray of the War of 1812; the idea was revived, and the Second Bank of the United States was chartered in 1816. It was destroyed by Jackson's veto of the bill to extend the bank's charter. The nation was returned to a system of state and private banks until the Congress passed the National Banking Act in 1863. This step and the subsequent taxation of state bank notes established the dominance of the national system. It enhanced deposit banking rather than note issue banking and established stringent requirements for chartering and examination.

Although the national bank legislation was a positive measure, it lacked the capacity to provide an elastic currency and mobile reserves; economic swings were frequent and severe. During the time before the creation of the Federal Reserve System, there were central reserve banks in only three cities, New York, Chicago and St. Louis—national banks with reserves held only in vault cash. There were three types of national banks: central reserve city banks, reserve city banks and country banks. Texas had reserve city banks, according to the classification, in Dallas, Fort Worth, Galveston, Houston, San Antonio and Waco. All other national banks were classified as country banks.

Although the totality of the reserve depositories was large, it was spread through the country; it lacked centralization, and so its effectiveness was hampered. Reserves were not easily shifted from one part of the country to another. When the 1893 depression and the Panic of 1907 struck, the problem was highlighted.

Something had to be done.

Congress first began with the Aldrich-Vreeland Act in 1908, an effort toward currency elasticity for temporary relief. It created the National Monetary Commission to study and make recommendations for changes in the banking system.

When the Democrats regained control of Congress in 1910, the proposals of Senator Nelson Aldrich, Rhode Island Republican, were viewed as favoring the moneyed interests of financial centers. Strong opposition arose from such populists as William Jennings Bryan.

The Congressional hearings by Representative A. P. Pujo of Louisiana on the banking and finance situation concluded that the concentration of money and credit control rested with only a few men. The results of the hearings moved the country to action. With the help of Colonel House of Texas, a friend of Bryan, Wilson secured Bryan's support at the 1912 convention. Meanwhile, Carter Glass, a newspaper publisher in Lynchburg, Virginia, had risen as a veteran member of the U. S. House of Representatives. Interested in monetary reform, he had become chairman of the House Banking and Currency Committee, and he led the Virginia delegation to support Wilson, a native of the Old Dominion. Glass was to become the leading figure in the creation of the Federal Reserve System. Others were Aldrich, Senator Robert Owen of Oklahoma, William G. McAdoo and H. Parker Willis, along with Colonel House.

Journeying to Princeton, New Jersey, on December 26, 1912, along with Willis, committee staff specialist and former professor of economics at Washington and Lee University, he called on the president-elect. The three discussed currency problems and a plan that envisioned a system of regional reserve banks. Wilson thought the idea was sound, but wanted to add a central board to control and coordinate the work of the regional banks. At first Glass disliked the concept, thinking it resembled the Aldrich proposal to create excessive centralization in banking. Much discussion followed; it was obvious that the new president would opt for legislation in currency reform, along with tariff reform.

The new Senate Banking and Currency Committee had been formed with Senator Robert Owen of Oklahoma as its chairman. He was viewed as being more favorable to the Bryan concept of monetary control.

President Wilson appeared before a joint session of Congress on June 23, 1913, and presented his plan for currency reform, with the support of Glass. Most bankers feared the program because it lacked banker control such as provided in the Aldrich proposal. In an astute agreement and compromise, working with bankers, the political mechanism for passage of the bill was engineered. Colonel House, the president's chief advisor, was instrumental in lining up votes and planning.

The Glass-Owen bill hit some rocky shoals from the beginning. Representative Robert L. Henry of Waco, Texas, struck out against it, demanding that Wilson destroy the "Money Trust" before tackling banking and currency reform. He was typical of many Democratic agrarians who saw no relief for agricultural credit, and he felt the bill was "wholly in the interest of the creditor class, the banking fraternity and the commercial world, without the proper provision for the debtor classes and those who toil, produce and sustain the country."

Wilson held his ground, assuring the agrarians that he would take care of their opposition by covering many of their grievances in later legislation. Henry refused to give up. Having been defeated in the House committee, the Texan turned to the Democratic caucus. But Bryan, then Secretary of State, took a stand for the modified bill. Democratic caucuses in both House and Senate approved it; passage was assured.

Meeting in Chicago in late August at the time of the raging political controversy over the Federal Reserve Bill, a commission of the ABA and the presidents of 47 state bankers associations posed many objections to it. But Glass kept the bill moving through the House. On September 18, 1913, it passed by an overwhelming vote, 287–85, on a largely partisan vote. The Senate committee under Owen held prolonged hearings. Meanwhile, the ABA had resolved against the legislation at its Boston convention, condemning the bill in the strongest of terms. In the Senate Elihu Root described it as "financial heresy."

The bill passed the Senate on December 19, 1913, by a vote of 54–34, although its survival over a substitute proposal had prevailed by only three votes. Conferees worked out the differences; both houses adopted it. Before a group of its supporters, President Wilson signed the Federal Reserve Act into law December 23, 1913. It was his Christmas present and the chief accomplishment of his first term of office, the establishment of a central bank.

Intense efforts were launched by various cities to secure one of the 12 banks established by the law. Texas joined the quest.

Texan Colonel House made important contributions to the Federal Reserve and to banking by strongly recommending to President Wilson that he select people for the first board who would have the confidence of banking and business. The president accorded House wide latitude in consulting with banking and business leaders to get their recommendations. Bankers were pleased with the choices; progressives were shocked. William P. Harding, Birmingham banker, was the only Southerner named.

Meanwhile, back in Texas Herbert Eldridge of Houston was elected TBA president in 1912. He changed jobs in January 1913, became a banker in New York City and wanted to step down as TBA leader. His friends in Texas would not hear of it, so he returned to the state for the 29th convention in Galveston in May. In his address to the delegates he stressed currency reform.

Delegates approved a graduated schedule of TBA dues, beginning with the $5 membership that had been in place since 1885.

Nathan Adams of Dallas was elected president. At a special meeting in that city a resolution was adopted asking J. W. Hoopes, TBA secretary, then a Galveston banker, to urge bankers to oppose the compulsory membership feature of the Glass-Owen bill and to favor banker membership on the Federal Reserve Board. Also opposed was compulsory par clearing of checks.

Intense efforts were launched by various, cities to secure one of the 12 banks established by the law. Texas joined the quest.

The 1913 First District TBA meeting attracted
many bankers to Houston on February 13.

At the ABA convention in Boston in 1913, J. W. (Fred) Hoopes, secretary of the
TBA, was elected treasurer of the ABA. He was the first Texan to hold a general
office in that association.

2
THE BIG PUSH—
TEXAS SEEKS REGIONAL BANK

*In the presentations for the bank, Texans supported the idea of 12 regional banks instead of
eight, for it was felt that if fewer banks were established, the nod might go to New Orleans.*
SUMMARY CONCLUSION OF ARTICLE IN *TBR*

"TEXAS WANTS RESERVE BANK," proclaimed the *TBR* in February 1914. To
support the feverish efforts to get one of the branches, bankers and business and civic
leaders entered the push and appeared before the committee designated to hold hearings throughout the country to hear the various proposals. Secretary of the Treasury
William G. McAdoo, a Californian, and David F. Houston, Secretary of Agricul-

ture, held the hearing in Austin. Houston, a native North Carolinian, had lived in Texas, where he taught at The University of Texas and was dean of the faculty and president of the university. He had moved to St. Louis in 1908, but still had many strong connections in the state of his former residence.

The Austin hearing was held February 9, 1914, and delegations from three cities—Dallas, Fort Worth and Houston—appeared to make powerful pleas for the location of one of the eight branch banks of the Federal Reserve.

The full report of the hearing and presentations was given in the *TBR*.

At the Austin meeting, held in the Federal building, Secretary McAdoo explained that since this was "Secretary Houston's native heath, it was only right that he should state the duties of the committee and purpose of the hearing." The session was penetrating and precise, and witnesses were restrained from steering off course with extraneous issues. Many of the stalwarts of banking leadership appeared. Not only was there strong in-state competition for the bank, but New Orleans was also a vigorous contender for it, and the struggle was fierce.

In the presentations for the bank, Texans supported the idea of 12 regional banks instead of eight, for it was felt that if fewer banks were established, the nod might go to New Orleans.

Then the weeks of waiting, the speculation as to the choices and the anxiety of cities whose economic development would be greatly aided by a favorable decision seemed like an eternity.

3

DALLAS SELECTED:
GOLD PENS for the SIGNERS

The Record *takes off its hat and makes one of those Lord Chesterfield bows to the*
GREAT SOUTHWEST. . . . The phrase "Texas has come into her own," long since
worn threadbare by the spell-binders, is no less trite than true.
EDITORIAL COMMENT, *TBR*, April 1914

THE DALLAS BANKS maintained their liaison with Colonel E. M. House. A political strategist of the first rank, House was very much interested in the Fed. Tom Love of Dallas, also close to Wilson, and Albert S. Burleson, Postmaster General and a Texan, had the interest of Texas at heart.

It has been said that G. B. Dealey, Dallas newspaper executive, along with his paper's Washington reporter, worked out a way to communicate secretly between Dallas and Washington. According to the report, the code word for President Wilson was "Allah," Secretary McAdoo, "Croesus," and Colonel House, "Tacitus."

While visiting the office of John Skelton Williams, Comptroller of the Currency, supposedly Love saw a map with the 12 bank locations, and Dallas was circled as the place for the Federal Reserve Bank.

"TEXAS GETS REGIONAL BANK," the headline in the *TBR* announced in April 1914. The big news came by telegram on April 12, 1914, from Burleson to Dealey. Dallas had been chosen for the Federal Reserve Regional Bank! Although disappointed at not being selected, bankers in other cities of Texas joined in the accolades and congratulations. Movements started immediately to secure branch offices.

The establishment of 12 districts provided banks in Boston, New York, Philadelphia, Cleveland, Richmond, Atlanta, Chicago, St. Louis, Minneapolis, Kansas City, Dallas and San Francisco, in that numerical order. Dallas was in Federal Reserve District 11.

State Banking Commissioner W. W. Collier, who had supported the Fed for Texas, urged state banks to join the system and to participate in the organization of the regional banks.

The Federal Reserve Organization Committee, having established 12 districts, asked five banks in each district to be representatives to sign the certificate of organization. For the Dallas region the signers were: James R. McKinney and B. A. McKinney, Durant National Bank, Durant, Oklahoma; J. G. McNary and E. W. Kayser, First National Bank, El Paso; T. C. Dunn and DeWitt C. Dunn, Union National Bank, Houston; T. C. Frost and Ned McIlhenny, Frost National Bank, San Antonio; and Andrew Querbes and W. J. Bayersdorffer, First National Bank, Shreveport.

The signing ceremony was held in the directors' room of the City National Bank,

Dallas. Each signer was given a gold fountain pen. The Dallas Clearing House gave a luncheon at the Adolphus Hotel.

At subsequent meetings the various directors were named. Oscar Wells, Houston banker, was selected as one of the Class A directors. Class B directors included three Texans: Frank Kell of Wichita Falls; Marion Sansom, Fort Worth; and J. J. Culbertson, Paris. Class C directors, all Texan bankers, were E. O. Tennison, Dallas; W. F. McCaleb, San Antonio; and Felix Martinez, El Paso. Tennison was selected chairman of the Dallas board of governors. The board established the bylaws and created an organization. R. L. Van Zandt, national bank examiner, Fort Worth, was elected vice governor (as they were designated at that time), and J. W. (Fred) Hoopes was elected cashier and secretary of the board of governors.

All 12 Federal Reserve Banks opened for business November 16, 1914.

4
JOIN the FED, the TBA URGES

We are, whether we like it or not, a part of this great regional banking system.
NATHAN ADAMS, TBA president

THE 30TH TBA CONVENTION, held in Fort Worth in May 1914, concentrated on the Federal Reserve Act, the Dallas Reserve Bank and the prospects for banking. President Nathan Adams, one of the leading movers for the selection of Dallas, noted, "We are, whether we like it or not, a part of this great regional banking system." He urged eligible banks to join.

But J. A. Pondrom of Texarkana, the incoming president, warned that establishment of the Fed might result in a crisis for the TBA because it might be desirable for bankers to group in a regional association of the Federal Reserve District configuration, an area that included parts of Louisiana, New Mexico, Oklahoma and Arizona. This concern did not prove valid.

No sooner had the Federal Reserve Bank of Dallas been established than Governor O. B. Colquitt proposed that Texas create a central state bank, with capital up to $70,000,000, to be known as the "Bank of Texas." He suggested the bank serve as fiscal agent for Texas, its counties, cities and towns, and provide a "safe and lucrative investment for the permanent school fund . . . and a reserve bank in aid of the general banking system."

James E. Ferguson, Temple banker, Democratic nominee for governor in the 1914 election, opposed creation of the bank. The bill was dealt its death blow October 8, 1914, by the Texas House of Representatives, 81–31.

Big issues are commonplace in Texas.

Big issues are commonplace in Texas.

115

The TBA held a special meeting in Dallas on October 23, 1914, to investigate a cotton loan plan and to devise ways to aid the reduction of cotton acreage for the next year. A tense situation over cotton had developed. No specific agreement was reached then, but at a later meeting bankers agreed to cooperate in a movement to prevent the sale of cotton at less than 8 cents a pound, with acreage reduction at least 50 percent, along with a loan fund to carry over the 1914 crop. Each county was to have a banker to coordinate activities for the TBA. In a change of attitude, the Farmers Union applauded the bankers.

The banker-farmer movement had taken hold in the state for the diversification of agriculture. It helped to solve a big problem of imagery for bankers and to provide practical information for farmers. Nowhere were the results more evident than in the Rio Grande Valley. The Mercedes *Tribune* gave a glowing account of these activities "that should be an object lesson to the rest of Texas."

In the election of 1914 James E. Ferguson was elected governor. An important issue in the election was prohibition. The Temple banker stood on the anti-prohibition side. A self-made man, he refused campaign contributions. The Ferguson name was to play a major role in Texas for years.

5

TBA MOVES HEADQUARTERS to DALLAS: THE PHILPOTT ERA BEGINS

We need a capable secretary. . . .
JOE HIRSCH, TBA president, 1915

THE FIRST MOVE of the TBA headquarters took place in December 1914, going from Austin to Dallas. It was necessary to have the small office near the association's elected secretary, J. W. Hoopes, who had been named cashier of the Dallas Federal Reserve Bank. The Dallas office was first located in the Federal Reserve Building.

This move established Dallas as the TBA headquarters until its removal back to Austin in 1964 upon the retirement of William A. Philpott, Jr., and selection of Sam O. Kimberlin, Jr., as his successor.

War in Europe claimed the attention of the association at the 31st convention in Waco, May 1915.

President Pondrom noted the hostilities: "During the midsummer of last year, with scarcely a moment's warning, there was precipitated the greatest war in human history involving all the most populous and enlightened nations of Europe. . . .there was panic everywhere, financial, industrial and commercial," he said.

War was knocking at the doors of America. Texas bankers knew it. Woodrow Wil-

William A. Philpott, Jr., TBA secretary, in his
sporty heyday in his Dallas home.

son, basking in the creation of the Federal Reserve as the greatest accomplishment of
his first term, would soon be consumed in diplomacy.

The world's dislocation had not caused bank failures in Texas. After the shock
wave had subsided bankers realized that Europe at war needed Texas products. A
near-hopeless situation had resulted in the cotton industry when panic forced can-
cellations of purchases and shipments abroad; cotton prices had dropped as low as
1 cent or 2 cents per pound for a day.

TBA memberships decreased slightly, to 1,388.

A Corpus Christi banker, Joe Hirsch, was the newly elected president. Known as a
tireless promoter of a mutually protective relationship between banking and agriculture, the TBA year reflected his interest.

The TBA secretary's office having already moved to Dallas, the executive committee approved the move of the *TBR* to that city in July 1915.

When the convention met in Houston in May 1916, President Hirsch suggested a
significant action. "We need a capable secretary who will keep in touch with legislation, both national and state, affecting the banking business," he observed in his ad-

117

dress. He laid the plan for the employment of the TBA's first full-time secretary. After nine years as secretary, Hoopes was stepping aside. His official duties with the Fed would not allow further service as a volunteer. The convention noted his long service with appreciation.

William A. Philpott, Jr., managing editor of the *TBR*, was elected by the executive committee to serve in the dual capacity of secretary and editor. Thus, on May 11, 1916, began his long record of service to the association as managing officer.

6
PAR CLEARANCE and STRONG DISSENT

Prominent men in banking and the law everywhere have taken sides. . . .Of those bankers in Texas who have expressed themselves, 95 percent of them are protesting against the plan. . . .
EDITORIAL COMMENT, *TBR*, June 1916

T HE TBA MET TO REVIEW the proposal by the Fed to impose par clearance beginning July 15, 1916. Strong dissent arose against the proposal which appeared to "threaten the very existence of many banks that are members of this association."

To ascertain the association's policy the executive committee directed a mail poll of the 1,400 members. The canvass resulted in 556 replies voting yes for a TBA meeting of protest; 148 voted no. The special meeting was called for Dallas on May 24. The association was authorized to develop a national protest, with all state banking associations to send delegates to a meeting in St. Louis on June 10. Secretary Philpott sent the invitations to all the state secretaries. A vote of protest resulted; the conference decided to convene again in Kansas City; and Nathan Adams, former TBA president and Dallas banker, was selected as national chairman to coordinate efforts against the Fed action. The ABA joined in the effort to amend the Federal Reserve Act for relief against the par order.

The uproar was heated; the Fed legislation was amended July 21, 1917, to permit the handling of checks drawn on nonmember banks in the same manner as checks upon member banks, "provided the nonmember banks would agree to remit to the Reserve banks at par."

In late 1916 a contest developed for a regional office of the Federal Farm Loan Bank. It was announced that Houston had been selected as the bank's location, narrowly beating out Fort Worth.

The round of the seven TBA district meetings in February 1917 featured talks on foodstuffs, cotton and other agricultural products in possible wartime; agricultural preparedness and live-at-home hints; and the new Federal Home Loan Bank Act.

A highlight was the new TBA feature, educational work by correspondence courses, using the American Institute of Banking texts for "junior bank men."

The entourage of the TBA officers and bankers who made the circuit of district meetings had been dubbed by Secretary Philpott as the "Flying Squadron," and interest grew in taking part in the trip.

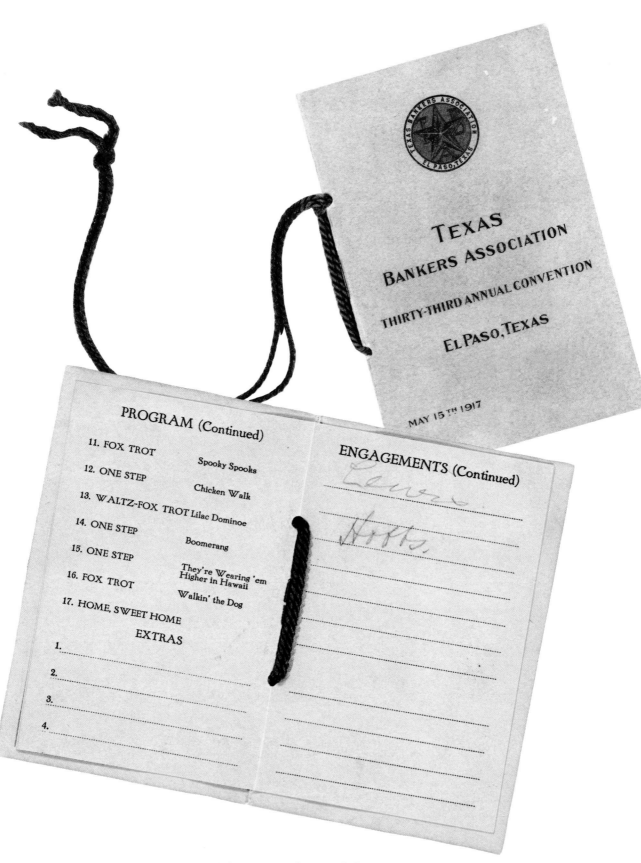

TEXAS BANKERS ASSOCIATION

THIRTY-THIRD ANNUAL CONVENTION

EL PASO, TEXAS

MAY 15 TH 1917

PROGRAM (Continued)

11. FOX TROT Spooky Spooks
12. ONE STEP Chicken Walk
13. WALTZ-FOX TROT Lilac Dominoe
14. ONE STEP Boomerang
15. ONE STEP They're Wearing 'em Higher in Hawaii
16. FOX TROT Walkin' the Dog
17. HOME, SWEET HOME

EXTRAS

1. _____
2. _____
3. _____
4. _____

ENGAGEMENTS (Continued)

The Grand Ball of the TBA in El Paso, 1917,
was typical of the elegant entertainment of the
association.

PART SIX

World War I and
A Turbulent Postwar Era

1

PATRIOTISM and PERFORMANCE

War is upon us. It will hurt us deeply.
J. W. BUTLER, TBA president, 1917

W ORLD WAR I CAME IN APRIL 1917. At the El Paso convention in May President J. W. Butler, Clifton banker, opened his address by remarking: "War is upon us. It will hurt us deeply. It will help us greatly. War is like childbirth, a terrible pain at the price of a clean, new life. Let us remember that all existence is warfare of some sort, a ceaseless struggle of the spirit forward to a finer freedom."

In a patriotic vein the leader continued: "This war that now impends was forced upon us because we have insisted that human rights and decencies must be respected."

The Clifton banker was prophetic: "In fighting for this faith, in fighting for the land that is ours, some of us will die on the fields of battle. That is as high a death as men may attain. I would rather live in the golden sunshine of a glorious heart expanding optimism for one single moment, than to grovel in the misty miasmatic shadows of pessimism through the eternal years," he said.

He appealed for banker support of the Liberty Loan War Bonds Drive. The 1,200 bankers assembled at the convention in quick succession adopted a resolution endorsing President Wilson and "his aims in peace and war. . . ."

In every way the convention felt the patriotic urge for Texas to be out front.

Quickly responding to the national appeal for support of the Liberty Loan Drive, they agreed to accept their part. "Our cooperation will be continuous," Butler wired treasury Secretary McAdoo. There were now 1,502 members to back up this pledge.

One of the tragedies of banking supervision happened in Teague, August 28, 1916, when John S. Patterson, commissioner of banking, was shot and fatally wounded in the line of duty. The account of the tragedy reported that the shooting took place about 6:30 that evening in the Farmers and Merchants State Bank. Patterson died the next day in a Waco hospital.

The *TBR* reported that T. R. Watson, president; J. E. Watson, vice president; and W. R. Watson, cashier of the bank, were placed under arrest. The trouble occurred after banking hours when Patterson, with J. E. McKinnon, bank examiner, "were in the act of putting up a notice announcing the bank to be in charge of the commissioner."

To promote the Liberty Loan Drive, many banks resorted to novel ways of support. For example, the First National Bank and the Citizens State Bank of El Campo used newspaper ads, circulars and billboards to promote the campaign. "War is a business with us now," the banks proclaimed, "and, like any other business, it cannot be carried on successfully without money." So these banks agreed to make loans for bond purchases by the public at 3 ½ percent interest. "We are free born Americans and we want to remain free, and we shall remain free: But we must be up and doing!" the ads said.

Texas had been asked to furnish $36,000,000.

TBA President Howell E. Smith, of McKinney, urged bankers to express their patriotism and "to enlist as soldiers of finance."

The first issue of the Liberty Loan Bonds was subscribed one and a half times, $3 billion. The Eleventh Federal Reserve District, chiefly Texas, oversubscribed its quota of $40,000,000 by $9,000,000. J. W. Hoopes, deputy governor of the Dallas Fed and former TBA secretary, headed the Liberty Loan Drive.

The war raged in Europe. Battlefield losses included bankers; sacrifice spanned the spectrum of service. The *TBR* urged bankers to get out in the streets and promote the Second Liberty Loan Drive of 1917 for the stupendous amount of $3 billion. Also in place was the Treasury Department's Thrift Stamps and War Savings Certificate campaign for the people of small means.

A group of state bankers gathered for a conference in Dallas, December 13, 1917, to discuss various matters. Several of the 30 present expressed a desire to organize a State Bankers Association, separate from the TBA which had to represent all banks. It appeared that a resolution for that purpose would be quickly adopted, but J. W. Butler, former TBA president, asked for time in which to consider so important a resolution "since of the 875 state banks in the state, only 30 were represented." A vote was delayed until after a hearty luncheon. Returning to the session, Butler offered a substitute motion, arguing for unity. He suggested that the executive committee of the TBA organize a state bankers' section, wherein "matters pertaining to the state banks' welfare could be cared for."

Debate, considerable and heated, continued. The Butler motion prevailed by the narrow margin of 17 to 15.

2
DROUGHT, VICTORY and POSTWAR PROBLEMS, SOME NEW and SOME OLD

We may achieve climate but weather is thrust upon us.
O. HENRY

ALTHOUGH DROUGHT AND INSECTS had reduced production of many staple crops in Texas in 1917, the drumbeat for food and feed for war production had almost calloused the eardrums of Texas farmers. "You can't eat cotton," farmers were told, and "we must have food for ourselves, our stock, our armies and our allies."

"Still," observed the *TBR*, "cotton was selling for 30 cents."

But, having suffered from a "drouthy" year in 1917, farmers were urged to increase food, feed and livestock production in 1918. It was hard to convince a Texas farmer to abandon cotton in favor of corn at $2 per bushel.

Wartime inflation sent prices soaring.

In the midst of bloody wartime an incident happened in Fentress, Texas, which could not have been predicted. The town's bank was demolished when a big water storage tank gave way and tons of water came crashing down on the building. Cashier J. W. Lipscomb was in the bank when he heard the first noise of the falling tank. He ran into the vault, and the vault walls probably saved his life. The building, only two years old and made of brick, was a wreck. Lipscomb moved the bank into temporary quarters.

Now Texas had to turn its attention to another severe problem.

Drought!

Certain sections of the state were suffering from the worst drought in history. The dry period had resulted in stringent conditions in southwest Texas. "Farmers had their fields prepared for months and ready for planting, but the skies remain as brass," wrote one banker. "It is evident that we must see them through. They must have feed for their hogs and cattle and horses and we have purchased this for them and taken their notes for it." The drought area banks hard hit, they appealed to other areas of banking to support the war drives since their short funds were needed to aid the farmers at home.

President Smith took up the war theme at the 1918 convention in Galveston.

"The question in this country today is whether or not a man is a loyal American citizen, and is he willing to support this great government to the last ditch and with his last dollar, and if he will not do it he is against this government, for the time has come when there is no half way ground upon which he can stand.

"He who is rich in dollars and poor in patriotism and loyalty, is poor indeed, and

Wartime inflation sent prices soaring.

should not be permitted the privilege of American citizenship," the McKinney banker stated strongly.

The association was expanding—1,548 members: state banks, 794; national banks, 450; and private banks, 165; associate members totaled 49.

In a contested election for president W. W. Woodson of Waco was the victor.

The 1918 convention disbanded the Texas Women Bankers Association because of the pressures of war.

But the association created a State Bank Section the following day, selected J. W. Butler of Clifton as the first chairman and gave him authority to name one representative from each of the seven TBA districts to the administrative council of the section.

June 17, 1918, was a banner day in the financial history of El Paso. The branch of the Federal Reserve Bank of Dallas opened. Bankers from all parts of Texas and surrounding area attended. By noon 5,000 checks had passed through the bank. A gala banquet closed the eventful day.

The devastating drought continued in west Texas; a major crisis had developed. Governor William P. Hobby headed a movement for volunteer contributions. While the drive for funds faltered, bankers joined the effort. Banks in the most favored parts of the state agreed to make loans to the banks in the dry areas for a year at 6 percent; the subscription asked was a sum not less than 5 percent of their capital and surplus. A committee was formed, worked out details and suggested a total of $5,000,000 for the purpose. The TBA asked member banks to participate. Patriotism took on an additional armor—helping the people of Texas—and it worked.

President Woodson, as his predecessors in the war period, asked banks to continue to support the war loan drives, support of "my government in its most critical hour." Said he, "Tell Mr. Nathan Adams, director of sales, to wire the boys at the Front: 'We have done our best,'" the TBA leader said.

Soon the war ended—November 11, 1918.

Texans had supported the fight for victory. By "Wheatless Mondays" and "Meatless Tuesdays," and by providing nearly 200,000 service people, putting a vast amount of money in the bond drives and countless other ways, the battle had been won.

At the 35th convention in Galveston, May 1919, there were far different emotions than in the previous year when the war was at its most crucial point.

Said President Woodson, "Out of the travail of war, America has been reborn; her days of seclusion and isolation are past."

But another threat stalked the nation. Inflation.

The expanding economy gave Texas a good year in 1919; the devastation of dry weather had abated with the coming of a better season.

Woodson believed that the Federal Reserve could liquidate the enormous public debt gradually and "that business need feel no resultant shock."

He was pleased to report that the legislature had passed a uniform negotiable instruments act and a uniform warehouse receipts act, attributing the success to Austin's Dr. E. P. Wilmont.

Membership was up to 1,602.

Woodson supported the formation of a League of Nations "to derive the full benefits of victory."

F. Marion Law of Houston was elected president.

Monday, August 4, 1919, the Houston branch of the Federal Reserve Bank of Dallas was opened. Houston had 110 member banks in its territory.

In the latter part of 1919 the par battle with the Fed broke out afresh.

"To par or not to par," the *TBR* put it.

The Fed had launched a campaign for universal parring of bank checks. TBA President Law, realizing the significance of the issue to the association, called a special meeting of the executive committee in November to discuss the question. A full, frank discussion lasted for several hours. No agreement was reached, so the questionnaire approach was used. Of 854 replies, 724 members voted no on the Fed plan. The association was besieged by letters against the proposal. No issue had brought such frank and vitriolic condemnation.

One writer burst into verse, quoting in his response:

"Things are coming to a h— of a pass

When a man can't club his own jackass."

The Fed stuck to its guns, focusing upon the nonmember banks. As of January 1920 the Dallas Federal Reserve Bank reported that all but 90 have "signed on the dotted line and are remitting for all checks at par. . . ." But the *TBR* pointed out that "most of the nonmember banks are parring over their protest—many of them being of the most vigorous sort."

Law addressed the 36th convention in Galveston in May 1920, knowing that the 1,666 TBA membership was at its peak—only 59 banks in the state were not members—but recognizing the uneasy situation that prevailed among the assembled delegates over par exchange and other matters.

Said Law: "If the Texas Bankers Association is anything, it is democratic."

Because the TBA State Bank Section had been so successful, it was suggested that a Trust Section be established. There were some 50 trust companies within the TBA membership.

The Houston leader urged the bankers to restrict inflationary credit. "Credit is dangerously high," he said. "This country must get down to earth once more in its ways of living and doing business, and it is up to the banker to see that the descent is made in a gradual and orderly fashion."

A severe credit crunch in the fall of 1920 resulted in strained conditions, and many businesses urged the Federal Reserve to assume credit control and force more credit availability. Texas bankers feared increased inflation by excess governmental reaction. Knowing the stringent situation with respect to cotton, the bankers joined in forming the Southern Federal Finance Corporation. President Eldred McKinnon of Austin, who had won a contested election for president of the TBA, urged the members to invest at least 3 percent of their capital and surplus in stock of the corporation to promote cotton markets.

Another event of 1920 was the naming of Miss Iva M. Aday as the first woman deputy Texas banking commissioner.

If the Texas Bankers Association is anything, it is democratic.

125

Total resources of Texas banks in 1920 were $1,171,373,000; deposits climbed to $844,000,000; and the 1920 census had kept the state fifth in national rank. A drop in the value of cotton produced, along with declines in other agricultural production, marked 1920 as the beginning of the postwar recession.

Texas bankers found Federal Reserve membership an advantage for rediscounting service. The farm price slump caught many banks in an extended position, and 702 of them in the Eleventh District used the rediscounting facilities. As the economic recession increased in 1921, 82 percent of the member banks in the Dallas district rediscounted notes with the Fed. This resulted in increased rates; extension of credit to country banks was cut drastically.

3

DECADE of the TWENTIES—
READJUSTMENT, CONTRACTION and
the GUARANTY FUND LAW TERMINATED

To be a good banker is to render a great service to one's fellowman, and I should rather be a good banker . . . than the richest man in the world.
JESSE H. JONES, Houston banker, 1923

THE PROSPERITY OF THE DECADE of World War I resulted in general good times for banks. The numbers increased; failures were few.

But a period of readjustment began with the decade of the 1920s. It would change the face of banking in Texas and the nation.

TBA conventions, from 1918, feared galloping inflation. As pointed out by Grant and Crum, wholesale prices increased 22 percent by 1920. The inflationary period was followed by the major economic contraction. From May 1920 to the following June, wholesale prices dropped 56 percent, "the sharpest decline in prices on record in the history of the United States," they observed.

The nation was in a period of wild expansion and contraction. Bankers were concerned about the quality of credit and portfolio management in the fast-changing conditions.

The Federal Reserve discount rate fluctuated from 7 percent in 1920 to a low of 4.5 percent in late 1921. The economic plunge was quickly reversed, however, and by 1923 another boom period had reached its peak. This upturn produced substantially stable conditions for Texas bankers during the easy money years until 1928, the beginning of trouble, and the debacle of 1929 and subsequent years.

Clearly, the storm clouds were gathering.

Texas depended on cotton, oil, cattle and other livestock, as well as a growing diversification in produce and grain, for its primary economic base. During the decade agricultural prices failed to regain the relatively high levels expected; the fluctuation in prices was a constant source of concern to banking.

The highest level of cotton prices was reached in 1920 at 36.2 cents per pound; the decline dropped the price to 9.2 cents by April 1921.

The recession led to a number of bank failures and resulted in the repeal of the Guaranty Fund law in 1927.

As pointed out by Sam O. Kimberlin, Jr., during 1921 a total of 22 state banks in the Fund failed, followed by another 27 in 1922. This resulted in heavy assessments on the other state banks in the system to pay off depositors. And the trouble did not stop there. Between 1923 and 1925 an additional 34 banks in the fund failed, causing concern about the profits of surviving banks and possible impairment of their capital. To alleviate the problem the legislature amended the act to permit state banks to switch from the Guaranty Fund to the Bond Security System. According to Kimberlin, 300 state banks switched within 90 days. Also, several state banks switched to national charters. Liquidations of others reduced the number of state banks from 1,008 in 1921 to 677 in 1930.

Commenting on the events of the decade, TBA secretary William A. Philpott, Jr., said: "After the . . . plan was adopted there began the period of the wildest promotion, the greatest bank expansion Texas had ever seen, and that was the signal for numerous persons with no banking experience to open a bank and offer the depositing public the same degree of safety afforded by the old, well-established, conservative banker with ample capital and seasoned experience. Banks were organized in every town and hamlet until a peak of more than 1,000 state banks was reached. Every one hung out the sign 'Guaranty Fund Bank' and was allowed to advertise the statement that no depositor had ever lost a dollar in a Guaranty Fund bank in Texas."

Many factors led to the bank failures, of course, but it was clearly a combination of over-expansion, incompetent management, fluctuating economic conditions and bank runs. At the outset the Texas banking law did not restrict chartering, a defect later cured.

TBA President R. L. Thornton of Dallas discussed the problem of deposit insurance in a *TBR* article, September 1925: "In my judgment and opinion . . . the system created too many banks and too few bankers . . . to handle and properly conduct the business of banking. . . . It also showed that many unscrupulous men had entered the business of banking for numerous reasons, the principal one of which was that the public was protected by the good and solvent banks and this offered a splendid opportunity to embezzlers and pilferers."

There were numerous changes in the State Banking Department—commissioners and bank examiners—and the department operated with inadequate facilities and equipment.

At the convention in San Antonio in 1921 Eldred McKinnon recounted the difficulties of banking during the year. "We live in the South and cannot escape the financial troubles that have arisen over the South's chief product upon which Texas largely depends, cotton," he said. With it all, the economic theory of supply and demand was not working, he told the bankers, as there was a surplus of 10,000,000 bales of cotton on hand. Cotton exports had been disrupted—and 85 percent of Texas cotton was for export.

It is interesting to note that the demand for cotton exportation was one of the prime reasons for adoption of the Edge Act by the Congress, a law that was to be used later by banks to operate businesses abroad.

The association continued to grow—a total of 1,684 in 1921. The magazine turned in a comfortable profit of $5,989.44 "without cost to the TBA."

Bank burglaries were occurring; yeggmen were involved in night robberies; two bank robberies had occurred in daylight without success, but one young cashier had been killed while resisting. Check swindlers were plentiful.

The TBA Trust Division traces its beginning to the 1921 convention. Delegates authorized a Trust Company Section, and incoming President Warren P. Andrews of Fort Worth was authorized to name a chairman of the section for the first year "in whose hands would be the work of organization. . . ." Appointed as the first head of the section was Dick Ansley, Commerce Trust Company, San Antonio. He was also authorized to draft bylaws and to appoint the members of the first administrative council of the section. One of the bylaws provided for the section to meet annually with the TBA convention.

The action in San Antonio established a trust group in the TBA which has continued to be recognized as one of the foremost in the nation. Duly organized, the new section met May 18, 1922.

President Andrews told the May 1922 convention in Fort Worth that "the tremendous decline in the value of farm products and live stock has brought about an acute lending and marketing condition in these lines of industry, and as a consequence the banking situation in the smaller cities of the state took an acid test." He reported the association's efforts in support of the War Finance Corporation which had distributed $23,000,000 to banks and producers in Texas.

Defending the Federal Reserve, Andrews deplored the "unwarranted and flagrant attacks" made upon it.

With improving economic conditions, Texas bankers planning to attend the ABA convention in New York City were offered a cruise via Havana. The one-way special rate was $117.

At the Dallas convention in May 1923 the normal run of affairs returned. Previous meetings had dealt in crisis issues. President M. C. Driscoll of Yoakum confirmed the more placid year: "Your association . . . has sought to pursue the even tenor of its way in a somewhat quiet and peaceful manner."

One of the sad notes of the convention was the memorial to Mrs. William A. Philpott, Jr., wife of the TBA secretary, who had died December 23, 1922. F. M. Law made the motion for a page to be set aside in the *TBR* in memoriam to her.

Houston's Jesse H. Jones, president of the National Bank of Commerce, spoke briefly at the 1923 convention since the scheduled speaker was unable to attend. Jones had already achieved status as one of the leading citizens of his city and Texas. He was later one of the foremost leaders of the Roosevelt administration, powerful as head of the Reconstruction Finance Corporation and as Secretary of Commerce and director of War Mobilization.

"The calling of banker is second in importance only perhaps to that of the ministry. The dearest and most sacred thing to man is his soul, and the next is his money; so I put the minister first and next to him the banker. Money is the measure of all things material, and we all work for money. . . . The bank is the institution established by society for the care and safe-keeping of money and for the convenience in carrying on business and trade," Jones said.

"To be a good banker is to render a great service to one's fellowman, and I should rather be a good banker . . . than the richest man in the world."

The issue that aroused bankers around the country—par clearance—had moved to the U. S. Supreme Court. The court declared a North Carolina statute allowing an exchange on checks constitutional. The 1923 case caused the Federal Reserve to abandon its efforts to require nonmember banks to clear at par.

At the 1924 convention in Austin President A. M. Graves of Clarksville discussed important issues facing banking, including the McFadden Bill expected to pass Congress. One of its major provisions dealt with branch banking. The bill, as Graves explained it, would prohibit a national bank from branching in any state which did not permit branches.

An indicator of the conditions in 1924 was reflected in the announcement by two of the larger Houston banks that the rate of interest on savings accounts was being reduced from 4 to 3 percent.

The banker who had argued effectively against the Guaranty Fund, R. L. Thornton of Dallas, now was TBA president. At the Houston convention in mid-May he told the delegates that the law, after being in operation for 14 years, was "economically unsound, unworkable and unfair." Texas bankers flooded the TBA office with support for their leader.

The August 1925 *TBR* mentioned the death of Mrs. Anna Martin, pioneer woman banker of Texas, at her home in Mason. She and her sons had established the bank in 1901, and until her death at 81 she remained the active president. "She was one of the first, if not the first, among women bank presidents in the state," the story reported.

The frequent problem of drought again rose in the south central sections of the state. President Francis H. Welch of Taylor asked bankers to meet in Dallas to coordinate help, a leadership role the association assumed in periods of dry weather crises.

The TBA executive committee abolished the third district and absorbed it into the surrounding districts in 1925, but did not reconstitute the other districts.

President Welch supported the McFadden bill in Congress before the 42nd convention in 1926 in Galveston.

Commissioner of Banks Charles O. Austin, speaking frankly at the 1926 convention, deplored the weaknesses of the Guaranty Fund Law and the ease with which the "job hunter" could secure a bank charter and operate as a Fund bank, and urged revision of the act. "Self interest is the curse of the age," the regulator said, "but it should be kept out of the legislative halls."

The repeal of the Guaranty Fund and Bond Security Plan law by the Texas legislators on February 2, 1927, was for banking the event of the year and the decade.

An innovation introduced by some Texas banks in 1926 was the service charge. Several had imposed a 50 cents a month charge on balances of less than $50.

Self interest is the curse of the age, but it should be kept out of the legislative halls.

129

4
TBA BANK ROBBERY REWARD
PROGRAM is DEAD SERIOUS

. . . the Association will willingly pay a reward . . . for each dead bank robber, killed while in the act of robbing a member bank in Texas.
OFFICIAL TBA REWARD NOTICE IN *TBR*, 1926

A BOLD AND CONTROVERSIAL STEP was instituted by the TBA in 1926 in an effort to reduce bank robberies in Texas. The *TBR* carried a one-page announcement of a money payment of $500 (later increased to $5,000) to reduce bank robberies in Texas.

Under the morgue photos of two bandits, the story announced: "The Texas Bankers Association has paid Capt. Tom Hickman, Texas ranger, $1,000 for the killing of the two men pictured above. They were shot down after holding up and robbing the Red River National Bank of Clarksville of $33,125.00 on September 9, 1926. The men were killed after leaving the bank and before they could reach their waiting automobile. The $1,000 gift represents $500.00 for each dead yegg."

The announcement continued: "$500 for Each Dead One in the Future. The Texas Bankers Association has not paid a money reward for bank criminals for 20 years until now. No rewards have been offered. No robbers have been killed before. However, from this date on, the Association will willingly pay a reward of $500.00 for each dead bank robber, killed while in the act of robbing a member bank in Texas. The Association will not pay one penny for the arrest or conviction of bank robbers in this state. But the reward of $500.00 will be paid very promptly for every dead bank robber, who is killed while robbing a member bank of the Texas Bankers Association.

"This seems a little cold and hard—but the robbers are more so when they have the drop on the bank officer and employee; and when the bandit is shot down while robbing a bank he deserves no sympathy or compassion. This reward is not calculated to increase murder—but only intended to deter the robber who may be planning to rob and kill. It is also expected to cause bankers to be more careful and officers more eager to shoot bandits off the job.

"Remember: $500.00 for each dead bank robber, killed while robbing a member of the Texas Bankers Association. The good robber is the dead one; the Association promises to pay $500.00 for each good one."

The announcement urged bankers to show the notice to local law officers and have local papers reproduce it.

Accompanying the reward notice was a long article by Secretary Philpott about the problem, observing that bank robbery had become one of the simplest arts. Good roads had assured fairly easy escape by automobile. He suggested these steps: cash

MONEY REWARD

For DEAD Bank Robbers

A cash reward will be paid for each Bank Robber legally killed while Robbing this bank

THE Texas Bankers Association, a corporation, offers a standing reward for each bank robber legally killed while robbing and holding up a reward subscribing member bank in Texas with firearms during the daytime. Limits of the place and time of such killing are: in the banking house, or as the robbers and holdups leave the bank, while the robbery and holdup and threats are being committed within the bank; and as they flee from the bank with the property taken, and are resisting legal pursuit and arrest, within five miles of the bank robbed and within one hour after the robbery and holdup.

¶ The amount of the reward for each dead robber will be the total collected from subscribing member banks at $5 per subscriber, but the total amount, in any event, shall not exceed $5,000.00.

¶ This reward does not apply to night attacks on Texas banks.

¶ The Association will not give one cent for live bank robbers. They are rarely identified, more rarely convicted, and most rarely stay in the penitentiary when sent there---all of which operations are troublesome, burdensome and costly to our government.

¶ In order to protect the lives of people in such banks and to protect the property of such banks, the Association is prepared to pay for any number of such robbers and holdups so killed, while they are robbing and holding up its reward subscribing member banks with firearms in the daytime.

¶ It is expressly provided that only the Texas Bankers Association shall determine whether or not payment of this reward shall be made hereunder, and to whom (if anyone) such payment shall be made, and such determination and judgment shall be final, conclusive and not reviewable.

¶ This reward is effective January 15th, 1933, and all other rewards, offers and statements are cancelled and superseded hereby.

TEXAS BANKERS ASSOCIATION

The TBA fought the rampaging bank robbers by promoting a program that was controversial but effective.

$5,000 REWARD

For DEAD Bank Robbers

$5,000 cash will be paid for each Bank Robber legally killed while Robbing this bank

THE Texas Bankers Association, a corporation, offers a standing reward of $5,000 for each bank robber legally killed while robbing and holding up a reward subscribing member bank in Texas with firearms during the daytime. Limits of the place and time of such killing are: in the banking house, or as the robbers and holdups leave the bank, while the robbery and holdup and threats are being committed; and as they flee from the bank with the property taken, and are resisting legal pursuit and arrest, within twenty miles of the bank robbed and within six hours after the robbery and holdup. This reward does not apply to night attacks on Texas banks. It is expressly provided that the Texas Bankers Association shall determine whether or not payment of this reward shall be made hereunder, and to whom (if anyone) such payment shall be made, and such determination and judgment shall be final, conclusive and not reviewable.

q The Association will not give one cent for live bank robbers. They are rarely identified, more rarely convicted, and most rarely stay in the penitentiary when sent there --- all of which operations are troublesome, burdensome and costly to our government.

q In order to protect the lives of people in such banks and to protect the property of such banks, the Association is prepared to pay for any number of such robbers and holdups so killed, while they are robbing and holding up its reward subscribing member banks with firearms in the daytime, at $5,000 apiece.

q This reward is effective April 1st, 1930, and all other rewards, offers and statements are cancelled and superseded hereby.

TEXAS BANKERS ASSOCIATION

$5,000 in cash will be so paid for the legal killing of any robber and holdup WHILE ROBBING THIS BANK with firearms in the daytime

Important Notice

¶ Your good bank is a subscribing member of the Dead Bandit reward plan, and as such is protected by the terms of the enclosed sign. Please destroy all signs you now have displayed. They are out of date. Please display these new signs prominently in your bank lobby. You will note that the reward plan as it now stands is effective January 15th, 1933, until further notice.

¶ Many banks have these cards in a neat frame under glass. This protects the cards from weather stains and wear. We suggest that you frame your cards and display them prominently in your lobby.

¶ Be certain that all the old reward cards are removed from public display, and destroyed.

EXECUTIVE COMMITTEE
Texas Bankers Association

covered by burglary insurance; at least three pistols placed around the bank in strategic places, and in the vault, a sawed-off shotgun and pistol; all employees trained in firearms use; the bank closed during lunch hour and an employee never left alone; and caution taken.

The crusade against bank robbers was to become a major issue in 1927.

The exciting news of the 1926 ABA convention in Los Angeles was that the 1927 convention would be held in Houston. F. M. Law and A. D. Simpson had spearheaded the drive to land the big meeting.

Also Secretary Philpott was elected first vice president of the ABA State Secretaries Section and was elevated to the presidency of the important national element in 1927 at the Houston convention. Exactly 50 years later (1977) Sam O. Kimberlin, Jr., TBA executive vice president, served as head of the ABA State Association Division.

Cotton problems continued to plague the economy. The TBA took action through its agricultural committee to organize each cotton county in an intensive action to reduce cotton acreage to work out of the "distressing slump in the price of cotton," and to prevent a "recurrence of the present debacle."

One humorous Texas banker wrote the TBA: "As I see it, the whole trouble is with the ladies. I have noticed that since the ladies stopped wearing clothes the demand for cotton has gone to thunder." He suggested replacing silk stockings with cotton ones. The suggestion was not well received.

The repeal of the Guaranty Fund and Bond Security Plan law by the Texas legislators on February 2, 1927, signed by Governor Dan Moody on February 11, caused rejoicing. The TBA had kept the issue alive in its editorials in the *TBR*, efforts backed by the banking department of the state. The repeal bill was drafted by a former state senator and banker, Paul D. Page of Bastrop, chairman of the TBA legislative committee.

The McFadden bill passed Congress and was law. It prohibited banks from branching in states where branching is not permitted for state banks. That was the policy for banking in Texas, and bankers were pleased when President Calvin Coolidge signed the bill into law February 25, 1927.

More good news for Texas bankers came from the Federal Reserve Board in Washington—a branch of the Dallas Federal Reserve was approved for San Antonio. Efforts for the branch had been under way for more than 13 years, and the bankers were jubilant. The new branch, which would serve 240 or more banks, opened July 5, 1927.

More than 800 delegates converged on El Paso for the 43rd convention of the association in May 1927. President Charles A. Fisk of Amarillo was buoyant in his review of the successful TBA year, including repeal of the Guaranty Fund law. Among the accolades he shared was recognition of Texas Ranger Captain Tom Hickman for his help in the protective work of the association.

F. M. Law of Houston, general chairman of the October 24–27 ABA convention for that city, urged at least 1,000 Texans to attend. The first to be held in Houston, it was a notable success—more than 4,000 people came to Houston for the convention—and those attending gave the city credit for doing "the thing up brown!"

The McFadden bill passed Congress and was law. It prohibited banks from branching in states where branching is not permitted for state banks. That was the policy of banking in Texas, and bankers were pleased when President Calvin Coolidge signed the bill into law February 25, 1927.

134

Declared the *TBR*: "The god of conventions is proud. Houston is proud. Texas is proud."

The program to reduce bank robberies in Texas, launched in 1926, became a major effort in the administration of TBA President William M. Massie, Fort Worth banker. A program to up the reward to $5,000 for dead bank robbers was inaugurated November 10, 1927. Reporting in the magazine in January 1928, Massie gave the status to date. Three robbers had been killed while in the act of robbing banks; two more were wounded, one probably fatally, he said. And only one successful bank heist had occurred during the six weeks. Massie made it clear that the program would be aggressively promoted and that "not one cent would be paid for the apprehension of one alleged bank robber alive."

Citing the robbery record, he said 140 successful bank robberies had occurred in the previous eight years; that very few of the robbers were ever apprehended or convicted; that often they were pardoned and "soon at liberty and free to commit more bank robberies." The only way to stop a robber, he insisted, is to kill him. And the TBA members agreed.

Answering the critics of the reward program, the association pointed out that the purpose of the effort was to stop bank bandits in Texas. "The object was not to incite murder or to hire anyone killed," the *TBR* said.

The issue was heightened on March 12, 1928, when Captain Frank Hamer of the Texas Rangers held a news conference in the Texas State Capitol. He handed a prepared statement to the reporters which asserted: "This reward has aroused the greed and desire of a small group of men who have more love for money than for human life, and who are besides unscrupulous enough to do anything that will bring them money without too much risk of personal danger. . . . Here is a perfect murder machine as can be devised, supported by the Bankers Association, operated by the officers of the state and directed by a small group of greedy men who furnish the victims and take their cut on the money."

His was a serious charge, carried in front page headline stories in the daily press of Texas.

In the April 1928 *TBR* the following appeared: "Some papers and enforcement officials have criticized the reward program of this Association for dead bandits. They charge it incites to murder and ask for an investigation. An investigation of how bank robbers and other convicts can escape at the rate of 75 a month might be in order."

Continuing in the May issue: " . . . daylight holdups are a thing of the past—not one in two months. . . . The $5,000 reward, despite the country newspapers, publicity seeking peace officers and cheap politicians, has turned the trick."

Bankers were urged to attend the May convention in San Antonio to hear and applaud President Massie. "He believes it is not so important the manner in which a bank robber meets death as it is that he is dead," the *TBR* reported.

At the 1928 convention Massie reported on other matters before taking up the bank robber issue.

Prosperity was widespread in the state. "Prices have stimulated real estate and securities prices are advancing; private building operations and public improvements are going forward at an astounding pace. All of this has been made possible by a plentiful supply of credit at low interest rates. Owing to the large amount of money in the country it is evident that rates of earnings by banks must be correspondingly lower. Such a condition is apt to lead us to take greater risks in order to increase our earnings and the danger should be constantly kept in mind," the leader warned.

Convention speaker James Shaw, Commissioner of Banks, reported the net loss in the Guaranty Fund banks from 1909 to 1927 was $12,257,972.74, "nearly one fourth of the working capital of all state banks in Texas today."

Reporting on the state banks, Shaw said that 1,560 had been chartered since 1905; and 740 were in operation. "Over one half of the state banks chartered have voluntarily liquidated, converted into national banks, or have failed outright," he reported. "Bankers should realize that they are on trial before the bar of public opinion in Texas, and the verdict will be largely of their own making," he said. In many ways the Texas commissioner was lecturing on the basics of banking on the eve of the great economic debacle. He urged bankers to remember the mission of banking, to confine their loans to short term, liquid paper, and shun loans that were capital in nature. "Banks fail . . . from incompetence of officers and directors. The days of ' one-man banking' had passed to the day of banks run by collective minds," he said.

President Massie defended the bank robbery reward program before the delegates, asserting that it was working well. He noted that "some reformers" believed that bank robbers were only impulsive, "unfortunate individuals whose better natures are temporarily mastered by hunger, rage or sudden temptation. The fact is, however, that crime in this country has become a highly organized profession," he asserted. His successors were urged to carry on the reward program. Prolonged applause greeted his remarks about the program and the suggestion that it be continued.

At the meeting of the executive committee the "reward program for dead bandits was discussed very minutely." Two modifications were made: the $5,000 reward was to cover those bandits "slain in daylight holdups . . . and bandits killed while robbing subscribing banks only will be paid for." To eliminate the bank robber from the state was the TBA mission. "Only dead robbers wanted," said the *TBR*. The association held its ground. Numerous eliminations of bank robbers were reported through the years until the program was discontinued in 1964, no rewards having been paid for several years.

5

THE "SANTA CLAUS BANK ROBBERY"
in CISCO

C ISCO, TEXAS, IS A PLEASANT PLACE, situated between Fort Worth and Abilene. It was in Cisco that a bank robbery took place which became nationally famous, even with a state historical marker designating it as the place where the "Santa Claus Bank Robbery" occurred on the afternoon of December 23, 1927. Four bandits entered the First National Bank, one dressed in a Santa Claus suit.

Several children had spotted "Santa" on the street and trailed him gleefully to the bank. Noting that he carried no sign or advertisement, a lady inquired, "What store do you represent?" Quickly came the answer, "You'll find out soon enough."

Once inside the bank, the bandits drew their revolvers and ordered all officials and employees to lie on the floor. A local mother with her small daughter, caught up at the excitement of seeing Santa Claus, went to the bank as the robbery was about to begin. When the shooting started she pushed her daughter out a side door to the alley, ran out herself and rushed to the nearby City Hall to alert officers.

"They're robbing the First National Bank!" she exclaimed.

Great excitement prevailed; a violent gun battle erupted; one of the robbers was killed; the other three escaped. Two of the children who had gone to the bank with "Santa" were taken as hostages by the fleeing bandits. Obviously shaken by the sudden violence of their hero, they were soon released. The chief of police died that night of gunshot wounds. Others died later.

"Santa Claus" was identified as a local bandit. Captured and convicted, while awaiting further action he shot a jailer. The popular officer was dying in the hospital, when an aroused crowd stormed the jail, took the bandit, tied a rope over a guy wire and lynched him. "His form dangled in the moonlight, and slowly it swung in the chilling wind," the account said, remaining there for 20 minutes before being cut down and taken to the undertaker's.

The joy of the Christmas season was dampened that day in Cisco by a robbery described as perhaps the most daring and bloody in the history of bank banditry in Texas. It involved many people—a total of 11 casualties—with violent death and enough high adventure for a metropolis, not to mention the quiet small city of Cisco in Eastland County.

An account of the tragedy by James P. McCracken, president of the First National Bank, was published in 1958. Dedicating the booklet, he said, "We desire that this booklet shall be dedicated to the memory of those fearless and devoted peace officers who gave their lives in bringing lawlessness before the bar of justice in this unforgettable event."

Such bold acts against banks gave substantial public support to the TBA in its crusade for dead bank robbers.

The nation's press carried a feature story from Uvalde in 1982 about an 81-year-old former bank and train robber who recalled his escapades in the heyday of banditry. Described as "one of the last remaining desperadoes from the Bonnie and Clyde era of the 1920s and 1930s," Joe Newton spoke freely about his life as a robber. For his escapades he served 11 years in prison. After a life of crime he settled down, and the news feature described him as a "beloved figure about town, something of a local celebrity" in Uvalde as a law-abiding citizen. Newton was pictured as having a horror of today's crime and criminals, the drunken and dope-crazed types. "There may have been a few like that back then, but not like today," he was quoted as saying. Newton's "career" included 74 bank robberies, mostly small banks, with safes blown late at night. He confirmed that it was fairly easy to rob a bank back then "because of slipshod security, poor communications and the ease of traveling with wads of cash in a time when virtually everything was bought for cash."

Once inside the bank, the bandits drew their revolvers and ordered all officials and employees to lie on the floor.

PART SEVEN

The Great Depression, Banking and the TBA In a Period of Financial Crisis

1

DISARRAY in the MARKETPLACE

"There is a crash coming . . . and it may be a terrific one."
ROGER BABSON, September 5, 1929

THE TBR NOTED THE EXCELLENT BUSINESS YEAR of 1928. "There was a slight applying of brakes with the appearance of the presidential election detour; but that narrow turn in the road once passed, every human seemed to step on the gas, and 1928 whizzed by in a glaze of new high records for producers, distributors and consumers. The year was one of incomprehensible speculation, high money rates, new high levels of production, and unheard of mergers in all lines of business," the story said.

"Does anybody dare say much about 1929? Well, hardly," was the question that soon demanded an answer.

The 1920s produced a new order of things in America. The coming of radio, improved highways, business development, growth of cities changed the nation in many respects. Buoyed by business and technological progress, the country nevertheless had seen the defeat of Wilson's peace efforts, moral disarray, labor unrest and disobedience to Prohibition. It was the flapper age with all of its free-wheeling attributes.

Prominent figures such as Charles A. Lindbergh and Admiral Richard E. Byrd caught the imagination of Americans. And it was the decade of the last hurrah of William Jennings Bryan in the Scopes Trial. Texans in remote places tuned in the world on the magic of radio, and a few bold bankers were enticed to speak on the air. Henry Ford abandoned the Model-T for the Model-A, rumble seat and all, with four-

It was the flapper age with all of its free-wheeling attributes.

139

wheel brakes. Other, fancier autos boasted of speed and luxury. The old buggy was forever relegated to the barnyard shed or to oblivion. Tractors replaced the mule and horse in the beginning of the machine age, but cotton, the big Texas money crop, still had to be picked by hand, and the boll weevil had to be reckoned with, although new chemicals appeared to reduce its propagating capacity.

This was the setting when the TBA met for the 45th convention in Galveston in May 1929. President W. A. Williams of San Antonio recalled the service of the association since its beginnings, consistent and constant service through the cooperation of its membership.

"The business attitude of the state, generally, is one of confidence in the future," he declared. But he warned that bankers should employ business principles and conservatism in the management of their banks.

A. A. (Buck) Horne of Galveston was elected to the presidency with the first signs of an approaching storm on the economic horizon.

Speculation, rapid rise in securities—many bought on margin—pyramided virtually out of control without regulation. The raw economics of the marketplace was in full bloom; human avarice undergirded the "get rich now" mentality.

The economy was as hot as the Texas sun in the summer of 1929. The boom was worldwide.

Banks made loans to speculators. Loans for securities appeared to be in order, as the record of the stock market was an upward spiral of bull enthusiasm for most of the 1920s. In 1927 the market advanced sharply. The Fed's low discount rate dropped to 3.5 percent. Purchase of government securities pumped the burgeoning economy to new peaks and provided funds for speculation in securities and real estate.

Plenty of money and plenty of takers, from the lowest to the highest echelons of American economic society. Even the old critics of free enterprise saw in the boom the epitome of opportunity for all.

Storm clouds and warnings!

Conservative bankers and the Fed viewed the situation with mixed emotions. To impose restrictive monetary measures might slow down the boom, and there was little inflationary pressure accompanying the upward ride. But the boom was out of control in stocks.

Even President Herbert Hoover campaigned on a note of good times. "We shall soon with the help of God be in sight of the day when poverty will be banished from this nation," he said.

Roger Babson on September 5, 1929, gave a dire prediction: "There is a crash coming, and it may be a terrific one." It might even involve a drop "from 60 to 80 points in the Dow-Jones barometer," he warned. Wall Street and America paid little attention to the prophets of caution, who were viewed as discreditors and scaremongers. But the Babson prediction did slow down market speculation.

Thursday, October 24, 1929—the day the bubble burst.

The previous day the stock market had plunged, wiped out months of gain and created a wild scramble to salvage whatever was possible from the plunge. When the market opened Thursday morning, pandemonium reigned. The ticker tape ran behind; near panic and confusion prevailed in New York. That was calmed somewhat

140

by noontime at the New York Stock Exchange when bankers met with J. P. Morgan to stop the plunge. But the downward trend continued from "Black Thursday" to the weekend, resumed the decline on Monday. Tuesday, October 29, 1929, was the day that shattered all optimism. The bottom fell out of the market; the average dropped 49 points and set in motion a downward slide that lasted till mid-1932.

The stock market crash in October was the precursor of the Great Depression, a violent contraction of the economy worldwide. The toll was severe. In 1929 AT&T dropped from 301¼ to 193¼; General Electric from 403 to 168⅛; U.S. Steel from 261¾ to 150.

The 1926–1929 boom and ensuing crash left in its wake an economy in near collapse, resulted in political changes of major magnitude, and established government as a leading force in management of business and banking.

The serious economic contraction, even with the advent of the New Deal and Franklin D. Roosevelt years, did not disappear until late 1939 when the nation began its rearmament program for World War II.

Business and bank failures mushroomed. Texas shared the sufferings of the Great Depression.

Bankers greeted 1930 with concern. TBA President Horne and the association leadership carefully reviewed their responsibilities. At the 46th convention in Fort Worth in May, six months after the stock market debacle, things were in a status quo condition, described by Andy Gidley of Lytle as meaning, in the words of an old country preacher: "Status quo . . . is Latin for we are in a hell of a mess!"

Delegates laughed; few disagreed.

Horne presided at the convention that devoted most of its attention to what was likely to happen to the crossroad bank, the small country bank. Branch banking was suggested as one solution, but Texas bankers "did not relish the trend." Others spoke of service charges. Horne supported unit banking as best for Texas. The convention record reveals very little panic about the economy.

When John Q. McAdams of Winters assumed the presidency in 1930, he probably viewed the honor with mixed emotions as the prospects for economic upheaval deepened.

Bank auditors were given an Audit Section with the TBA, "along the lines of the TBA Trust Section." H. F. Comfort, San Jacinto Trust Company, Houston, was selected as first chairman.

The association's protective committee discussed a $100,000 civil suit filed on November 2, 1928, by the mother of one of the men killed in the robbery of the Citizens National Bank, Odessa, in 1927. The TBA, 30 state and national banks, and the sheriffs of Ector, Midland and Upton counties, were named in the suit which was filed in District Court in Rains County. Representing the TBA were Judge Nelson Phillips, Dallas, former chief justice of the Texas Supreme Court; Judge L. A. Clark, Greenville; Judge O. H. Rodes of Emory; and the TBA regular attorney, R. G. Smith of Dallas. Judge Charles Gibbs of San Angelo represented the lawmen. The suit was tried and appealed to the Supreme Court of Texas, where the plaintiff lost.

As the economic gloom spread more attention was given to articles on the subject in the *TBR*. Alf Morris, Winnsboro banker, asked the question, "Is American busi-

ness sick unto death?" He answered with an emphatic no. Said the *TBR*: "Let's look
forward confidently, use our imaginations in visualizing the glorious future that lies
ahead, and work hard to speed its coming. We are sick of the pessimist. We would
like to boot every prophet of gloom where the booting is best."

President McAdams, after appraising the condition of Texas banking, concluded
that it was in generally sound condition and "for the most part bank failures within
recent months have been due to local causes." Efforts to squeeze the water "out of
fictitious values in real estate, stocks" had prepared the banks for the depression with
improved note cases. But it was recognized that falling farm prices and recent drought
had created distress. Deposits in Texas banks on September 24, 1930, were at a new
low. Speculation reduced, more funds were available for traditional use, and banks
had an ample supply of money. "Be sure the pendulum will swing back," McAdams
prophesied.

In 1931 the association broke its meeting cycle to hold the 47th convention in
San Angelo in May. In preconvention promotion it was suggested to bankers to quit
fretting and let Atlas do the worrying—he's supposed to carry the world. "It's time to
reason together in the fair city of San Angelo."

Not since 1903 had the convention met in a city that size, but San Angelo was
"little but loud," a city of 25,325 in 1931, with adequate hotels. And the convention
was a success—1,125 delegates attended.

Increasing bank robberies occupied a portion of the meeting.

Farm prices had dropped to 40-cent wheat, 18-cent oats, 25-cent corn and 6-cent
cotton. Red Cross relief was being distributed.

J. W. (Fred) Hoopes of Dallas was elected president. He summoned the TBA
membership to that city on October 20, to help relieve the critical cotton price situation. The Federal Farm Board had suggested a plan to withhold 7,000,000 bales.

The impact of the depression had struck in Texas.

In the November 1931 issue of the *TBR*, this "eruption of fear" was discussed.
Noting the high nervous tension "which has characterized the public mind in these
United States has erupted in . . . frenzied runs on banks and the loss of public confidence. . . . Thriving communities have suffered the first bank failures in their histories. Solvent as well as weak banks have succumbed."

Bank suspensions, consolidations and voluntary liquidations in the state totaled
112 from January 1 to October 31, 1931. Since Texas had 1,300 banks at the beginning of the year, the percentage was not as severe as it sounded—and Texas was
suffering fewer bank suspensions than most states. The nation's failure rate was 10.9
percent.

Wrote O. P. Newberry of Gorman: "In these days of five-cent cotton and thirty-
cent cigarettes the matter of bank management is a problem which confronts everyone whether he operates a large or small institution." He argued that no individual,
firm, bank or other corporation which was out of debt ever went broke.

Published in the *TBR* in February 1932 was a compilation of banking in 1931.
Nationally, only about 2 percent of total bank resources were tied up in closings.
Nearly 20,000 banks were operating at year's end, despite the 28,275 business failures,
unprecedented declines in real estate values and loss of confidence among depositors.

142

The crossroads bank in America had been the largest victim. Texas had lost 10.7 percent of its banks by closings or merger, reflecting a trend of states with a larger number of small banks. South Dakota, for example, had lost 21.3 percent.

As bank closings increased a flood of guaranty deposit bills were introduced in Congress. The Texas experience became a point in the consideration of the legislation.

"The Texas Bankers Association has been through many a rough sea, but perhaps the past year has claimed a larger toll of seasick passengers than any voyage we have taken since our organization in 1885," President Hoopes told the May 1932 convention in Austin. Texas ranked sixth in the number of banks in the nation in 1931, third in April 1932. He praised the conservative bankers of the state.

Congress had before it many bills regarding banking. The Revenue Act of 1932 required banks to impose a 2-cent tax on each bank check.

2
HOW ABOUT SERVICE CHARGES?

I do not expect my barber to put hair tonic on free, gratis, for nothing.
COMMENT OF A BANK CUSTOMER ON BANK SERVICE CHARGES

THE TBA LAUNCHED its schedule of uniform service charges—suggestions only for use by individual banks—in 1932.

Service charges for banks in Texas began in the early 1930s when bankers were blamed for nearly everything bad that was happening in the world of business. Banking revenues were declining; confidence in banking had reached a new low. New sources of earnings were sought. Banks analyzed costs and decided on an "activity" charge to be levied.

The origin and development of the movement for service charges in Texas banks can be traced clearly to 1929, when widely separated banks began applying certain charges in checking accounts. "At the beginning it was only the hardy, the daring, the courageous banker who advocated the service charge, and undertook to install it," reported the *TBR*. In 1929, the record shows, not more than 50 banks were selling service to their customers. One of these was the Lubbock National Bank, whose cashier was John D. Mitchell. He talked customers into the idea of a fee for certain transactions—at least to cover costs. Tough going at first—but once the customers understood a bank could only be sound when it is profitable, as is true of all business, the depositors responded. Cashier Mitchell received much attention for his actions and was invited to address the TBA convention in 1932 on the subject, "Modern

Banking Necessitates an Activity Charge." He made a rousing address, moving the delegates to action. The South Plains Bankers Association, meeting earlier, submitted a resolution for a uniform schedule of service charges for Texas banks. The TBA adopted the resolution unanimously—and set in motion a uniform schedule under the administration of President Melvin Rouff of Houston.

Mitchell's powerful address was spiked with humor. Said he, "Previous to the installation of bank service charges in Lubbock, we performed about as many free services as a centipede has legs—but today we have cut so many of these off that we have that same old centipede limping around on crutches."

President Rouff named Mitchell chairman of the Uniform Services Committee. On August 2, 1932, the TBA committee mailed to the membership a small booklet with an accompanying letter from President Rouff, urging that the charges as suggested, or similar ones, be installed in Texas banks. Wrote Rouff, "Unprofitable banking practices are the most unsound tendencies in modern banking. The failure of banks to collect adequate charges for services rendered has been, no doubt, the dominant cause of bank suspensions during the period of stress. The Texas Bankers Association now pleads for unified action on the part of every Texas banker in putting banking on a profitable basis in our State. . . . Some of these schedules, especially those pertaining to activity, analysis, and float, may at first seem complicated. A slight study, however, will convince you of their soundness, clearness and practicability," he wrote.

Some of the service charges suggested were: Accounts with average daily balance below $50, with five checks or less, a minimum monthly service charge of 50 cents; each check in addition to the five free checks, 3 cents. Above $50 average daily balance, one check free for each $10 balance; additional checks 3 cents, with minimum charge of 50 cents.

Accounts of churches, lodges, municipalities and charitable organizations were excepted.

The schedule for float charges was 5 cents for all items under $25, increased to 15 cents for all items $100 to $200, and 17 cents per $1,000 per day of float. On non-depositors on all out-of-town items cashed, a minimum rate of 25 cents per $100, with a minimum charge of 10 cents for handling any item, was required.

The booklet covered many other charges, such as overdrafts, charge backs, stop payments, various drafts, escrows, loans, buying and selling securities (stocks, one half of the broker's commission), credit reports, safe deposit box rentals (minimum annual charge of $2 and no free boxes), and trust department charges set forth in the 1930 schedule for Trust Section, TBA.

The booklet had numerous paragraphs that might be included in letters to bank customers: "Banking is like any other line of business, to be stable it must make a profit. . . ."

According to the *TBR*, "The movement went off with fervor. The service charge gospel was preached and practiced. Immediately county and sectional banking organizations became active. The TBA schedule of charges was taken as a basis—many groups adopting the charges as recommended without change. Others made minor changes in the charge schedule."

One banker reported that his bank lost two customers who had an "antagonistic attitude," and these two had been unsatisfactory accounts for months, "whose business we were glad to lose, and whose ill-will we already had."

Concluded the *TBR*, "It seemed that customer-resistance was only a bugaboo figment . . . and that the layman did not expect his banker to handle his banking business at a loss, or even without a fair profit."

One fellow quipped, the story continued, "I do not expect my barber to put hair tonic on free, gratis, for nothing!"

With the coming of the Roosevelt presidency in 1933, there was a banker's code for fair trade practices late that year. It specified service charges to all banks, effective January 1, 1934. There was a lot of confusion about the various codes of the NRA (National Recovery Act). Bankers often bristled over the confusion. But in the matter of service charges Texas bankers had the jump on Washington.

3
THE ROOSEVELT ERA BEGINS

I am prepared under my constitutional duty to recommend the measures that a stricken nation in the midst of a stricken world may require. . . .
FRANKLIN D. ROOSEVELT, first inaugural address, 1933

IN THE LATTER MONTHS of his administration President Hoover had recommended to Congress the Reconstruction Finance Corporation (RFC). Enacted, it provided public funds for lending to railroads, banks, agricultural agencies, industry and commerce. The action helped soften the pain of the depression, but the political tide was running against the incumbent. Hoover lost the 1932 election to Franklin D. Roosevelt.

Texas had a keen interest in the campaign. Roosevelt's running mate for vice president was John N. Garner of Uvalde, longtime member of Congress and Speaker of the House. He continued as vice president through the second FDR term.

As expected, the Roosevelt-Garner ticket swept Texas in 1932, 760,340 to 97,959. Elected governor again was Mrs. Miriam A. Ferguson, succeeding Ross Sterling.

Roosevelt was inaugurated March 4, 1933, at age 51, in the depth of the depression. At his side was "Cactus Jack" Garner. (In an effective maneuver at the Chicago convention in 1932, Sam Rayburn of Bonham had been asked to offer the vice presidency to Garner for Texas's support, sorely needed to put Roosevelt across on the fourth ballot.)

In office Roosevelt acted quickly. His first step was to declare a banking holiday,

In office Roosevelt acted quickly. His first step was to declare a banking holiday.

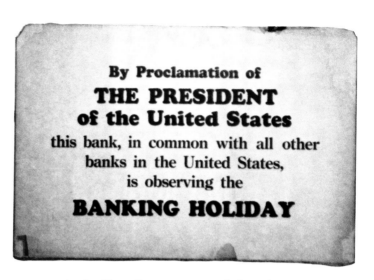

By Proclamation of
THE PRESIDENT
of the United States
this bank, in common with all other
banks in the United States,
is observing the

BANKING HOLIDAY

As the Great Depression spread throughout
the nation, Governor Ferguson and President
Roosevelt declared banking holidays in March
1933. It was the beginning of a new era in
bank regulation.

March 4–9. Then he summoned Congress into session March 9. From that date until June 16, the famous 100 days of action, the president and Congress put together a series of acts which embodied the New Deal. The Senate and House were overwhelmingly Democratic; action was quick.

"The clouds of the financial horizon of this country, which have been gradually darkening and lowering during the last three years, suddenly broke with a fury of a hurricane, during the last days of February and first days of March," wrote editor Philpott. "Men, able and strong, mean, ignorant and weak rushed to the safe-deposit storm cellars with all available cash clutched in trembling hands . . . no human was untouched by the panic. Fear gripped the minds and hearts of the populace," he wrote.

The banking bill quickly cleared Congress March 9. Bankers clamored for information. On March 11 it was announced that the banks would be reopened as quickly as their soundness could be determined.

Roosevelt addressed the nation by radio Sunday night, March 12, to explain his plan for financial reorganization. He focused the address on the common man.

Many Texans thought the banking holiday was unnecessary. They were far removed from the money centers and avoided much of the severe shock of the monetary panic.

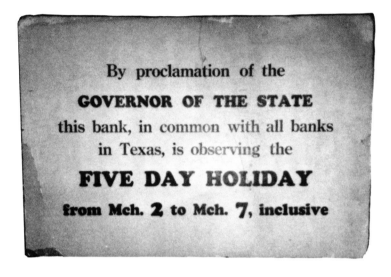

By proclamation of the

GOVERNOR OF THE STATE

this bank, in common with all banks
in Texas, is observing the

FIVE DAY HOLIDAY

from Mch. 2 to Mch. 7, inclusive

4
TEXAS and the BANKING HOLIDAY

"We left mother in Galveston."
JOHN M. GRIFFITH of Taylor, recalling the excitement of March 2, 1933

TEXAS WAS THE 22ND STATE to declare a bank holiday. March 2, 1933, was a state holiday, Texas Independence Day; all banks were closed. The deteriorating situation was watched closely by banking leaders in the state, including TBA President Rouff. These leaders came to Austin to meet with Governor Ferguson. She was advised of the gravity of the situation as other states were closing banks. At 4:30 p.m. on March 2, Governor Ferguson, after the session with banking leaders, issued a proclamation declaring a banking holiday for all Texas banks from March 3–7, inclusive. The Texas Legislature, in session, quickly enacted legislation empowering the commissioner of banking, with the governor's approval, to reopen all Texas banks when and as he saw fit, with the proper restrictions and regulations. Texas bankers had a major role in writing the law. Austin was a beehive of activity.

But President Roosevelt's action immediately after his inauguration proclaimed the national banking holiday March 5–9, inclusive. Tension was relaxed, and the 200 or so bankers who had gathered in Austin returned to their homes.

Monday, March 13, banks were reopened in the Federal Reserve cities. Tuesday,

At 4:30 p.m. on March 2, Governor Ferguson, after the session with banking leaders, issued a proclamation declaring a banking holiday for all Texas banks from March 3–7, inclusive.

147

March 14, all sound banks in clearinghouse cities opened. Other sound banks opened March 15. Order was restored without major disruptions, and banking resumed its important service.

The traumatic days of the banking holiday are still remembered by many of its survivors. In almost every instance there were moments of high crisis and, in some cases, examples of humor.

When three prominent Texas bankers such as Marcus Greer, Virgil Patterson and John Griffith sat down to talk about their banking experiences, their stimulating conversation often included many humorous episodes.

At the TBA convention in El Paso on April 30, 1981, these convivial fellows discussed a wide range of banking history they experienced before, during and after the Great Depression. In addition to each being a banker, Greer and Patterson had at one time been bank examiners, and all revealed vivid memories. (The session was recorded for the oral history archives of the TBA. Since that 1981 session, John Griffith has died.)

They discussed the Flying Squadron train trips, the gathering storm of depression that most bankers thought would be only temporary, the agony it brought, and the emergence of the postwar prosperity and banking changes.

Each of the three was a college graduate—Griffith and Patterson from SMU and Greer from UT—and had entered banking in the early 1920s. They jokingly recalled the "hard money" salaries as bank clerks of from $25 to $60 per month. Although college-educated, they began—as everyone else in those days—at the bottom and worked up to the top.

There is a classic story about the banking holiday that Griffith and Greer experienced.

It was March 2, 1933, a banking holiday for observance of Texas Independence Day. John Griffith's mother had gone to Galveston from Taylor to be with her daughter, Mrs. Marcus Greer, sister of John, for the birth of a son to the Greers. So John and his father decided that the holiday was a good time to drive to Galveston to bring John's mother home.

"The storm clouds were heavy and low, heavy over the economy of the nation, especially financial institutions," said Griffith. Banks were closing, lines of depositors were forming, some even in Texas, he recalled.

"We went to Galveston, had a nice visit in the morning. Buck Horne, executive vice president of the City National Bank where Marcus was cashier invited me to play golf. We had played three or four holes when we saw Dad and Marcus come running," John related. They reported that the Galveston Clearing House had received a call from Governor Ma Ferguson seeking advice on whether or not she as Governor of Texas should close the banks to avoid bank runs.

This was alarming information; it was more important than golf.

"We didn't even pick up our drives. Marcus and Mr. Horne went to the Clearing House meeting, and Dad and I got in our car and headed for home," John remembered.

"Dad and I had gone about 100 miles without saying a word, and finally I said, 'My God, Dad, we left Mother in Galveston!'"

During the banking holiday Governor Ferguson called a meeting of the bankers of

148

Texas to discuss plans for reopening the banks. Virgil Patterson, who was then assistant to the Chief National Bank Examiner, attended the meeting in Austin in place of his superior. The major bankers attended.

"Mrs. Ferguson was Governor, but Jim Ferguson (Pa) really ran the thing," Virgil remembered. "I sat on the back row. Jim Ferguson opened the meeting by saying that the purpose was to decide how to reopen the banks. There was great concern about what would happen," Virgil recounted. He recalls that the fear of runs on the banks led bankers to suggest that depositors ought to have a withdrawal limit, perhaps a dollar limit of something on the order of $20 to $100 per day.

Said Patterson, "Jim Ferguson took charge. 'I don't agree with any of you. The way to reopen the banks in Texas is to say COME AND GET IT! When you do what you fellows are talking about they will still be afraid of you.' He was the only one in the room that felt that way, but he dominated it and the banks were opened that way. He was right. Events proved it. There were no more runs."

One of the techniques used by some banks was to bring out stacks of vault cash and bags of coin and place them in clear view of anxious depositors who generally gained confidence after seeing the cash at the window. Some depositors withdrew their funds, took them to the U. S. Post Office for Postal Savings; the postal people then brought the money back to the bank for deposit. In all of the crucial days of the Great Depression fewer banks failed in Texas as a percentage of total banks than in most states. Much of the credit for this record was due to the soundness of most of the banks, conservative banking policies, and the cooperation of banking regulators who on occasion would go to a community where a bank was in trouble and urge local business people to put up more capital. In one instance a local business executive bought about $400,000 of a bank's delinquent notes to keep the institution open.

George G. Matkin, chairman of The State National Bank of El Paso, recalls many hair-raising experiences of the bank closing days. One small-town banker, fearing a run that would wipe out his institution, came to see Mr. Matkin, wept openly at his desk at his dilemma. Whereupon Mr. Matkin went to the vault and counted out a few thousands of dollars, adequate to withstand a run on the small bank, put them in a bag. The small-town banker left with the feeling that his burden had been lifted. A few days later he returned to El Paso, brought the money bag and returned it to Mr. Matkin unopened. No run had developed.

From experiences such as many old-time bankers tell, it is clear that those who survived the fire and ordeal of the banking holiday period emerged as even stronger bankers. Only 26 Texas banks failed to reopen.

Bill Kirkland in Houston tells of the time that the city's bankers met far into the night with Jesse Jones, nobody leaving the meeting until agreement was reached for Houston banks to support one another. That took a lot of arm-twisting in a few instances; banks were very competitive.

A veteran Midland banker, John P. Butler, when interviewed, commented, "The people didn't panic." Although bank customers could not draw money from their accounts during the holiday, merchants accepted checks from established customers. "Business went on," Butler said. He had been in banking since 1918, and had become a Midland banker in 1927, " . . . a town of around 3,000 when I came here."

In all of the crucial days of the Great Depression fewer banks failed in Texas as a percentage of total banks than in most states.

149

Banking in Texas soon got its second wind. Its story of growth and service in many ways defies the imagination. Incidentally, the first bank in Texas to cross the $100,000,000 was the First National Bank in Dallas. At the close of business on December 18, 1935, the stupendous total was reached, as reported in the *TBR*.

Continuing the rapid-fire action, President Roosevelt took the nation off the gold standard. Congress quickly ratified the Roosevelt proclamations; it was an era of emergency; actions were swift, often thought too hasty.

After the storm had subsided it was estimated that less than 2.6 percent of the banks in Texas failed to reopen. The public wanted banking; mass meetings were held urging support for reopening the banks.

To Mineral Wells went the bankers in May 1933 for the convention; there was plenty to discuss. President Rouff was pleased that 600 bankers attended at a time of banking crisis. Said the TBA leader, "The country has found the road away from disaster."

5

CONGRESSIONAL ACTION, ALPHABET AGENCIES, and GOLDEN JUBILEE

*On June 16, President Roosevelt signed the Glass-Steagall bill, and the Banking Act of
1933 became effective immediately.*
NEWS ITEM, *TBR*, 1933

MEMBERS OF CONGRESS HURRIED TO WASHINGTON in March 1933. Nine hours after convening on March 9 the Emergency Banking Relief Act was passed into law and signed by Roosevelt. Taking to the air on March 12 the president paid tribute to the people for their patience during the banking holiday. Stressing the role of banks in putting money to work for industry and agriculture, he said: "We do not want and will not have another epidemic of bank failures."

The Glass-Steagall bill was before Congress. One of its provisions was the Federal Deposit Insurance Corporation. The bill, quickly passed, was signed by President Roosevelt on June 16, and the Banking Act of 1933 became effective immediately. Texas did not like deposit insurance, but now it was the law. The same act divorced commercial and investment banking; it marked the change in the old concepts of banking. Henceforth, government regulation would impose a heavy hand on banking.

Temporary FDIC insurance was provided on deposits with balances less than $2,500 until July 1, 1934. Each Fed member had to apply for membership in the corporation and pay into it one-half of one percent of its deposits under the insured amount.

Nonmember banks were permitted to apply for membership with approval by the state authorities. The permanent FDIC insurance would become effective July 1, 1934. After that, all deposits not exceeding $10,000 were insured at 100 percent.

TBA President D. E. Blackburn of Victoria took the lead in holding appropriate meetings with state bankers to see what legislation was needed in the state banking law to conform with the new national legislation.

To aid the recovery, the Fed began a series of reductions in the discount rate, dropping it to one percent in 1937.

Although recovery was slow, it was visible. Confidence returned. Texas had fared much better than most states in the dark night of depression. Its diversified agricultural base had produced well, although at a lower price level. Adding to the picture was a growing oil production. Even with low prices nearly everything had a relative position.

An interesting development took place in October 1933, when the Texas Legislature passed a bill to create a Bank Deposit Insurance Company for state banks. With membership optional, it was a counterpart to the FDIC. It never got off the ground and was later disbanded.

Texas bankers whooped it up in Chicago, September 6, 1933. At the ABA convention Houston's F. Marion Law was elevated to the presidency of the ABA, the first Texas banker to head the large association. About 100 Texas bankers and members of their families sat up front to cheer the distinguished banker.

High in the leadership of the Roosevelt administration was another Houston banker and business leader, Jesse H. Jones, chairman of the RFC and later Secretary of Commerce. The powerful role he had in the economic recovery of the country and the speed with which it was achieved stands as a tribute to the man. Jones had the confidence of the nation's business community. His forthright manner convinced many a bank to take the government in partnership through capital stock purchases.

A provision of the National Recovery Act (NRA) startled some people. It required banks to set service charges and interest rates, and banks were given until December 31, 1933, to perfect the schedules in compliance with the code established for banks. A section of the code made possible uniform charges on all banking services in a given locality. Each bank account was supposed to pay its own way. Some bankers thought it was the first good hand "the banker has picked up in this new deal. It looks like four aces to us—let's play it hard," was the suggestion.

Getting out information on the NRA code was a major chore for the TBA. Many small banks in small towns thought the code would not apply to them. Said the association, "All banks . . . big and little, old and young, state and private and national are subject to the code." Along with the Banking Act of 1933 came the notable "Regulation Q" which set rates and banned interest on demand deposits.

R. E. Morrow, president of the Grapevine Home Bank, announced that he was tired of the banking business after 33 years and wanted to devote his time to farming and livestock interests. Proud of paying a dividend each year, he asked all depositors to come by and pick up their money. The course of governmental involvement in banking made many bankers of the old school consider a similar course. They did not relish Washington's alphabet soup of regulation.

Texas had fared better than most states in the dark night of depression.

151

The Golden Jubilee convention of the TBA was held in Dallas, May 15–17, 1934. President Blackburn presided at a more happy time since the economy was beginning its slow recovery, and bankers felt more like celebrating than in recent years in the depths of the depression. They danced to the music of Herbie Kay's orchestra and laughed at the comedy of Wheeler and Woolsey. ABA President Law addressed the convention. Sam R. Greer of Tyler was elected president. For the Golden Jubilee the Dallas Clearing House Association rolled out the red carpet for three days of "pleasure and profit."

Observed the *TBR*: "In the history of the universe 50 years is but a fleeting moment. But as banks, bankers and banking go, a half century span is several epochs. In 1934 banking no more resembled the old 40 percent, private banking of the 80s than will the 50th annual convention of the association in Dallas resemble the first meeting in Lampasas. The only similarity in the ages is the perplexities: we have the banking act of 1934 and the new deal; they had panics, talk of deposit guarantee and free silver. Man's vexations remain unchanged: then it was mustache cups, now it's diurnal shaving."

The convention program was printed in a gold-colored cover.

Blackburn reviewed the association's progress. Its peak in membership was reached in 1921 with 1,684. At the 1934 convention membership was 946, about the size of the TBA in 1909. Most of the drop was because of the mortality rate of banking in Texas—1,725 down to 1,000 in the same period.

At the 1934 convention 20 private bankers met and organized an association of private banks to consider and act on problems solely of interest to private banks "and cooperate with the Texas Bankers Association on all matters." J. D. Oppenheimer of San Antonio was named president.

During midsummer 1934 bankers rejoiced at the repeal of the 2-cent check tax, effective January 1, 1935. The repeal was put through by R. L. Doughton of North Carolina, a banker and chairman of the House committee, and President Roosevelt signed it.

Some uneasiness was being expressed at the increasing national debt which stood at $27 billion. Senator Carter Glass was concerned: "Pay day is coming and it will be pay for all this federal aid. . . .We need sound money . . . I'm never going to vote for any greenbacks," he declared.

It was the era of federal agencies. The *TBR* listed 42 new ones, known by abbreviations, beginning with the AAA to USUS.

Regulation F of the FDIC was issued August 2, 1934, requiring the display of the membership sign.

For Texas banker F. Marion Law, the ABA convention in Washington in October was a triumph. President Roosevelt was a speaker, along with Jesse H. Jones, RFC chairman. Several bankers were disturbed by Roosevelt's "fireside chat" of September 30 in which he scolded bankers for not helping their government as much as the British were helping theirs. Said President Law, "There is hardly a sane banker in the country who is not only willing, but eager to make good loans." Law had been in close touch with Roosevelt during the year of his ABA presidency and did much to keep banking in the support group of banking changes.

Some uneasiness was being expressed at the increasing national debt which stood at $27 billion.

152

Speaking at the ABA convention October 24, Roosevelt reminded the delegates: "Government should assert its leadership in encouraging not only the confidence of the people in banks, but the confidence of banks in people." He said the time was ripe for all forces intent upon the business recovery to form an alliance to accomplish it.

President Law returned home to Houston to a grand welcome November 16. He had performed in "super-man style, and as a real confidant of the president of the United States. . . . Houston is proud of 'Brother Law,' as Franklin D. calls him. Texas is proud of him—and so is the nation," the *TBR* said editorially.

President Greer presided at the May 1935 convention in Galveston. An entertainment feature was "two high-powered song and dance men, R. E. Shepherd and Jack Garrett of Dallas."

Fred F. Florence of Dallas was elected president. He presented a positive banking picture, both in Texas and in the nation. "The only semblance of a cloud to be seen on the business horizon at this time is a nebulous, misty, shadowy thing we call 'inflation,'" he said. Calling it a sinister and ruinous cloud, he noted that the recovery had shown that it was possible to emerge from the depression without inflation.

In 1935 the bankers of Texas began the aggressive promotion of the Texas Centennial Exposition. The first observance of the year was held in Gonzales, where the first shot for Texas independence was fired October 2, 1835.

The Banking Act of 1935 eliminated the double-liability requirement for national bank stockholders, effective July 1. The TBA moved to do the same for state bank stockholders. But it would take a legislative act, signature of the governor and vote of the people to amend the constitution. Through the strong leadership of the association, voters approved the amendment in a special election August 27, 1937. Dan Lydick of Fort Worth led the TBA effort as head of the TBA State Bank Committee which had been established in 1935.

The act gave permanent status to the FDIC, gave monetary control as the main focus of the Federal Reserve, changed the Federal Reserve Board to Board of Governors and created an open market committee.

An innovation in banking education began with the Graduate School of Banking at Rutgers University, sponsored by the ABA, AIB and Rutgers, held June 17–29, 1935. Five students from Texas were in the charter class: John Franklin Austin, Jr., Frankston; F. M. Harriss, Jr., El Paso; Edwin Peter Neilan, Dallas; William L. Tandy, Houston; and William Floyd Worthington, Dallas.

New Deal legislation continued to rain down from Washington, including the establishment of the Social Security system. It covered two aspects, unemployment compensation and old-age benefits. Banks were covered. Tax on the employer and employee began at 1 percent from 1937 to 1939, escalated annually to 3 percent in 1949. That was said to be the absolute limit.

Concluding his year as president at the 52nd TBA convention in Houston in May, Fred Florence was pleased to report that the year "has not been marked by any great emergency or outstanding event."

One of the highlights of the 1936 convention was the reestablishment of TBA district three, the territory adjacent to Austin, which had been discontinued in 1925.

The Banking Act of 1935 gave permanent status to the FDIC, gave monetary control as the main focus of the Federal Reserve, changed the Federal Reserve Board of Governors and created an open market committee.

153

President Theodore H. Nees of Beaumont named a young Taylor banker, John M. Griffith, as chairman.

September 15, 1936, was Bankers Day at the Texas Centennial Exposition in Dallas. Special railroad cars were used to take the large crowd to the big event.

A member of Congress from Texas, Representative Wright Patman of Texarkana, long to be identified with banking legislation and regulation, began to appear in the news. In 1937 he introduced a bill to provide for government ownership of the Federal Reserve banks.

President Nees, at the 1937 convention in San Antonio, admonished the bankers to pay attention to the note case. On depressions: "I will tell you the worse thing about them . . . is that they have been coming with a periodicity of too close to seven to ten years to make me feel just as comfortable as I would like to. . . ." Delegates again voiced opposition to branch banking.

While J. E. Woods of Temple headed the TBA, the chief issues were double liability, proposals in the Congress for branch banking and the Patman proposal for Fed ownership by the government. In his address at the Fort Worth convention in 1938, Woods waved off recession talk. "In Texas, by reason of our favored position, the business recession is probably more threatened than real," he declared.

One of the grand events of the year was the ABA convention in Houston, returning for the second time, November 14–18.

President Oral Jones of Wichita Falls presided at the 1939 convention in Dallas. Attendance at the TBA conventions had leveled off at about 1,500, the figure for that meeting.

A new member of the TBA headquarters staff, Milton Boswell, 22, a June 1939 graduate of The University of Texas School of Business Administration, became associate editor of the *Texas Bankers Record.* His name appeared on the masthead in July. A native of Plainview, his university studies had included journalism and trade association work.

Boswell was welcomed to the staff by Editor Philpott, who predicted: "Bankers of Texas will like Milton Boswell, and they will be pleased with his work."

When Philpott retired January 1, 1964, Boswell became editor of the *TBR*, served as acting secretary of the TBA and continued the editorship full time until his retirement in September 1981. Under his direction the *TBR* became the foremost state banking magazine in the nation. As did Philpott, Boswell spent a lifetime career in service to the TBA.

Another major step was taken in 1939 by the creation of the TBA Educational Conference, September 4–7, at The University of Texas in Austin. President Dan E. Lydick of Fort Worth named an impressive committee to plan the conference, consisting of J. Lewell Lafferty of Fort Worth; F. R. Barney of San Angelo; John M. Griffith, Taylor; and W. J. Evans, Dallas. A heavy registration—197—was present for the first conference, assembling in the sizzling heat in Hogg Memorial Auditorium.

Official Program

WARTIME
CONFERENCE

59th Annual Meeting

of the

Texas Bankers
Association

FORT WORTH
May 26-27, 1943

With national emphasis on World War II, the
TBA held its annual meeting in Fort Worth
and called it a Wartime Conference instead of
a convention. Speakers covered the pressing
issues caused by war.

PART EIGHT

World War II—America An Arsenal of Democracy

1

FINANCING GLOBAL CONFLICT— TEXAS BANKING on the LINE

War, he sung, is toil and trouble; Fighting still and still destroying . . . .
JOHN DRYDEN

A NEW WAR WAS RAGING IN EUROPE. Memories of World War I were fresh in the minds of many Texas bankers. Would the United States be involved? This was forefront in the thoughts of delegates as they gathered in Galveston for the 56th convention in 1940. The forces of Adolph Hitler were threatening to cross the English Channel. Each newspaper headline was anxiously read.

President Lydick noted the sadness caused by the death of Earl Noble of Texas City, the TBA treasurer. It was the first time the association had a convention with one of its general offices vacant.

The fate of London appeared in the balance as Nazi planes began their onslaught in September. America, strongly divided in war sentiment, began a crash defense program. President Walter P. Napier of San Antonio, addressing the convention in 1941, called on banking and business to "support every intelligent proposal to finance properly the contemplated increase in production and consumption to the end that dangerous inflationary trends are limited and excessive reserves controlled."

The march to World War II appeared inevitable when France fell to Germany in 1940 and Japan joined the Axis. The U. S. adopted selective service. Lend-lease followed in 1941. Germany invaded Russia. U. S. peace efforts collapsed.

Sunday, December 7, 1941, the Japanese attacked Pearl Harbor; the war was on for the U. S. Everything must be aimed toward victory. That was the position of the TBA. Bonds for victory! President Roosevelt estimated it would cost $86 billion to prosecute the war through 1943.

The association continued with plans for the district meetings and for the convention in San Antonio in May. The ABA canceled its annual convention in favor of a National Conference on Wartime Finance, held in Detroit.

The TBA and the World War II years can be summarized briefly:

1942—P. R. Hamil, Bay City, was president; the convention was held in San Antonio with the emphasis on wartime banking and war effort. No meetings were canceled. Texas banks were deeply involved in selling Defense Bonds; the TBA supported Governor Coke Stevenson in his opposition to gasoline rationing. Membership stood at 892. Women were "manning" banks, as Friona State Bank became the "first 100 percent all-woman bank in the nation." In November E. M. Longcope, Sr., died in Houston, remembered as one of the founders of the TBA in 1885. P. R. Doty of Beaumont was elected president.

1943—Banks in five of the six TBA districts voted not to hold annual meetings because of the war and lack of gasoline, but Dallas in the fifth district met. President Doty led the association in a "let's win the war in 1943" cry; banks began handling ration coupons; civilian goods diminished. The new Texas banking code was adopted, pushed by the TBA State Bank Committee. Bankers viewed with alarm the spread of government credit to farmers. The 59th convention in Fort Worth in May was streamlined, called the TBA Wartime Conference. The TBA Conference at The University of Texas was canceled. Nathan Adams of Dallas continued to lead in war loan drives, the third, with a quota for Texas of $420,000,000. Milton Boswell, *TBR* associate editor and assistant secretary of the TBA, had been given leave of absence to serve in the U. S. Air Force for the duration. J. O. Gillham of Brownfield was elected TBA president.

1944—Seven district meetings were held in February. The 60th convention met in Dallas in May. TBA supported the Fifth War Loan Drive on the theme, "Back the Attack, Buy More than Before." Deposits in Texas banks reached a high of $3,636,290,000 at the end of 1943. The TBA constitution was changed to provide for a vice president to succeed to the presidency in 1945, and DeWitt T. Ray of Dallas was elected to the vice presidency. Marvin C. Ulmer of Midland was elected president. There were prayers for the D-Day landing in Normandy. "Put national welfare above everything else," urged Ulmer, and numerous meetings were canceled. A quota of $414,000,000 for the Sixth War Loan Drive was given Texas. The "G.I. Bill of Rights" was adopted, and the TBA studied amendments necessary in Texas law for G. I. loans. Prospects for victory in Europe and the Pacific brightened as the year ended. Texas bankers continued to be numbered among the fallen and the wounded in far-flung areas of combat.

1945—The impact of three years of war on Texas banking, soaring deposits, involvement in war work, prayers for victory and durable peace absorbed the TBA members. But the year was to restrict meeting activities.

2
THE TBA CONVENTION
is CANCELED for the FIRST TIME

Japan, we are after you and nothing short of utter destruction for you will satisfy us.
COMMENT, *TBR*, May 1945, following German surrender

ALL TBA DISTRICT MEETINGS WERE CANCELED at the request of War Mobilization Director James Byrnes. The 61st TBA convention was canceled because of a request of the Office of Defense Transportation, the first one missed in 60 years, and 1945 became known as the conventionless year. The Seventh War Loan Drive quota was $168,000,000. Germany surrendered on May 8. Commented the *TBR*: "Japan, we are after you and nothing short of utter destruction for you will satisfy us." He predicted that bankers would not fail their responsibility in the postwar period. Monetary storm signals were flying, as the U. S. budget reached $99 billion, with $88 billion going to the war effort in 1945. Virgil Patterson of Amarillo urged bankers not to give veterans the brush-off. Murray Kyger of Fort Worth was named chairman of the special G. I. Bill Committee. The Executive Committee asked President Ulmer to hold over as TBA president, along with all other TBA officers, since no convention could be held. He became the first president in the TBA history to serve two terms. The association noted that its legislative committee, headed by J. A. Elkins of Houston, scored 100 percent performance in the legislature.

3
PEACE and PROSPERITY

While it is true that our past may be a pattern, it is axiomatically true that our individual future is a destiny.
MARVIN C. ULMER, TBA president, 1945

VICTORY IN THE PACIFIC—JAPAN SURRENDERED. Veterans returned to their banking posts in Texas. Now the "marching home" wish had become a reality. "All of us are tired to death of war and thoughts of war," was the popular saying. Women bankers had served well, a total of 415 women held officers' positions in Texas banks, including 13 presidencies.

Banking deposits in the nation's 14,500 banks had climbed to the great sum of $140 billion—and Texas bankers were amazed. "Just how high can deposits go?" was a question often asked. The wartime increase of bank deposits had given Texas banks their share. Eight banks had deposits of more than $100,000,000: First National, Dallas, $291,500,000; Republic, Dallas, $221,100,000; Commerce, Houston, $156,100,000; Fort Worth National, $140,400,000; First National, Houston, $138,500,000; Mercantile, Dallas, $133,200,000; First National, Fort Worth, $110,400,000; and Second National, Houston, $104,200,000, all end-of-year-1944 statements, described as "staggering figures."

Texans were pleased with the fast rate with which wartime restrictions were being removed. Coupled with peace and prosperity, the return to normalcy was soon achieved.

Roosevelt's fourth-term election in 1944 produced another landslide in Texas over Thomas E. Dewey. Upon FDR's death April 12, 1945, Harry Truman became president. He promised to "pitch out the window" many of the restrictions, regulations and emergency activities as quickly as possible.

On December 31, 1945, there were in Texas 434 national banks and 409 state banks. Total deposits in the national banks were $5.166 billion; state banks, $952,200,000.

Looking ahead, bankers projected a downward trend in deposits, but an increase in loan demand to support the widespread industrial development.

A movement to permit banks to operate on a five-day schedule began; farmers and ranchers objected.

Texans were pleased with the fast rate with which wartime restrictions were being removed.

160

PART NINE

A New TBA Era–
The Movers and Shakers

1

LEADERS, ISSUES and INVOLVEMENT

Government . . . must quit tinkering with our economic clock.
DEWITT T. RAY, TBA president, 1947

POSTWAR TEXAS CONTINUED TO VOTE for Democrats, including the election of Representative Lyndon B. Johnson for the U. S. Senate. Upon the death of Governor Beauford H. Jester in 1949, Lieutenant Governor Allan Shivers took over the office. Although Truman defeated Dewey in 1948 with Texas's support, voters began to make the Democratic-Republican contests closer. In 1952 and 1956 Governor Shivers refused to support Adlai Stevenson, and native-born (at Denison) Dwight D. Eisenhower, the Republican nominee, carried Texas and the nation in both elections. Senator Johnson and Representative Sam Rayburn, through their senior Congressional leadership, gave Texas a double dose of political astuteness and national recognition. The issue of tidelands oil and his successful fight for Texas on that issue projected Senator Price Daniel into the governorship in 1957.

In 1960 the Kennedy-Johnson ticket helped the Democrats carry Texas, a crucial state, over Richard M. Nixon. With the assassination of President Kennedy in Dallas in November 1963, Johnson became president, the second native Texan to hold the office. John M. Connally had succeeded Daniel as governor in 1962 and was seriously wounded in the Dallas tragedy. The Democratic structure of Texas, largely conservative, had widespread support among bankers. But Ralph Yarborough, a liberal, won a special election for the U. S. Senate in 1957 and served until defeated by Lloyd Bentsen. John Tower, a Wichita Falls Republican, succeeded Johnson in the U. S. Senate in 1961. Senator Bentsen's father, Lloyd M. Bentsen, had developed widespread banking and business interests in the McAllen-Mission area of the Lower Rio

Grande. His son has always counted bankers among his supporters, including in his reelection campaign in 1982.

President Johnson was reelected in 1964. He did not seek reelection, and in 1968 Texas voters supported Hubert H. Humphrey, but nationally Nixon won. President Nixon carried Texas over George McGovern in 1972, and Democrat Dolph Briscoe was elected governor, keeping the state's top elective office in the hands of Democrats. Briscoe had long been connected with banking in the state as a bank executive in Uvalde. Nixon's resignation over the Watergate controversy put Gerald Ford in office. Democrat Jimmy Carter defeated Ford in the 1976 election, with Texas overwhelmingly supporting the Georgian. Governor Briscoe was reelected and held the office until 1979, when William Clements, a Republican, became governor. He was defeated for reelection in 1982 by Democrat Mark White who was inaugurated in 1983. Meanwhile Senators Tower and Bentsen continued in office, giving Texas two-party representation in the Senate. That pattern was reflected in several of the House seats. Throughout the post-World War II period much of the state and national leadership of Texas had banking connections in one way or another. Too, Texas bankers were more involved in political affairs, and the TBA formed and operated a political action committee.

As the third "generation" of bankers became the movers and shakers after World War II, they brought to the TBA innovations, activities and new strategies that necessitated a broad-based involvement of the membership. The three rather clearly identifiable "generations" are the presidents from James F. Miller in 1885 to H. P. Hilliard in 1902; from Hilliard to DeWitt T. Ray in 1946; and from Ray to the present. Each of these leaders faced significant issues and led the association exceptionally well in their times.

DeWitt T. Ray of Dallas succeeded M. C. Ulmer of Midland as TBA president at the 1946 convention in Galveston. As mentioned, this generation of postwar bankers marked a new phase of TBA activity and launched four decades of positive change of the role and function of the association.

In 1947 Houston could boast of 500,000 population; it could handle easily the 1,760 delegates and guests of the 63rd convention. President Ray told the delegates: "The period in which we are now living will undoubtedly be designated by historians as the 'Atomic Age.'" He and other bankers were becoming concerned about the "huge public debt" of $285 billion. "Government, through its multiplicity of bureaus, must quit tinkering with our economic clock," he said.

W. A. Kirkland, Houston banker, was elected president. He had recently returned from duty as a naval officer in World War II (he also served in World War I) and had worked with fellow Houstonian Jesse H. Jones in the RFC in Washington. Bill Kirkland, a great-grandson of B. A. Shepherd, one of the founders in the Civil War days of the First National Bank, Houston, helped to establish the TBA retirement system, which became effective in 1948.

When the 1948 convention assembled in San Antonio, Kirkland pleasantly surprised delegates by becoming the first president to refrain from a long and detailed address. Instead he prepared a few succinct paragraphs, including emphasis on the soundness of the two "great systems of unit banking in Texas," and praise for the country-city bank relationship including his appreciation for the "great correspondent banking network."

A sad note of 1948 was the death of J. W. (Fred) Hoopes, former secretary of the TBA and founder of the *Texas Bankers Record* in 1911. He had been president of the TBA and treasurer of the ABA as well.

Milton Boswell, associate editor, reported that William A. Philpott's book, *In Praise of Ignorance*, was being bound and would soon be ready at $5 a copy. Only 500 copies were printed.

Texas banks continued to show increases in deposits for 1949. Houston banks had $1.1 billion; Dallas, $1.08 billion; Fort Worth, $400.7 million; San Antonio, $390 million; El Paso, $148.3 million.

The proposal for five-day banking created a furor in 1949. The TBA directed a survey: Question—Do you favor or oppose Saturday closing for Texas banks? Results: 432 opposed; 266 favored. Divided opinion? Yes, but the TBA had managed it before.

The 1949 convention in Fort Worth in May will long be remembered as one that almost didn't come off—due to high water! Two thousand bankers and guests were expected. Then, on Monday night, May 16, the heavy rains flooded the Trinity River, broke the levees, and Fort Worth suffered with thousands homeless. Plans were changed, all entertainment canceled by the Fort Worth Clearing House Association, and messages were dispatched to the registrants. The convention—beginning May 23—was reduced to one and a half days, with a compact business session daily. Attendance was 604 bankers who sat through the speeches "as there was nowhere else to go."

President John T. Yantis of Brownwood, noting it was the 65th convention, said that was the normal age for retirement, "but such is not the case with this association."

Fort Worth, pretty well flooded out for the 1949 convention, got the conclave again in 1950. Eighteen hundred delegates and guests arrived May 15. President Tom E. Acker of Jacksonville reported that 6,500 had attended the round of district meetings and that TBA membership was 977, every commercial bank but four having joined.

The May 1951 issue of the *TBR* was dedicated to a number of former TBA presidents who were asked to give their views. There were 25 of the former leaders living.

President C. E. McCutchen of Wichita Falls told the 1951 convention in Dallas that the rise of inflation, "greater now than any we have known since the time of the thirteen original states," was a reality. But he noted some signs of abatement.

"There isn't a Yes Man in the crowd," President A. E. Dabney, Jr., Corpus Christi, told the 68th convention in Galveston, May 1952. It was his way of praising the association. During the year the First Annual Texas Farm and Ranch Credit School for commercial banks was announced. It was held December 9–12 at Texas A&M campus.

Another major change during his administration was the move to charge a registration fee for all TBA meetings, the first time this policy had been approved by the council. Effective for the 1953 convention, it was justified on the preference of convention quality to attendance. Host cities were being pressed to handle the conventions, which meetings were famous nationally. For 68 years no fee had been charged;

The proposal for five-day banking created a furor in 1949.

163

how would the bankers react? The convention fee was set at $10 for each man and $5 for each woman. The funds collected would be expended by the local clearinghouse association.

W. Guy Draper of Temple, TBA president, reported to the 69th convention in Houston in 1953, that the registration fee was understood and accepted by the delegates.

The TBA Installment Credit Section was created; it held its first meeting in Fort Worth January 17, 1953. Record attendance was reported by nearly all of the elements of the association.

W. Neal Greer of Houston, TBA president, urged action for career development and opportunity to recruit bright young people for banking's top management. His views were stressed to the 1954 convention in San Antonio in May. "It is agreed that in many banks throughout the country the ranking officers are elderly men," he said. He urged swift promotion of the qualified.

Turning to the association, Greer asserted: "The TBA, while old, is not senile or palsied—it is still growing strong." And the older it got, the stronger it would get, he predicted.

Delegates endorsed Fred F. Florence of Dallas for vice president of the ABA, putting him in line for the presidency at the ABA 1954 convention.

The TBA president at the 71st convention in Fort Worth in May 1955 was a Taylor banker, a precise and orderly leader. John M. Griffith started the proceedings on time, finished ahead of time. Special entertainment featured the George Gobel Show. The 1,880 registrants confirmed the wisdom of the advocates of a convention registration fee—it had not reduced attendance at all.

Griffith told the delegates that the gross national product stood at $370 billion; the nation had fully recovered from the recent recession; recent rains had given comfort to the farmers of Texas; and there was little unemployment. The association was in good order, and members were paying the same dues they did in 1925. He noted the work of the TBA Trust Section in the passage of the new Texas Probate Code, "a model code for the country."

Efforts to secure enactment of a permissive five-day week law for the state were successful in 1955. Immediately 98 banks filed resolutions with the authorities to observe the new law, effective April 2. The remaining 875 or so banks kept their customary banking days. As far back as 1951 Harris McAshan of Houston had argued strongly for a five-day week law. The difficulty of getting bank employees to work six days a week was advanced as a major reason for change. Thirty-six states had already made the change to provide a choice.

The campaign for Fred Florence's election as ABA vice president produced favorable results—he was elected at the 1954 convention in Atlantic City. And September 28, 1955, was a happy day for Texas bankers at the ABA convention in Chicago—Florence was elevated to the ABA presidency. Some 425 Texans were on hand to applaud the Dallas banker, who became the second Texas banker to head the ABA with a membership of 14,000 banks. (Houston's F. Marion Law was the first.)

Florence was born in New York City in 1891 to immigrant parents, moved with his parents to Texas when only six months old and lived in Rusk. He had a successful banking career that took him to Dallas. Along the way he took time to serve as TBA president. To the cheering delegates he said: "Our strength in providing constructive financial leadership lies in our unanimity and wisdom." He believed banking would keep pace "with ingenuity in science and business."

A Texas banker with theatrical flair and a storyteller of acclaim took the TBA gavel as president at the 1955 convention. P. B. (Jack) Garrett of Dallas was dubbed the "Texas edition of George M. Cohan." Although trained in law and having practiced, he chose banking. He had been a flyer in World War I. There was never a dull moment around Jack Garrett. He drove across his points with good stories, well told, and a feature of his year was banking education. The state approved the TBA's manual on money and banking for use in the high schools to encourage young people to make banking career choices.

Association members elected at the Dallas convention Joe A. Clarke of Fort Worth. As had his predecessor, Clarke had musical talent; he was a performer, a trumpeter of note.

The TBA convention met in Galveston in 1957, the first convention to be held in the new Moody Civic Center. President Clarke affirmed the good financial condition of the association; for the first time it had assets in excess of $50,000. The dues (ranging from $10 to $150) was reported as the lowest in the country for any banking association.

Under the leadership of President Roy Selby of Ganado, the administrative council approved the 1958 "Flying Squadron Trip," and the Audit Section, established 27 years previously, was changed to the Bank Operations Section. W. A. Philpott, Jr., was elected secretary for the 42nd year; Milton Boswell was reelected association manager; and Mrs. J. O. Tyler was reelected office secretary.

In 1957 the TBA turned its attention to the newly founded Southwestern Graduate School of Banking at Southern Methodist University in Dallas, a school called SWIGSBIE. Fred Florence recommended its support to the TBA council.

The first session was held in 1958. It was the outgrowth of an idea advanced by a Tyler banker, Roger Harris. The Dallas Clearing House Association agreed to underwrite the school financially up to $10,000. Dr. Richard B. Johnson of SMU was asked to be the school's first director. DeWitt T. Ray, Dallas banker and former TBA president, was named the first banker dean. Johnson and Ray organized a blue ribbon advisory committee of Dallas bankers. The first class had an enrollment of 196, including seven women. A young El Paso banker, Sam Young, Jr., was its first president. Also a member of the first class was Charlie Childers, as Young, a future TBA president. Fred Korth of San Antonio was the baccalaureate speaker.

As noted by President Selby at the 1958 convention in Houston, interest rates were declining. With 90-day bills bringing "in the neighborhood of 1 percent, surely we have cause to become alarmed." Although he believed in credit availability at "reasonable cost" to support economic recovery, "I believe that money can become too cheap," he said.

2
FIESTA TIME for the OLD TBA—
the DIAMOND JUBILEE

*Truth is, the good ship TBA is more seaworthy now, even amid the typhoons and
maelstroms of our modern world, than when it timidly set out from the shore at Lampasas
Springs in 1885.*
HOWARD HAMBLETON, TBA president, 1959

THE TBA, HEADED BY HOWARD HAMBLETON, Waco, set about planning for its
75th anniversary, the Diamond Jubilee celebration to be at the convention in San
Antonio in May 1959.

It was another active year. Texas bankers applauded Frank Price of Houston, who
had become president of the National Association of Bank Auditors and Comptrol-
lers (NABAC) July 1.

Hambleton prodded bankers to pay attention to legislative matters in Austin. One
issue dealt with the escheats law, and it was the subject of intense legislative battles.

When the Diamond Jubilee Convention met in May, about 1,800 bankers and
guests were present, representing some 625 different Texas banks, along with more
than 100 out-of-state institutions. It was fiesta time for the old TBA. From the time
Dan Oppenheimer of the host metropolis presented the "keys to the city" to the last
gavel sound, there were noted speakers and lavish entertainment to make the convention memorable as one of "many carats."

President Hambleton reviewed the traditions of the TBA: "Its steadfast course for
conservatism as opposed to the radical and controversial position, has kept its sails
spread to tempered winds that have borne the craft straight forward, so that even the
stormy weather gales have not torn the canvas, neither has the hull been scarred by
rocks and reefs. Truth is, the good ship TBA is more seaworthy now, even amid the
typhoons and maelstroms of our modern world, than when it timidly set out from the
shore at Lampasas Springs in 1885."

Delegates endorsed the candidacy of I. Frank Betts, Beaumont banker, for treasurer of the ABA. He was elected without opposition at the ABA convention in
Miami, the second Texas banker to hold the office. It was a vintage year for Texas
bankers in organizational leadership. Charles Hamilton of Houston was elected president of the ABA Trust Division. Reed Sass of Fort Worth was elected president of the
Financial Public Relations Association, later the Bank Marketing Association.

Ben Wooten, Dallas banker, was given the Horatio Alger "rags to riches" award in
New York. It noted that he had been born on a small farm outside Timpson in east
Texas and had worn homemade clothes while doing farm work and picking cotton
and cutting cordwood with his father. His success story was well known to Texas
bankers; many of them had come from similar backgrounds. At the Miami conven-

It was fiesta time for
the old TBA.

166

tion of the ABA in October 1959, Wooten appeared on the program since he had been appointed chairman for the observance of the 100th anniversary of the national banking system in 1963. The TBA had a special train to the convention.

A Tyler banker, W. A. (Abe) Pounds was the TBA president in May 1960, preparing for the convention in Fort Worth, but he was stricken with a heart attack while sitting at his desk only one week before the meeting. He had taken the association through a rigorous year. Unable to attend, Pounds asked W. Dewey Lawrence, also of Tyler, to read his prepared address.

"I may be a bit down—but not out. And if they will just let me have my cigarettes I'll get out of here, and quick," the ailing president wrote the 1,786 delegates.

In the decade of the 1950s—now passed into history—there was the war in Korea, authorization of the H-bomb by President Truman, and the launching in 1954 of *Nautilus*, the first atomic submarine. The U. S. Supreme Court had struck down racial segregation in public schools on May 17, 1954. The bill creating the interstate highway system had been signed by President Eisenhower in 1956; the same year the first orbital satellite had been launched; the first jet airline service had been inaugurated; and in 1959 Alaska had been admitted as the 49th state and Hawaii as the 50th. Also enacted by Congress was substantial banking legislation, including bank holding company activities.

As Texas began the decade of the 1960s, it numbered a population of 9,579,000, 24.2 percent gain over the 7,700,000 of 1950. Texas banks had total resources of $12.296 billion, and deposit totals were equally impressive.

El Paso's Thomas C. Patterson, TBA president at the 1961 convention in Dallas, listed a year of accomplishment, including attendance of 6,500 at the district meetings. He urged bankers to help elect good men as lawmakers. Delegates were pleased to see W. A. (Abe) Pounds. Now recovered, he was asked to preside at one of the sessions.

Farewell to Galveston! The 78th convention assembled in the island city in May 1962. It was the last of the long series of meetings held in Galveston, going back to 1887 when the third meeting was held there. President Lawrence S. Goforth, Comfort, discussed the fast growth of "politically aided credit unions." Delegates agreed that credit unions should be "confined to the purpose for which they were intended . . . proper and constructive [was] the original concept under which a group of persons with a common bond may organize and operate a credit union. . . ."

It was at Galveston that Virgil P. Patterson, Amarillo banker, was elected TBA president. Another of the new breed of postwar leaders, he addressed the Panhandle Bankers Association in his home city and put forth a basic tenet: Modern banking requires and gets good talent. He affirmed that the beginning of modern banking followed World War II. Describing the banker of 1962, the one-time national bank examiner stated these characteristics: Younger, better educated, not tested by depression, a "team man" who likes people, who works well with his associates and is active in local and state affairs. In a way, he was describing himself. While the affable Amarillo banker was TBA president, there was the fruition of a movement considered for some time—the creation of a separate association for state chartered banks.

167

3
A DECISIVE ACTION—
STATE BANKERS ORGANIZE

. . . the new association will in no way conflict with, or take the place of, any function or
activity of the Texas Bankers Association.
P. B. (JACK) GARRETT, Association of State Chartered Banks

IT WAS A DECISIVE PERIOD FOR THE TBA. A meeting was held in Austin on September 7, 1962, attended by some 400 state bankers. The Association of State Chartered Banks (ASCB) in Texas was organized. P. B. (Jack) Garrett of Dallas, former TBA president, was elected chairman.

In the September issue of the *TBR* he stated: "I want to stress . . . that the new association will in no way conflict with, or take the place of, any function or activity of the Texas Bankers Association. On the contrary, the new association of state chartered banks will be helpful to the TBA in many ways, especially on legislative matters, in which we have common interests with national banks."

Advocates of the new association felt that efforts for branch banking would jeopardize the dual banking system. Commissioner of Banking J. M. Falkner attended the meeting and gave it support. Berle E. Godfrey of Fort Worth was elected vice president; C. Truett Smith, Wylie, secretary; and Tom Joseph, Austin, treasurer. The executive committee included 31 of the top state bankers, including TBA Vice President David Blackburn.

The next step of the fledgling association was to name a managing officer. Sam O. Kimberlin, Jr., was the choice of the group, and he became executive director October 24, 1962. Since 1956 he had been counsel to the Department of Banking in Austin. "He is thoroughly familiar with all problems confronting state banks," the announcement said. The young Kimberlin established offices in the Perry-Brooks Building in Austin. The headquarters of the TBA, first in Austin, had been in Dallas for many years and was located at 2118 Adolphus Tower.

Branch banking issues had been around for years. As far back as 1929 Fred Florence suggested branching for banks in the larger Texas cities. In 1949 a bill for branching was before the legislature, reported on favorably by committee but later tabled. In 1951 a bill for branching was on the way to enactment when the TBA rallied strong opposition to it. The bill was defeated, but the issue remained alive. The TBA took a strong position against branching in 1965, against both state and federal branching proposals.

One of the first accomplishments of the new association was the legislative removal in 1963 of state banks from sales and corporate franchise taxes for parity with national banks.

So TBA President Virgil Patterson was at the helm in a decisive time.

Meeting in Houston in May 1963, he reflected on a busy year. In his admired style of directness, he alluded to the TBA as the "effective organization" with its 1,100 member banks. "Ours is an alert and efficient group," he declared. Speaking of legislation, he said: "Our association does not ask for special legislation, but we must remain on the alert to keep harmful legislation from being passed."

Delegates numbered 2,100. They elected David R. Blackburn of Victoria as president. President Patterson yielded to David E. Blackburn, father of the incoming president and himself TBA president 1933–1934, to affix the president's pin on his son's lapel. To his junior the senior Blackburn remarked: "Son, this pin was attached to my coat thirty years ago." It was a ceremony "surcharged with emotion and sentiment."

Ben Wooten traveled around the nation for the ABA Centennial Commission. DeWitt T. Ray served as chairman for Texas; A. E. Dabney was vice chairman. Texas celebrated the event widely. President John F. Kennedy inaugurated the celebration in Washington.

Our association does not ask for special legislation, but we must remain on the alert to keep harmful legislation from being passed.

4
THE TBA:
CHANGE to MEET NEW EXPECTATIONS, NEW CHALLENGES

The secretary, W. A. Philpott, Jr., . . . informed the council of his plans to retire . . . no later than January 1, 1964.
DAVID R. BLACKBURN, TBA president, 1963

IN PRESIDENT BLACKBURN'S ADMINISTRATION significant changes were started that changed the association's initiative and emphasis, and which signified the beginning of a new era for the TBA.

Meeting in Dallas June 4, 1963, he announced to the Administrative Council that Tom C. Frost, Jr., San Antonio, was being appointed to head the TBA Committee on Constitution and Bylaws.

The council met again September 6. Considerable discussion was held on the location of the association's headquarters office which had been in Dallas since 1914. The decision was to continue its location in Dallas. Another session was held in October. After transacting some legislative committee matters, the council went into executive session.

Reporting to the TBA membership the following day, President Blackburn told of the meeting. He said: "The secretary, W. A. Philpott, Jr., who has served the association as secretary for 48 years, informed the council of his plans to retire in accordance with the association's retirement program. He asked the council to approve his

169

plan, and that his retirement become effective no later than January 1, 1964. The council granted the secretary's request, with an expression of regret."

The statement continued by informing the membership that "Mr. Philpott's plans for retirement create the need for an immediate reorganizational study." He promised that the council, acting as a committee of the whole, would undertake immediately a "comprehensive reorganization study of the affairs of the association."

At the meeting November 25 the council authorized a committee of President Blackburn, Vice President James Aston and Past President Virgil Patterson to recommend a successor to Philpott.

A series of major decisions was made at the council meeting December 16, 1963. Milton Boswell was advanced from associate editor to editor of the *TBR*, effective January 1, 1964. He was also elected acting secretary, effective January 1. Boswell had served the TBA since 1939. In addition to being associate editor, he had been association manager for a number of years. The retirement arrangement with "Mr. Phil" called for his being available as a consultant on associational matters.

In the October 1963 *TBR* was a brief notice of the planned retirement by Secretary Philpott. He was inundated by messages of good wishes. The venerable gentleman who had been associated with the TBA since 1913 wrote: "On this page, through the years, we have put out many thoughts on the topic at hand: withdrawal from a regular business life. Now, for us, the time is here."

At later meetings the council voted unanimously to move the TBA headquarters from Dallas to Austin "as soon as practicable."

Chairman Tom Frost, Jr., and the committee to study the constitution and bylaws, met April 15, 1964, announced several important changes to be recommended to the next convention in San Antonio in May. Proposed changes included designation of Austin as association headquarters; giving the administrative committee nominating powers; reconstituting the council to consist of 14 members plus the president, vice president and treasurer, with each of the TBA districts to elect two members for staggered terms of two years each; providing for employment of the secretary by the council and other such employees as deemed necessary. They were adopted at the convention.

President Blackburn rounded out the year as TBA president at the San Antonio convention, a year of dramatic proportions. A resolution expressing "profound gratitude for his service . . . respect and admiration for his long and distinguished record . . . esteem and best wishes for his retirement years" was adopted honoring W. A. Philpott, Jr.

Incoming TBA president James W. Aston of Dallas immediately set in motion plans to carry out the newly expanded association program. The administrative council met May 13, 1964. One of the significant actions was the immediate discontinuance of the TBA "$5,000 Reward for Dead Bank Robbers," ending the much discussed and often controversial program which began in 1927. The council met July 10 in Austin, approved the interpretation of the purpose and objectives of the association: "This association is, in fact, a facility and extension of each member institution, working through a central office on association-approved objectives, which will help to preserve and promote the welfare of banking with the public interest." Objectives:

By 1958 the marvel of electronic bookkeeping had made its debut in banking in Texas. Citizens State Bank, Corpus Christi, displays its machine.

"To preserve and promote sound banking law. To provide information, educational facilities for discussion of laws, regulations, procedures, systems, and developments, affecting banking. To provide management aids which are not readily available to individual members. To assist banking in building its reputation with the public."

To continue the study, Aston named a special committee, with H. K. Allen of Temple as chairman.

At the call of President Aston the administrative council met in Austin August 8, 1964. A new era for the association was launched. More about that later, but here let us review the remarkable service of William A. Philpott, Jr., who had retired as of January 1, 1964.

William A. Philpott, Jr., TBA managing
officer and editor of the *Texas Bankers Record*,
retired on January 1, 1964, after 51 years with
the association.

172

PART TEN

The TBA and the Philpott Era

1

MORE than HALF a CENTURY— the MAJOR DOMO

Fortunately for us poor uninformed cusses, the Omnipotent One has us by the hand all the days of our lives. With His protective guidance, we untutored ones survive and thrive more serenely and contentedly than those who depend on knowledge for power.
WILLIAM A. PHILPOTT, *In Praise of Ignorance*, 1948

FOR 51 YEARS WILLIAM ALBERT PHILPOTT, JR., had a major role in the Texas Bankers Association, a record that stands as a tribute to the man and his era.

Born in St. Jo, Montague County, September 17, 1885, he moved as a child, first to Rising Star and then to Bowie. After high school graduation he enrolled in The University of Texas, where he "excelled in scholarship, edited the college daily, established a humor magazine, and won the statewide gymnastic contest." He became a cub reporter on the *San Antonio Express* and later became night editor of the *Austin Statesman*. In 1913 he was selected as editor of the *Texas Bankers Record*, then in 1915 elected secretary of the Texas Bankers Association. He retired from both offices January 1, 1964.

In so many ways Philpott *was* the TBA for more than half of its first century. Born in the same year it was established, he was by nature a person who liked people, and the TBA gave him a significant opportunity to combine his talents and interests to the fullest.

On Sunday morning, October 10, 1971, at age 86, he met three golfing friends for a game. On the course he became unwell but refused to be attended. He drove home and died peacefully there a short time later.

His qualities of preciseness, accuracy and punctuality, developed during his news-

In so many ways Philpott was the TBA for more than half of its first century.

173

paper days, became his hallmark. He practiced a spartan health routine of exercise, and to the end his golf score was lower than his age. At age 77, for example, he shot a 73. He accumulated six holes-in-one over the years.

Punctuality was his guiding star, and Texas bankers, whether at the annual convention or with the Flying Squadron, knew that the starting time was to be precisely announced and maintained.

Sorrow had come his way early. On December 14, 1914, he married Mary Bachman of Austin. J. Frank Dobie was best man at the wedding. Happiness flourished in the Philpott home for a few short years until, after losing their first child, a son, at birth, the tragedy deepened—Mary died on December 21, 1922, one day after the birth and death of their second son. Philpott was left alone.

Grief-stricken at the loss of Mary, whom he described as, " . . . loveable and gracious woman, unexcelled helpmate and sweetheart extraordinary. . . . But surely, nothing can so much disturb the soul or perplex the intellect of a man as the death of a tender helpmate. It is for him a separation, violent, sudden and entire from all that has hitherto comforted, delighted and engaged him." Commenting on the essays Philpott wrote for the *TBR*, Milton Boswell said: "His choice of themes ranged far and wide. He dwelt largely on life and how to live more abundantly. He wrote the way he felt and he usually felt fine. Much sadness, however, did enter his life and on occasion, Mr. Phil recorded his feelings of sorrow and grief."

He never forgot his brief life with Mary, and each Christmas season was a mixed memory—of his happy marriage in 1914 and her death in 1922.

At "Mr. Phil's" funeral in Dallas the minister noted his many achievements. Said he: "Mr. Philpott was a man of accomplishment and culture; of great and good deeds. Generous to a fault, he was always the first in meeting the needs of his family and friends. A man of high morals, in all his life he never drank, smoked, nor was heard to utter a single ungentlemanly comment or word. . . . He enjoyed memories of the past, but always looked with pleasant expectation to the future. He recently said, 'What the morrow promises has always captivated me.' He was not an ostentatious nor prideful man. Nor would he wish us to eulogize him. He would wish only to be remembered as a good and decent man, which he was."

One of his many published writings was written at the time of his 86th birthday in 1971. It said: "The yesteryears lay quietly in shrouds of sweet memories and contentment, as they should. As long as my future is kept in focus, life will continue to charm and invigorate me. The go-go attitude will preserve me as fresh, as pleasant, as free of complaints, even as rollicking as the flowers of Spring."

Three weeks later, without complaint and enjoying the fullness of life and his certain philosophy of it, he departed for "another and better state, in which all tears will be wiped from the eyes, and the whole soul shall be filled with joy."

The gentleman who was the major domo of the TBA, the austere product of Victorian times, talented writer and friend of Texas bankers, was no more.

2
HUMOR and PHILOSOPHY—
the CREATIVE MIND
of "MR. PHIL"

*We've seen all the vacancies—here's our refrain: There's nothing as vacant
as a vacant brain!*
From PHILPOTT'S "NOBODY HOME UPSTAIRS," poetry file

COMMENTING ON HIS REMARKABLE UNCLE, Bill Philpott, Cisco business executive, recalls the joy of visiting with him in Dallas. "He would gather us around him and read great stories and tell remarkable tales," he said.

Recognized as "one of the world's foremost authorities on the subject of U.S. paper money," the publication *Coin World* said his death "plunged the numismatic world into mourning for a man largely responsible for bringing paper money collecting to the unprecedented point in popularity it enjoys today. He was a member of the American Numismatic Association since 1918 and had served 10 terms on its board of directors, a record. He received the association's 50-Year Medal at the convention in San Diego in 1968. At first he started collecting metal coins, but he sold that collection in 1946. He became the dean of the paper money collectors and wrote many nationally published articles about it."

But his interest in collecting did not stop there. He had put together one of the finest collections of early Texas letters, manuscripts and historical documents anywhere. Interested in Texas folklore, he served as president of that society. His Dallas home was filled with his many collections, each assembled, catalogued and preserved in an orderly manner.

"Mr. Phil" penned many poems, in addition to his noted prose, and friends far and near sought his items, including *In Praise of Ignorance*.

Here are a few selections from his poetry file:

Ah, the Raven doth remember
   nineteen-forty-two's November,
With its grewsome, ghoulish ration
   of the gas to gallons four;
How he madly, sadly flutters,
   haunts me at my window shutters,
Gloats and croaks and darkly stutters,
   "You can have just gallons four"
"Please," plead I, "Plutonian Demon,
   can't I have a little more?"
Quoth the Raven, "Only four!"

In a spoof headed "Putting the Hart Before the Corse," Philpott, a fellow who never drank, saw the humor of the drunk:

Starkle, starkle, little twink
Who the hell I are, you think
The alco-ence of infiohol
Some thinkle peep I'm drunk, that's all;
I've only had ten drittle links
Sober I'll Sunday up, methinks
I feel so fleepy, but no regret
The drunker I sit here, the longer I get.

A more philosophical vein, untitled:

I'd rather be a could be
If I could not be an are
For a could be is a maybe
With a chance of touching par
I'd rather be a has been
Than a might have been by far
For a might have been has never been
But a has was once an are.

And "Is There a Doctor Syntax in the House" brings up the split infinitive:

If for a single noun the verb be plural,
Forgive the man,—he's unrefined and rural;
And if his writings show a variant tense,
Just pass it as a lack of bookish sense;
Excuse mixed metaphors and scrambled cases,
Such errors oft are writ in learned places.
But don't forgive the man with brain diminutive,
Who, cold and cruel, splits a poor infinitive!

Philpott let the vacant brain come in for consideration in "Nobody Home Upstairs":

Ponder the vacuum, study the void,
Consider the vast plain's barren spread;
Of unfilled things that ever have annoyed
Vacuity's top is an empty head!
We've seen all the vacancies—here's our refrain:
There's nothing as vacant as a vacant brain!

His 51 years as editor of the *TBR* gave him an opportunity to write a page each month. The magazine was never late, with the exception of one time when he was involved in an automobile accident in Mexico.

Writing in his last year before retirement, he said: "Men will have various things entered on the credit side of the ledger. . . . Here is a recap of the things none of us can possess too abundantly: affectionate and considerate relatives; faithful and fond friends; an exuberance of health; a sense of humor; contentedness and peace of mind; complete unselfishness, and thoughtfulness of others; compassion for those less fortunate than we; and a righteous longing for humility."

Just before he died, "Mr. Phil" wrote a letter to a friend who was preparing for retirement. "Remember," he wrote, "each year it gets easier to shoot your age in golf because you get an extra stroke."

The friend, saddened by Phil's death, commented: "That seems to sum up the philosophy by which he lived all 86 years."

Sam O. Kimberlin, Jr., TBA executive vice
president, began his long tenure on September
15, 1964. The association launched a new era,
a leadership posture that rounds out the TBA's
first century at the zenith of organization and
management.

PART ELEVEN

Consolidation and Expansion: A New TBA Vigor

1

BEGINNING the KIMBERLIN ERA—the RIGHT COMBINATION for a NEW TBA THRUST

Mr. Kimberlin is eminently qualified as chief executive officer of this organization . . . .
JAMES W. ASTON, TBA president, 1964

AT THE ADMINISTRATIVE COUNCIL MEETING in Austin on August 8, 1964, Sam O. Kimberlin, Jr., of Austin was named executive vice president, a newly created title for the managing officer of the TBA. A native of Wichita Falls, he was educated at The University of Texas. He received his law degree in 1953 and was a U. S. Marine Corps veteran. As counsel to the Texas Department of Banking, beginning in 1956, he was named executive director of the Association of State Chartered Banks upon its founding in 1962. He had also served as former division head of the office of attorney general of Texas.

On September 15, at age 36, he began as TBA executive vice president in the new TBA headquarters in the International Life Building in Austin. Said President Aston: "Mr. Kimberlin is eminently qualified as chief executive officer of this association. . . . We know that he will help greatly the association to achieve its goals."

The TBA had found a man with the right combination for present and future challenges. The Kimberlin era had commenced.

Milton Boswell, acting secretary until Kimberlin's selection, continued as editor of the *TBR.*

The Kimberlin choice had been worked out with the ASCB in discussions on common objectives of both associations, starting August 21 with a luncheon session in Dallas. The TBA and ASCB leadership hammered out a plan for putting the two organizations together. President Aston appointed ASCB's Jack Garrett chairman of the TBA legislative committee, and members of the ASCB committee were invited to attend each meeting of the TBA council.

Many positive suggestions for consolidation were advanced, including strengthened state and national bank divisions. The TBA agreed to purchase the physical assets of ASCB. Legislative committee representation was worked out, providing for a state and a national banker from each of the 31 senatorial districts. After all details were completed, bankers in Texas were united, and ASCB merged into the TBA, carrying on its activities as the state banking section.

With the consolidation of the two associations, Kimberlin entered his TBA management era with the confidence of the elected leadership of both groups. He began immediately to put together the enlarged staff and broadened services of the association.

In 1953 the administrative council had approved the desirability of having a full-time counsel to work on legislative and regulatory matters. Appointed as associate counsel and secretary, effective December 1, 1964, Leonard Passmore of Austin began a long tenure of service to the TBA. Born in Picton in Hopkins County, he did undergraduate work at The University of Texas and East Texas State Teachers College, receiving a bachelor of science degree from the latter institution in 1941. He graduated from The University of Texas School of Law in 1949. In World War II he was involved in combat operations in the China-Burma-India Theater. Passmore practiced law in Mount Vernon for eight years before becoming assistant attorney general of Texas on January 1, 1958. On being appointed first assistant attorney general, he was acting attorney general in the absence of his superior, and he possessed a wide background of experience with banks and state agencies. He at once began detailed reports to the TBA membership on legislation, regulation and judicial decisions of interest to Texas banking. Passmore retired in September 1983.

Addressing the 1965 TBA convention in Fort Worth in May 1965, President Aston told the 1,747 bankers and guests that "the association is moving strongly forward. There is no room for division among ourselves, pitting state banks against city banks, or unit banks against multiple-office banks. The financial system is too competitive to permit any of us to erect a wall of isolation around our institutions with any hope of survival." He urged a progressive approach for Texas banking.

The delegates resolved against branch banking and supported nationwide par banking as recommended by the ABA; they resolved against the proposal to change the structure of the Fed as advocated by Representative Wright Patman.

Elected TBA president at the 1965 assembly, Jeff Austin of Frankston, a record-holding track star in his college days, literally hit the ground running. One of the first acts of the council was to approve the location of the TBA in the Vaughn Building in Austin. The TBA was moved from Dallas to Austin where it has remained.

It was to Austin that the 1966 convention went in May. President Austin had a note of progress for the delegates and guests. Never known for long speeches, he said:

The delegates resolved against branch banking, supported nationwide par banking as recommended by the ABA.

"We open this 82nd convention on a bright, prosperous, and happy note. Among us, there is a feeling that all is well although we are somewhat apprehensive of profits at the year's end." Speakers included Governor John Connally and Murray Kyger, former TBA president and president of the Association of Reserve City Bankers. For the first time under the new procedures, the administrative committee had served as the nominating committee.

Delegates elected Walter F. Johnson of Abilene president, and to strengthen the new union, Jack Adams of Austin was elected chairman of the national bank division, and C. Truett Smith of Wylie was elected to head the state bank division.

President Johnson's administration set the policy of scheduling the TBA convention date and place more than one year in advance. The policy started in 1967 with the convention in Dallas and in San Antonio in 1968. The council provided classroom literature to teachers and worked to build a closer tie with banking faculties in colleges and universities. The convention registration fee was set at $30 for men and $20 for women.

Past President Jeff Austin headed a committee to study the TBA districts. Its report recommended the association be divided into eight districts instead of seven.

A career national bank examiner, William B. Camp, from Greenville, was selected by President Lyndon Johnson as Comptroller of the Currency. He succeeded James J. Saxon. Joining the comptroller's office in February 1937 after graduating from Baylor University, he became assistant examiner in 1941 and was commissioned national bank examiner in 1949.

2
TBA GOES to WASHINGTON— EMPHASIS on LEGISLATIVE and REGULATORY ISSUES and on EDUCATION

Seldom, if ever, has a single session of the legislature produced so much sound and beneficial legislation.
SAM O. KIMBERLIN, JR., 1967

THE TBA PURSUED ITS EMPHASIS ON INVOLVEMENT in banking legislative and regulatory matters, including the modernization of the Texas banking code. Legislation to accomplish this was introduced in 1967. Beginning in 1966, the association made its visit to Washington an annual event for conferences with officials on legislative and administrative developments. In 1967 the trip included ABA briefings, visits with regulatory authorities, including Comptroller Camp; coffee at the White House;

181

and a breakfast session with the National Association of Supervisors of State Banks. A dinner and reception was held for the Texas Congressional delegation. At the ABA briefings the bankers heard information on federal legislative matters from John Holton, ABA federal legislative counsel, a native Texan and former administrative assistant to Speaker Sam Rayburn. In a way, it was like "old home week" for bankers and their friends from Texas. Texas was represented by the President of the United States Lyndon B. Johnson, by Comptroller of the Currency William B. Camp, by ABA Executive Vice President Charls Walker, and on through a long list of significant decision and policy makers on the banks of the Potomac.

At SMU and SWIGSBIE the trust bankers were proud of the development of the trust curriculum. John Barry Hubbard of Fort Worth called attention to the program under the leadership of Dr. Norman A. Wiggins, Wake Forest University professor of law, with the assistance of the man known as "Mr. Trust Business," Dr. Gilbert T. Stephenson.

The 1967 legislative session produced positive results. The consumer credit code bill passed and was signed. So were the banking code revisions. "Seldom, if ever, has a single session of the legislature produced so much sound and beneficial legislation," Sam Kimberlin noted.

The reorganization of the TBA produced cohesive action by bankers, and the role and service of the association grew immensely in the year.

President Walter F. Johnson rounded out his year at the 83rd convention in Dallas in June 1967. The program included an address by Nat Rogers, president of the ABA Savings Division. Rogers was a young banking leader from Jackson, Mississippi. Other speakers were John Holton of the ABA, Senator John Tower and FDIC Chairman K. A. Randall. Walter Heller, economist; J. M. Falkner, banking commissioner; and Norman R. Dunn, regional administrator of national banks, completed the list of speakers.

Paul Mason of Fort Worth, chairman of the committee on constitution and by-laws, reported several proposed changes, including the change from seven to eight TBA districts. "Tight money" was critical for the bankers, Johnson said.

During the year a committee on education and a committee on mortgage lending had been established.

The gavel was passed to S. R. (Buddy) Jones, Jr., Pasadena. He continued the policy established two years previously of holding the two-day meeting of the administrative council as a busy working session. At the meeting June 25–26 Cecil Culver of Groom was named as the first chairman of TBA district eight. Bankers were concerned about "Truth-in-Lending" legislation in Congress.

During the summer of 1967 some 1,200 bankers attended a series of seminars on the new consumer credit code, one of these being the 26th Bankers Conference in Austin at The University of Texas.

The association established a new membership dues schedule, changing from a capital stock basis to total resources. A retirement plan was approved to cover the administrative staff and employees.

While in Washington for the annual visit on February 8, 1968, the TBA council met. Paul Mason, chairman of a special committee to study the purposes and implementation of an educational program, announced that Dr. Lee Wilborn of Austin was suggested as educational director for the TBA. The council approved, and the TBA launched an aggressive program that captured national attention.

In 1967 Texas led the nation in number of banks with 1,146, followed by Illinois with 1,063. California had the most banking offices, 184 banks and 2,764 branches. Nationally the total was 14,255 banks and 17,561 branches.

In St. Louis on November 21 the Conference of Southern Bankers Association Executives elected Sam Kimberlin chairman. He announced that the 1968 meeting would be in Houston.

The foundation of SWIGSBIE announced that it would underwrite a program, the Assemblies for Bank Directors, with Dr. Richard B. Johnson as director. The first two assemblies were held at Hot Springs and Colorado Springs.

Speaking to the National Association of Bank Women (NABW) in Houston, President Jones noted the steady increase of the role of women in banking. "As banking grows, so the opportunity for success of the lady bankers enhances," he said.

Bankers and tourists alike swarmed to San Antonio in 1968 for the HemisFair, whose Tower of the Americas rose 622 feet for a view over the historic old city.

President Jones led the 2,510 bankers and guests at the 84th convention in May. Program Chairman Gene Edwards of Amarillo had put together an impressive list of speakers, including Allan Shivers, president of the Chamber of Commerce of the United States; Roger Blough, chairman of the U.S. Steel Corporation; Comptroller William B. Camp; and George Champion, chairman of Chase Manhattan Bank.

Jones paid special attention to the development of the educational program.

TBA Vice President Jack Adams of Austin had retired from banking. John F. Geis of Beaumont was elected president.

In August the attorney general of Texas ruled that banks could not accept deposits in off-premises machines. The TBA council approved sponsorship of the School of Banking of the South at LSU.

The council recommended that the Trust Section be made a division of the TBA, and that the Mortgage Finance Committee be made a section. The formation of a Marketing Committee was approved, and President Geis was authorized to make the appointments. In November 1968 the association scheduled five luncheon meetings around the state for legislators.

ABA Executive Vice President Charls Walker, Graham native, was appointed Under Secretary of the Treasury and took office January 27, 1969. Willis Alexander, Missouri banker and former ABA president, was named executive vice president of that association.

A major change in Texas banking leadership took place February 13 when Nat S. Rogers, ABA vice president, joined First City National Bank, Houston, as president. He had been a Jackson, Mississippi, banker and was widely known as one of the top men in banking. This put Texas in line for its third ABA president.

Bankers gathered in Houston in May for the 85th convention, with TBA President John Geis in the chair. A resolution was "cheerfully adopted" welcoming Nat Rogers to Texas. Jeff Austin observed that "Texas has a rich heritage of deeds and accomplishments by gallant men and noble women, many of whom came to our land from Mississippi . . . and other great states of our nation. . . . We are fortunate that

183

tradition continues. . . . Nat Rogers has become a citizen of our state and the City of Houston. . . ."

President Geis noted the success of the association's educational program and paid tribute to Jack Garrett in whose administration in 1955 the idea was born and to the committee who chose Dr. Wilborn. "Bingo," he said, "I come along and reap the rewards of one of the greatest programs your association has ever undertaken."

3
REMEMBERING HISTORY—
TBA HISTORICAL MARKER
for LAMPASAS

Thus was born a great trade association; now the oldest and largest of its kind in the United States.
JOHN F. GEIS, dedicatory address, TBA marker, 1969

DERRELL HENRY OF ODESSA became president at the end of the 1968 convention. He announced that a Texas Historical Marker would be dedicated in Lampasas, the place of the first TBA meeting in 1885. A formal program was set for 3:00 p.m., June 17, 1969, at the courthouse square, with TBA officials and representatives of the Lampasas County Historical Society.

After the meeting of the administrative council in Austin, June 15–17, President Henry and others of the group went to Lampasas for the dedication of the marker. Henry presided at the dedication, and Senator J. P. Word unveiled the marker. Immediate Past President John Geis gave the dedicatory address, tracing the history of the TBA. In conclusion, Geis said: "Thus was born a great trade association; now the oldest and largest of its kind in the United States. Today it speaks as the voice of more than 1,150 banks of Texas, vigorously helping its member banks to provide outstanding service to the people of Texas, and meeting the objectives and challenges presented so ably by those farsighted bankers in Lampasas Springs, 84 years ago."

A large group attended, responding to the invitation of President Henry, including William A. Philpott, Jr., of Dallas, longtime TBA managing officer and *TBR* editor. Geis noted Philpott's presence and recognized his keen interest in history and his diligence at collecting memorabilia.

Of the 12,000 registrants at the 1969 ABA convention in Honolulu, 1,129 were Texans. It was the first time the convention had been held outside the continental United States. The highlight of the meeting was the election of Nat S. Rogers of Houston as president.

The TBA remembers its founding in Lampasas. A historical marker recalling the founding in 1885 was unveiled in an official ceremony in 1969. Left to right are John F. Geis, Sam O. Kimberlin, Jr., and Derrell Henry. Henry was the incumbent TBA president; Geis was his immediate predecessor.

"This is for me a moment of commitment and of affirmation," Rogers said. "I begin a tour of duty as your elected president in the face of somewhat striking alternatives—the prospect of expanded, stimulating, and profitable opportunities on the one hand—or burdensome regulations, heavier taxation, and a communication block with the public on the other," he stated. To the delegates he announced a new "master-plan for bank public relations."

President Henry concluded his TBA presidency at the Fort Worth convention in May 1970. Said he, "We have tried to create among Texas bankers during our term of office a renewed awareness of the need for a continuous reevaluation of our banking services to meet the environmental requirements of our time—the necessity of becoming more effective politically."

Another long-time TBA leader, San Antonio's Tom C. Frost, a member of one of the leading banking families in Texas, became president in 1970.

In a letter to Texas bankers that September he noted the death on September 18, "just a few months before his 100th birthday," of L. A. Schreiner, chairman of the Charles Schreiner Bank of Kerrville. Praising his modesty and character, Frost said: "During his era, a man's word was his bond in contrast to the necessity to document in legal . . . form with several copies the agreements of today. In Mr. Schreiner's era, to do a kindness and help your fellow man did not have to be tax deductible . . . Mr. Schreiner's greatness lay in his living for the benefit of his fellow man. Few individuals sold personal assets at a sacrifice during the depression to make loans to their customers as Mr. Schreiner did," he said.

In October Texas bankers flocked to Miami Beach for the ABA convention presided over by one of their cohorts—Houston's Nat S. Rogers. And the good news was that Dallas would be the 1971 ABA convention city.

Although the 1960s had been turbulent with civil rights, political upheavals, assassinations, war, vastly expanded federal regulations on banking, the decision of President Johnson not to seek reelection, the expansion of America's space program at Houston, the landing of Apollo 11 on the moon in 1969—banking forged ahead in a heavily bureaucratic world of new challenges and rapid change. Total assets of Texas banks increased by 77 percent, and the asset mix reflected an even more phenomenal change. Computerized banking developed dramatically.

Texas banks fostered economic expansion by increases in the loans and discount, with consumer loans increasing more rapidly than any other type of major bank loan.

As of December 31, 1970, there were 530 national banks with total resources of $22 billion and deposits of $18.3 billion. State banks numbered 653 with resources of $8.9 billion and deposits of $7.95 billion. Total banks were 1,183, resources of $30.99 billion and deposits of $26.3 billion.

The myriad of problems and new opportunities caused banking to "bore with a big auger."

The 1970 president of NABW was a Texas banker, Bobbye Taylor of Lamesa. Speaking in Washington, D.C., she told the bank women, "It is clear that the responsibilities shouldered by these women bankers have increased tremendously in the past five years." Career advancement, she reported, was the cry she heard from women bankers in America as she traveled as their national leader.

Speaking before the first Texas International Trade Mission in Mexico City in November, President Frost discussed the profitable business opportunities Texas bankers were finding in Mexico.

Meanwhile, Texas bankers kept their eyes on Washington where the bank holding company bill was being considered by Congress. Finally adopted, President Nixon signed the bill December 31, 1970. Former Governor John B. Connally was appointed Secretary of the Treasury by Nixon, effective February 1, 1971.

Meeting May 2 in Dallas, the TBA administrative council held an extended discussion on the bank holding company act. It reaffirmed the dedication of the TBA to the dual and unit banking system of the state, took note of the development of registered bank holding companies in Texas, and recommended that the succeeding council "continue to closely study the further development of registered bank holding companies in Texas and of the necessity to be alert to any development which might jeopardize the dual banking system."

The myriad problems and new opportunities caused banking to bore with a big auger.

186

At the convention in Dallas in May 1971 President Frost used the titles of current popular songs and urged bankers to adapt to change "and to build a banking industry which will not only be of greater benefit to our stockholders and customers but the entire public. . . . Listen to the music," he said.

The issue of bank holding companies became a much-discussed topic, and TBA President Oscar Lindemann of Dallas and the administrative council met to develop an association policy. The headquarters staff was authorized to plan and hold a number of one-day seminars around the state at which the pros and cons of the holding company act would be explained.

The long-time Commissioner of Banks J. M. Falkner died April 18. On August 29 W. A. (Doc) Sandlin, retired chief national bank examiner, died. Both men were respected leaders of bank regulation and supervision.

And, as has already been mentioned, the sorrowful news of the death of William A. Philpott, Jr., in Dallas, Sunday, October 10, 1971, was received by Texas bankers and his many friends around the country.

4

THE TBA and POLITICAL INVOLVEMENT

Those who complain about the way the ball bounces are often the ones who dropped it.
LEON STONE, TBA president, 1973

I T WAS OBVIOUS as 1972 arrived that bank holding company activity in the state focused on applications of banks to become bank holding companies. Already a number of applications had been approved, and the acquisition of banks through stock acquisition was mounting, the Dallas Federal Reserve reported.

The Bankers Legislative League of Texas (BALLOT) was organized. TBA President Lindemann called it "potentially an effective vehicle for making the voice of banking heard." BALLOT's first chairman was C. Truett Smith of Wylie. A banker and newspaper publisher, he had served as chairman of the TBA's legislative committee. The first president was Gene Edwards of Amarillo.

"Texas Banking at the Crossroads" was the topic of President Lindemann's address at the San Antonio convention in May 1972. Said he, "I don't believe we're lost, but during this year we've been approaching the crossroads in Texas banking of a number of areas that are going to require bankers' involvement and decision rather quickly." The four areas he listed were: economic environment in the state and nation; form of the bank system that finally evolves and serves; the regulatory system that governs us; and our image with the public—our customer. "Step across the line and get involved," he urged.

187

One of the sad notes at the time of the convention was the death in Houston of Judge James A. Elkins, Sr. A leading banker and attorney-at-law, the 92-year-old Elkins had been a stalwart in banking and law, and had been one of the strong movers in the legislative activities of the TBA. Texas and its bankers knew his capacity for modesty and accomplishment, and often sought his counsel.

Leon Stone of Austin, the new TBA president, discussed the good economic outlook at the 31st TBA Conference at The University of Texas. Turning to the subject of bank holding companies, he noted that Texas had 13 multi-bank holding companies and 92 one-bank holding companies. He estimated that 65 percent of the deposits would be in holding companies by the end of 1972. "And it seems that the holding company process is just beginning," he said.

The ABA 1972 convention was held in Dallas in October. From far and near, 11,000 bankers and guests attended, and the city rolled out the red carpet as Texas bankers showed their traditional hospitality.

At the 89th convention in El Paso in May 1973, President Stone and 1,900 registrants enjoyed a top-level program of business and entertainment. It was the first time since 1927 that the association had met in that colorful city.

More banker involvement in governmental affairs was urged by Stone. "We are salesmen," he said. "We sell our banks and bank services. But at the same time we must realize that we are human and subject to all the weaknesses and foibles that are the enemies of full achievement and of full success. Those who complain about the way the ball bounces are often the ones who dropped it."

Bookman Peters of Bryan reported on the marked success of the educational program of the TBA, noting that 40,000 Texas teachers were involved in the economic education program.

C. Truett Smith of Wylie, the new TBA president, addressed the TBA Trust Division meeting May 17. A hectic legislative season was ahead, he pointed out, and he urged involvement in the political process: "Politics—a vehicle man rides to freedom."

Mrs. Marcella Perry of Houston was the dean of the 32nd TBA Bankers Conference in Austin.

A Dallas banker, Fred T. Brooks, was elected president of the Independent Bankers Association of America at its 43rd convention in San Francisco.

Another Dallas banker, Robert H. Stewart III, was elected vice president of the Association of Reserve City Bankers at the convention in Boca Raton, Florida.

PART TWELVE

Miracle on Tenth Street:
The TBA Gets
a Permanent Home

1

IDEAS and ACTION

It seems to me that attractive, adequate quarters located within the proximity of the Capitol in Austin should be provided.
C. TRUETT SMITH, TBA president, 1974

IN THE ADMINISTRATION OF PRESIDENT SMITH, the TBA began a study that produced what may be described as the "Miracle on Tenth Street."

Meeting on September 19, 1973, the TBA administrative council authorized President Smith to appoint a special committee to study the feasibility of the association constructing or acquiring its own office facilities within the city of Austin.

Acting quickly on the authorization—an idea he had fathered—Smith named S. Ross Greenwood of Temple as chairman of the special committee, along with Ed Wood, Jr., Dallas; Charles L. Childers, Tyler; Irby Metcalf, Jr., Fort Worth; Gene Edwards, Amarillo; A. C. Spencer, Huntsville; and John A. Wright of Abilene.

Although Smith had other important duties as TBA president, he had an idea that was not to be unduly delayed, and the special committee headed by Ross Greenwood acted quickly.

Before detailing the headquarters building story, it should be noted that the energy crisis was at hand "and expected to become critical over the coming months," according to the TBA leader. Other major events included the beginning of the Texas Constitutional Commission with its eight substantive committees dealing with various sections of the document. One of the provisions to be discussed was branch bank-

In 1973 the TBA began a feasibility study for the purpose of building or acquiring permanent headquarters in Austin. The committee and staff are shown at an early meeting. Seated, left to right, are J. B. Wheeler, Ed Wood, Jr., S. R. Greenwood and Truett Smith. Standing, left to right, are Jim Ed Waller, Milton Boswell, Charles L. Childers, Gene Edwards and Sam O. Kimberlin, Jr.

The architect's drawing of the proposed permanent headquarters of the Texas Bankers Association, located at 10th and Lavaca, Austin, as presented to the membership in a series of meetings around the state in November 1974. Overwhelmingly approved, the final steps were set in motion for the new facility built across the street from the Governor's Mansion.

ing. The TBA released figures on its survey, showing that 88.6 percent of the bankers opposed branching. A Stockdale banker, J. H. Bain, was chairman of the Texas Finance Commission. That body filed an objection to branching before the convention. Acting on the recommendation of the TBA legislative committee, Smith notified the Constitutional Commission February 27, 1974, that the prohibition against branch banking should be retained and that no percentage limitation on the size of holding companies be added to the new constitution.

When the 90th convention met in Fort Worth in May 1974, President Smith had much to report. There were "numerous clouds on the economic horizon," he told the bankers. Perils of inflation were present. Loss of confidence in government had taken its toll. Money costs were soaring. But instead of doom and gloom attitudes, "Let us as an industry rise to the occasion of new dimensions in leadership," he suggested.

The TBA president advocated the expansion of association services, including the idea of a home for the TBA and a history. Said President Smith: "It seems to me that attractive, adequate quarters located within the proximity of the Capitol in Austin should be provided. These facilities should take care of existing needs by providing proper office space, meeting rooms for committees and bankers on business in Austin, as well as provide space for a 'museum of Texas banking' in which could be displayed those items of historical interest across already 90 years of this Association. . . . Truly, 'A History of Texas Banking' should be a vital part of such a home office, and the inclusion of memorabilia of our industry should be a great inspiration pointing toward our centennial year ten years hence. I would hope that the great majority of the membership might enthusiastically approve of such a plan."

Now the impetus was obvious.

Gene Edwards of Amarillo, incoming TBA president, called the administrative council into a working session, June 2–4. One of the first reports on Sunday evening, June 2, 1974, was by Chairman S. Ross Greenwood of the New Facilities Committee, as it had become known. He detailed the committee's work, and the council approved the continuation of negotiations for a building site in Austin.

President Edwards, addressing the 33rd Bankers Conference in Austin, reviewed the history and growth of the TBA. He admonished the bankers to place restraints on the growth of credit in those days of double-digit inflation. Stated the Panhandle banking leader: "We should decline credit that is sought for speculative and non-productive measures."

He named Walter Johnson of Abilene, former TBA president, to head a committee to study the district meetings.

On November 13 Edwards wrote to the bankers that discussion of the proposed headquarters building for the association would take place at the district meetings. The consensus gained would enable the administrative council to act in December.

Not one to delay action, Edwards, along with Greenwood, took the message to the membership around Texas. The committee worked thoroughly and quickly.

The TBA president advocated the expansion of association services, including the idea of a home for the TBA and a history.

191

A happy day for the TBA was December 30, 1975, when the ground-breaking ceremony was held at the Austin site of the new TBA headquarters building. TBA officials watch as Committee Chairman S. R. Greenwood lifts the first shovel of dirt at 203 West 10th Street. Left to right are Phillip W. Shepherd, Archi- tect, Dallas; Christopher L. Williston, Austin; J. B. Wheeler, Plainview; C. Truett Smith, Wylie; Jim Ed Waller, Lubbock; S. R. Green- wood, Temple; Charles L. Childers, Tyler; Ed- ward A. Wood, Jr., Dallas; Gene Edwards, Amarillo; Sam O. Kimberlin, Jr., Austin; Larry Nelson, Contractor, Austin.

2

THE TBA COUNCIL
APPROVES the COMMITTEE REPORT

The New Facilities Committee reported that the consensus was overwhelmingly in favor of the project.
GENE EDWARDS, TBA president, advises the members, 1974

CHAIRMAN GREENWOOD filed a comprehensive report on the proposal for a head-quarters building, including an architectural concept, in mid-November. In the *TBR* for that month he gave the rationale for the building and presented the recommendations of the committee. The report said: "The present offices of the TBA are small (3,200′), inflexible, and quite inadequate to allow for expansion of services, provide for meetings and conferences, house a library and museum, and portray the true image of banking in Texas. . . . Since the activation of the committee more than 20 meetings have been held, always with candor and forthrightness, with final unanimity," he wrote. The final report from the New Facilities Committee, he pointed out, recommended expenditure of up to $1,200,000 for land acquisition and construction, projected on a building of 11,400 square feet and a parking garage of 10,000 square feet. The estimate also included landscaping, furnishing and all other costs.

The administrative council met December 9, 1974, in Austin and voted to follow the recommendations of the committee. President Edwards told of the progress this way: "The Administrative Council . . . met today in Austin to hear the final report of the New Facilities Committee. This report gave the results of the eight District Meetings that were held in November to explain the proposed headquarters building in depth to all Texas bankers who could attend. The New Facilities Committee reported that the consensus was overwhelmingly in favor of the project, more than 96 percent of the bankers attending the meetings voting affirmatively. Based on this report, plus the information that had been furnished at their three previous meetings, the Administrative Council voted to proceed with the project."

In his letter to the TBA membership, President Edwards discussed the method of payment for the building by the membership in up to three annual payments. The TBA dues were the lowest of 14 states examined. "In fact," he wrote, "the one-time assessment of three and one-half times a member bank's annual dues is less than the annual dues paid in three of these states for a bank with $37,500,000."

The successful effort was admired around the nation for its careful and studied approach. President Edwards and Chairman Greenwood had made the round of meetings to "sell" the idea on a systematic and realistic basis. It was a masterful performance by people who believed in association expansion.

Winding down a busy and impressive year, TBA President Edwards led 1,600 bankers and spouses at the 91st convention in Houston. Reporting on the status of

It was a masterful performance by people who believed in association expansion.

193

the building program, he announced enthusiastic support of the project and that $1,300,000 had already been committed "to acquire a beautiful piece of land directly across the street from the Governor's Mansion and to construct a building."

J. B. Wheeler of Plainview was elected president at the Houston convention in May. The bid of $575,750 for constructing the headquarters building at 203 West Tenth Street was accepted. Groundbreaking ceremonies were held at the Austin site on December 30, 1975.

At the 1976 convention in El Paso in May, S. Ross Greenwood, Temple, became president. As a leader of the effort for a headquarters building, he followed construction progress eagerly.

And at the December 1976 board meeting, Phillip Shepherd and Bob Boyd of Dallas, architects for the new TBA building, reported on construction work and indicated the tentative completion date as February 1977.

Said Texas Governor Dolph Briscoe, "The TBA building adds greatly to the neighborhood," at the formal dedication of the new TBA Headquarters Building at 203 West Tenth Street in Austin.

True. The impressive building across the street from the Governor's Mansion, a long-time dream of leaders of the TBA, was dedicated on the afternoon of July 23, 1977. LEFT TO RIGHT: Charles L. Childers, *TBA President*; S. R. (Ross) Greenwood, *Building Committee Chairman*; Governor Dolph Briscoe.

Enthusiasm for the handsome building was as hot as the sweltering weather. The facility, which provides for the increasing functions of the TBA, was constructed without debt with the support of the members of the association.

Here are photos of the "miracle," the headquarters building of the Texas Bankers Association.

195

From any view, the TBA Headquarters provides an excellent study in handsome architecture amid the beauty of the surrounding area.

This is the Lavaca Street side of the building, a facility with two stories, a basement and parking areas.

The entrance foyer is an area of impressive dignity, with the traditional stairway and the view through the foyer to the fountain and garden.

On this floor are offices of the TBA activities, along with the permanent museum. This area also functions as reception space.

ABOVE: Shown here is part of the first floor area including the space devoted to the *Texas Bankers Record*, the TBA's monthly magazine, published since 1911. Here are shelved the bound volumes of the magazine, a vital source of much of the association's history and of Texas banking history. BELOW: The spiral stairway, viewed from the second floor, is a striking feature of the design and interior decorating of the building. The second floor is also reached by an elevator.

ABOVE: The TBA building provides the staff on the second floor a full range of space usage, including a library, kitchen facilities and the Board Room. The stairway ties together the traditional theme, and the general impression is of spaciousness. BELOW: The northeast corner of the building is devoted to the office of the Executive Vice President, which has a lovely view across Tenth Street to the Governor's Mansion and beyond to the Texas Capitol.

The environs of the TBA Headquarters prove the wisdom shown in selecting its location. Looking across the building, there is the view of the impressive Texas State Capitol, and to the left the Governor's Mansion is visible. The large lot has protected the building's vista.

ABOVE: The President's Room is tastefully furnished and reflects the tradition of its first president, James F. Miller, whose portrait is a constant reminder of the heritage of the association leaders who have served since 1885. The roll-top desk was one used by Mr. Miller and his successors in Gonzales. BELOW: The large Board Room provides a gracious meeting place for many of the TBA's activities, including meetings of the Board of Directors and the many committees. On the walls are color portraits of the TBA presidents who have served since the establishment of the building.

The TBA Library is an ideal place for research, and small groups use it for conferences. Convenient to the senior staff offices, it is a depository for current financial information and a wide range of publications.

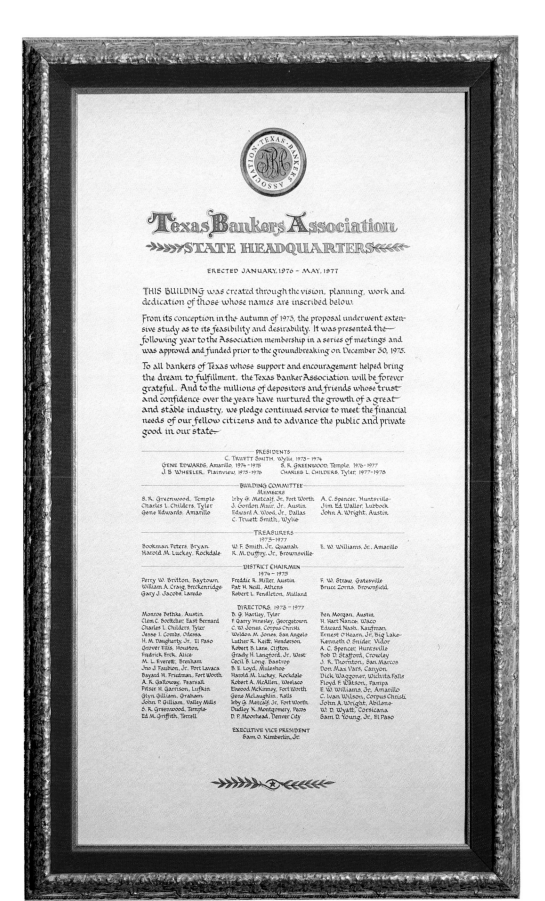

Texas Bankers Association

➤➤➤**STATE HEADQUARTERS**◄◄◄

ERECTED JANUARY, 1976 – MAY, 1977

THIS BUILDING was created through the vision, planning, work and dedication of those whose names are inscribed below.

From its conception in the autumn of 1973, the proposal underwent extensive study as to its feasibility and desirability. It was presented the following year to the Association membership in a series of meetings and was approved and funded prior to the groundbreaking on December 30, 1975.

To all bankers of Texas whose support and encouragement helped bring the dream to fulfillment, the Texas Banker Association will be forever grateful. And to the millions of depositors and friends whose trust and confidence over the years have nurtured the growth of a great and stable industry, we pledge continued service to meet the financial needs of our fellow citizens and to advance the public and private good in our state.

PRESIDENTS
C. TRUETT SMITH, Wylie, 1973–1974

| GENE EDWARDS, Amarillo, 1974–1975 | S. R. GREENWOOD, Temple, 1976–1977 |
| J. B. WHEELER, Plainview, 1975–1976 | CHARLES L. CHILDERS, Tyler, 1977–1978 |

BUILDING COMMITTEE
MEMBERS

S. R. Greenwood, Temple	Irby G. Metcalf, Jr., Fort Worth	A. C. Spencer, Huntsville
Charles L. Childers, Tyler	J. Gordon Muir, Jr., Austin	Jim Ed Waller, Lubbock
Gene Edwards, Amarillo	Edward A. Wood, Jr., Dallas	John A. Wright, Austin
	C. Truett Smith, Wylie	

TREASURERS
1973–1977

| Bookman Peters, Bryan | W. F. Smith, Jr., Quanah | E. W. Williams, Jr., Amarillo |
| Harold M. Luckey, Rockdale | R. M. Duffey, Jr., Brownsville | |

DISTRICT CHAIRMEN
1974–1975

Perry W. Britton, Baytown	Freddie R. Miller, Austin	F. W. Straw, Gatesville
William A. Craig, Breckenridge	Pat H. Neill, Athens	Bruce Zorns, Brownfield
Gary J. Jacobs, Laredo	Robert L. Pendleton, Midland	

DIRECTORS, 1973–1977

Monroe Bethke, Austin	B. G. Hartley, Tyler	Ben Morgan, Austin
Clem C. Boettcher, East Bernard	F. Garry Hinesley, Georgetown	H. Hart Nance, Waco
Charles L. Childers, Tyler	C. W. Jones, Corpus Christi	Edward Nash, Kaufman
Jesse I. Combs, Odessa	Weldon M. Jones, San Angelo	Ernest O'Hearn, Jr., Big Lake
H. M. Daugherty, Jr., El Paso	Luther R. Keitt, Henderson	Kenneth O. Snider, Vidor
Grover Ellis, Houston	Robert B. Lane, Clifton	A. C. Spencer, Huntsville
Fredrick Erck, Alice	Grady H. Langford, Jr., West	Bob D. Stafford, Crowley
M. L. Everett, Brenham	Cecil B. Long, Bastrop	J. R. Thornton, San Marcos
Jno. J. Faubion, Jr., Port Lavaca	B. E. Loyd, Muleshoe	Don Max Vars, Canyon
Bayard H. Friedman, Fort Worth	Harold M. Luckey, Rockdale	Dick Waggoner, Wichita Falls
A. R. Galloway, Pearsall	Robert A. McAllen, Weslaco	Floyd F. Watson, Pampa
Pitser H. Garrison, Lufkin	Elwood McKinney, Fort Worth	E. W. Williams, Jr., Amarillo
Glyn Gilliam, Graham	Gene McLaughlin, Ralls	C. Ivan Wilson, Corpus Christi
John P. Gilliam, Valley Mills	Irby G. Metcalf, Jr., Fort Worth	John A. Wright, Abilene
S. R. Greenwood, Temple	Dudley K. Montgomery, Pecos	W. D. Wyatt, Corsicana
Ed M. Griffith, Terrell	D. P. Moorhead, Denver City	Sam D. Young, Jr., El Paso

EXECUTIVE VICE PRESIDENT
Sam O. Kimberlin, Jr.

➤➤➤ ✦ ◄◄◄

Meeting of the Historical Committee in the TBA board room. Left to right are S. R. Jones, Jr., Pasadena; C. Truett Smith, Wylie; Sam O. Kimberlin, Jr., Austin; Leon Stone, Austin; Chairman Gene Edwards, Amarillo; Glen E. Lemon, Booker; Robert G. Greer, Houston; Derrell Henry, Odessa; R. M. Duffey, Jr., Brownsville; S. R. Greenwood, Temple.

Working with the TBA Historical Committee and meeting in Austin is the group charged with the preparation of the TBA history and museum. Left to right are Sam O. Kimberlin, Jr.; Jack Maguire; Mary Ellen Simpson; Harry Gatton; Lynn Singleton; Fred Whitehead; David Haynes; Sandra Carr; David Garrison; Al Lowman.

The Historical Committee is joined by others attending one of the many working sessions in Austin. Left to right are Harry Gatton; Mary Ellen Simpson; Robert G. Greer; S. R. Greenwood; R. M. Duffey, Jr.; Leon Stone; Chairman Gene Edwards; C. Truett Smith; S. R. Jones, Jr.; Derrell Henry; Sam O. Kimberlin, Jr.; Glen E. Lemon.

Sam O. Kimberlin, Jr., TBA executive vice president, is shown some of the memorabilia of William A. Philpott, Jr., by Bill Philpott, right, in Cisco. The latter is a nephew of the longtime managing officer of the TBA.

3
THE MIRACLE
on TENTH STREET DEDICATED—
WITHOUT DEBT

The TBA building adds greatly to the neighborhood.
GOVERNOR DOLPH BRISCOE, TBA building dedication, July 23, 1977

DALLAS WAS THE PLACE for the 1977 convention, and Charles L. Childers of Tyler was elected president. Writing to the association membership on May 18, 1977, he reported that "the construction of your TBA headquarters is now complete and all costs, including furniture and equipment, have been paid. It is so comforting to know that the finances of the TBA are excellent, and we are without debt."

He announced that a committee headed by former President C. Truett Smith was working on plans for the formal dedication.

The TBA moved to its new building from the 10th floor of the Vaughn Building at convention time 1977, always a hectic period for any association. But the pressures on the staff were relieved by the dignity, size and utility of the handsome new headquarters.

Chairman Smith told the board of directors, meeting in the new facility for the first time on June 19–21, that plans for the formal dedication were set for Saturday afternoon, July 23, 1977, 5:00 to 8:00 p.m. Governor Dolph Briscoe would cut the ribbon.

The Grand Opening Committee included, in addition to Smith, Gene Edwards, Charles L. Childers, Leon Stone, Charles E. Cheever, Jr., J. B. Wheeler, E. W. Williams, S. Ross Greenwood, and ex officio Alison Kimberlin and Mary Ellen Simpson.

It was a sweltering Saturday afternoon, July 23, 1977, for the building dedication. One person fainted from the oppressive heat. But still it was a perfect day for the bankers of Texas and their leaders, a day of accomplishment and the realization of an idea suggested by C. Truett Smith, TBA president in 1973–1974.

Governor and Mrs. Briscoe walked across West Tenth Street from the Governor's Mansion for the auspicious occasion. TBA President Charles L. Childers presided at the ribbon-cutting ceremony. S. R. Greenwood, cochairman of the committee for the building, introduced Governor Briscoe. The chief executive of Texas, a banker, brought laughter to the audience when he commented that the TBA building "adds greatly to the neighborhood." President Childers traced the history of the facility, a two-story brick structure with basement and parking facilities, and pointed with pride to the fact that it was fully paid for through the support of the member banks. Its total cost, including land, furnishings, landscaping and other improvements, was

It was a sweltering Saturday afternoon, July 23, 1977, for the building dedication.

206

$1,240,000, fully funded before construction began. Shepherd and Boyd of Dallas were the architects; Austin-Nelson Construction Company, the general contractors; Corporate Designs, Inc., Dallas, were the interior decorators.

In addition to Governor Briscoe, many dignitaries attended, including former TBA presidents and bank chief executive officers.

Commented Greenwood: "It is symbolic of all that's good in banking in Texas." The audience cheered.

The building on the knoll just south of the Governor's Mansion became the center of association and banking activities, providing the appropriate facilities for expanded service. No wonder all who worked to achieve it and who underwrote its construction costs would long remember that hot day in July 1977.

PART THIRTEEN

The TBA Rounds Out
The Last Decade
Of the First Century:
From the Colorado
To the Potomac,
Banking Reform and Equity

1

THE ART of CONSENSUS
and a LEVEL PLAYING FIELD

The delivery of financial services to individuals and business will never be the same.
R. M. DUFFEY, JR., TBA president, 1979

ON DECEMBER 9, 1974, the name of the TBA's top policy group, the administrative council, was changed to the board of directors, more in keeping with banking terminology. The following May at the Houston convention President Edwards had a long list of accomplishments for the delegates, in addition to his report on the new headquarters building. Actually, the association was now entering a crucial decade, the last of the first century of its existence. Edwards and his successors knew that it would not be an easy time for banking.

The 1975 legislative session, described as the "biggest log-jam on the Colorado," required constant attention by the association. As it was nearing completion, Sam

Kimberlin and Leonard Passmore were able to report the passage of several bills favored by the TBA and signed by Governor Dolph Briscoe. One dealt with banking facilities, allowing drive-in facilities located within 500 feet of the main banking house, connected to the latter in one of the ways now permitted by statute or by "closed television or other physically connected delivery service."

Electronic funds transfers—"the most discussed, the most misunderstood subject in banking"—was a topic of intense consideration around the country. President J. B. Wheeler wrote: "There never is any substitute, as we all know, for the assembly of all information available concerning any subject. CBCTs, EFT, POS and their use across the nation, and especially in Texas, are no exception." The TBA board endorsed the EFT program.

There was a note of Texas pride in the naming of Joe Selby, Ganado native and son of former TBA president, Roy Selby, as first deputy comptroller of the currency for operations.

Texas bankers went to New York City in October for the ABA Centennial Convention. In observance of the centennial the Smithsonian Institution opened an exhibit on the history of American banking. The U. S. Postal Service issued a special stamp.

The Equal Credit Opportunity Act became effective October 28, 1975.

President Wheeler and Vice President Greenwood toured various meetings in the state to acquaint bankers with the organization and the aims of the SouthWestern Automated Clearing House Association (SWACHA). George W. McAulay of Dallas was elected president of that group.

Another staff addition was announced. Edward A. Yopp was named executive director of the TBA Trust Division.

President Wheeler warned the bankers at the round of district meetings about the negative aspects of the Financial Reform Act pending in Congress. All-out opposition was launched—and the successful efforts were recognized by bankers around the nation. The Arkansas Bankers Association adopted a resolution thanking Wheeler and Sam Kimberlin for arousing the country to action to defeat the legislation.

At the El Paso convention in May 1976, Governor Dolph Briscoe warned that "neither man nor government can afford to live beyond their means."

S. Ross Greenwood, Temple, took over the presidency in El Paso. During the summer he testified before the Subcommittee on Financial Relations of the U. S. Senate at a hearing in Dallas and strongly opposed changes in the McFadden Act. He urged that finance be kept close to the people.

R. M. Duffey, Jr., of Brownsville was appointed to head a special committee to study the dues structure of the association. He was serving as TBA treasurer.

Greenwood identified EFT as a priority matter for the association during his administration. Said he, "Texas cannot be an island to itself with the other states having an advantage of participation." The association announced that an amendment to the Texas Constitution to permit EFT banking in Texas would be sought.

Competitive equality with the "thrift" institutions was a goal of the ABA leadership conferences on critical legislative and regulatory matters, and reports were made to the membership on such things as nationwide NOW accounts, proposed as an opportunity for parity between banks, savings and loans, and credit unions. This would provide equality of rate ceilings in both savings and NOW accounts, reserve requirements and other inequities as delineated by President Greenwood and ABA President Liddon McPeters.

Banking grew in Texas. Deposits increased at an annual rate of 12.5 percent in the first half of the decade, and Texas now ranked fourth in the nation.

President Charles Childers and the TBA board of directors met September 27, 1977, in the directors' room of the new headquarters building. Banking leaders from around the state hoped the voters of Texas would approve Proposition Six authorizing the legislature to permit Texas banks to use electronic devices off premises. The proposed amendment did not permit brick and mortar branches. But the voters turned down the EFT proposal.

The Foundations at SWIGSBIE and the TBA announced plans for a new Intermediate School of Bank Management at SMU, May 28-June 2, 1978. The old TBA Bankers Conference in Austin, a general banking curriculum held since 1939, was discontinued in favor of specific programs.

The 94th convention met in San Antonio in May 1978. It was the 13th time the association had gathered in the Alamo City since the first meeting held there in 1893. (The largest attendance at any TBA convention had been registered in 1968, the year of the HemisFair, with 2,510 in attendance.)

President Childers told of the many developments which had taken place in his year of the presidency, but one that would be remembered for a long time was the dedication of the TBA headquarters.

A San Antonio banker, Charles L. Cheever, Jr., was elected president.

At the June meeting of the TBA board of directors, he asked for and was given authority to create a special Bank Tax Task Force.

The association valued highly its nationally recognized education program under the direction of Dr. Lee Wilborn. President Cheever, noting that the program began in 1968, reviewed its exciting development under Dr. Wilborn for the decade. With accolades for his success, Dr. Wilborn retired from the TBA post January 1, 1979.

A banker and a professor at The University of Texas collaborated on a new book, *The Development of State-Chartered Banking in Texas*. Underwritten by the Association of State Chartered Banks in the late 1960s, the authors of the book were Joseph M. (Jody) Grant, a graduate student in finance, and Lawrence L. Crum, professor of banking and finance at the Austin campus. Published in 1978 by the Bureau of Business Research at the university, it was a significant contribution to banking and financial history. Grant, a Dallas banker, had been in banking in Texas since receiving his doctorate.

About 1,000 Texans flocked to Honolulu for the 105th ABA convention in October. More than 800 of the group attended the annual TBA breakfast, a longtime tradition.

Inflation and interest rates were increasing; bankers in Honolulu heard nothing to indicate an easing of the old dilemma. President Carter announced a program for

Banking grew in Texas. Deposits increased at an annual rate of 12.5 percent in the first half of the decade, and Texas now ranked fourth in the nation.

211

combating inflation, including restrictions on salary increases and prices. The nation had experienced valleys and peaks in the economy before, but it appeared that the current peak was lodged at a dizzy height which troubled bankers.

The TBA group went to Washington in January 1979 to tell the national leadership of their concerns over increasing paperwork, excessive regulation and the pending proposal to require mandatory reserves for all depository institutions. The TBA wanted reserve requirements reduced, with equal application to all financial institutions.

At the March board session the association policy was that of support of the ABA position of voluntary membership in the Federal Reserve for state banks.

President Cheever presided at the 95th convention in Fort Worth in May. Governor William Clements was the first speaker. The new governor had threatened to veto a bill increasing interest on residential mortgage loans from 10 to 12 percent, and the bankers listened attentively as he explained a change in his view—moving to a "floating" interest rate tied to U. S. Treasury bonds.

In his summary of banking events during the year, Cheever included such things as pre-authorized transfers from savings to checking; authorization for money market certificates; the passage of FIRA; and the Fed membership issue. It was clearly obvious that the agendas of TBA presidents were full—and the workload was increasing every year.

R. M. Duffey, Jr., Brownsville, moved up to the presidency of the TBA.

At the organizational meeting in June President Duffey announced the appointment for the first time of a TBA Community Banker Committee, with Shelley H. Collier, Jr., of McAllen, chairman.

Another significant action was the appointment of Gene Edwards of Amarillo, former TBA president, as chairman of the TBA Historical Committee.

The ABA Leadership Conference in Washington was a time for top-level discussions on the pending HR 7 issue on reserve requirements, transaction accounts, and efforts to ensure a more "level playing field" for commercial banks in competition with other financial intermediaries. Bankers supported the Stanton amendment to HR 7 which achieved equity and preserved a voluntary relationship between banks and the Fed.

To New Orleans went Texas bankers for the 1979 ABA convention, realizing that numerous critical issues, including the high rate of inflation and interest rates, would be discussed. On hand was Federal Reserve Chairman Paul Volcker. News of the drastic action by the Fed to restrict monetary growth arrived at the convention simultaneously with Volcker. Fighting inflation was a major effort for the ABA under its new president, C. C. Hope, Jr.

Bankers were obliged to act. The record of the 1970s had clearly established their assignments—and the TBA was heavily involved on all fronts. As Duffey said, "The delivery of financial services to individuals and business will never be the same."

Bankers were obliged to act. The record of the 1970s had clearly established their assignments—and the TBA was heavily involved on all fronts.

2
FINANCIAL REFORM:
NO TRANQUILITY for BANKING
and the TBA

Stay with the Procession or you will Never Catch Up.
GEORGE ADE, American humorist

A NEW DECADE! A FAST-MOVING PROCESSION!
January 1980 ushered in an era of dramatic changes in banking and finance. "Parity will be our watchword," President Duffey declared, "and inflation will probably remain 'public enemy number one. . . .'" He observed that the 1980s would not be tranquil.

As the TBA professional staff expanded, Mrs. Mary Ellen Simpson joined the staff on September 12, 1966. A native of Iowa, her husband, Captain Grant W. Simpson, U. S. Air Force, was killed in action in Korea in July 1951. She had been a resident of Texas since 1945. Mrs. Simpson rose through the ranks to her present office, Director of Administration and Finance.

Joining the professional staff of the TBA January 1, 1980, as associate counsel was James C. Lederer. A graduate of The University of Texas Law School, he had practiced law in Houston and had a thorough background of legal experience. His work would be in legislative, legal and regulatory matters. The association now had three attorneys: EVP Sam Kimberlin, Counsel Leonard Passmore and Lederer.

Scott A. Blech, named executive director of the TBA Trust Division, succeeded Edward A. Yopp, effective March 3, 1980. Yopp resigned to return to banking. Blech came to the TBA from the ABA Trust Division.

Christopher L. (Chris) Williston, director, Banking Professional Activities, joined the TBA in September 1975. He qualified for the professional accreditation by the American Society of Association Executives as Certified Association Executive (CAE).

At the end of March 1980 Congress passed and President Carter signed a far-reaching legislative package called the Financial Institutions Deregulation and Monetary Control Act, described as the most important banking legislation since the 1930s.

At the Houston convention, the 96th of the TBA, Sam D. Young, Jr., El Paso, became president.

A fairly new phenomenon—money market funds—had appeared in money circles only a few years prior to 1980, but by then the full impact of the growth of the funds was alarming to bankers.

The commencement date for NOW accounts nationwide for depository institutions was December 31, 1980.

213

The prime rate was at an all-time high of 20 1/2 percent, and the inflation rate in 1980 had been more than 12 percent. Banking and the TBA shifted gears and began a course to meet the challenges and to preserve its market share of business.

Among the first challenges President Young issued to the membership was to support Proposition One, the constitutional amendment on the November ballot to authorize banks to deploy unmanned teller machines on a shared basis countywide. He noted that S&Ls and credit unions already had the authority.

Joining the list of Texas bankers who have headed the Association of Reserve City Bankers was Paul Mason of Fort Worth.

For the first time the TBA began offering a group medical, life and accident plan, commencing August 1, 1980.

Dr. Richard B. Johnson, president of the SWIGSBIE foundation at SMU, director of the Assemblies of Bank Directors, died June 27 after a period of declining health.

A strong statewide campaign was launched in September and October to secure passage of Proposition One by voters November 4. Three former presidents of Texas banking organizations headed a Convenience Banking Committee to spearhead the project. They were Charles E. Cheever, TBA; William R. Simkin, IBA; and Derrell R. Henry, Texas Association of Bank Holding Companies, also a former TBA president. Proposition One was supported by Governor Clements, and the voters approved unmanned teller machines.

The Bank Marketing Association tapped a Texas banker, Ronald E. Hale of Bryan, as president. Selected to head one of the top ABA leadership posts was Charles Pistor of Dallas, appointed as chairman of the ABA Government Relations Council.

An event worthy of note took place in Cranfills Gap, Bosque County, at a board meeting of the First Security State Bank. The *TBR* reported that Hubert B. Viertel had been recognized for completing 33 years of service on the bank's board without ever missing one of the 400 meetings held in that time. His unbroken attendance was a "record probably unequaled in our state or nation."

The TBA board of directors decided December 12 to reaffirm its earlier position of seeking legislative repeal of the bank capital stock tax and replacing it with a corporate franchise tax.

Dr. Alan B. Coleman was elected president of the SWIGSBIE Foundation and director of the Assemblies for Bank Directors, as well as the Graduate School of Banking and the Intermediate Banking School.

Skyrocketing inflation and interest rates hammered hard on the people of the country—and on banks, particularly in Texas which had a restrictive interest rate structure. One of the big issues successfully pursued in President Young's administration was the passage by the Texas Legislature of an important interest rate bill that permitted an alternate rate of up to 18 percent. Governor Clements signed the bill.

As the bankers gathered in El Paso for the 97th convention, April 30-May 2, 1981, President Young was on home turf; nothing was spared to conduct a first-rate convention. Speakers included former President Gerald Ford, Senator Lloyd M. Bentsen and Robert H. Boykin, president of the Dallas Federal Reserve.

In his parting address to the 1,600 registrants, President Young described the banking industry, its opportunities and its problems, pointing out the change, contrast

Skyrocketing inflation and interest rates hammered hard on the people of the country—and on banks, particularly in Texas which had a restrictive interest rate structure.

214

and paradox present. He turned to the responsibilities of banking in the critical near future: to lead in the fight against inflation and against excessive government; to deal with market share limitation; and to work with the various banking organizations for the benefit of the public and banking. He described his experience as TBA president as "a shining highlight of my career in banking."

One of the first happy duties of incoming President Robert G. Greer of Houston was to tell the bankers that Governor Clements had signed the interest rate bill on May 8, culminating a long effort for rate relief by the TBA. He also told the membership that of the more than 100 bills "described in the TBA Bulletin this year, 33 passed, all with our blessings. Eighteen of the 33 directly affect banking in a beneficial way. No bill passed over our objection this Session," he said.

3

PREPARING for the TBA CENTENNIAL— A PUBLISHED HISTORY and a MUSEUM

Gene Edwards has done an outstanding job . . . .
ROBERT G. GREER, TBA president, commenting on the work of the Chairman of the Historical Committee

ON JUNE 12, 1981, PRESIDENT GREER REPORTED: "The Historical Committee is in the process of commissioning the writing of a book covering the history of the TBA, really a history of Texas banking as revealed through Association experiences and anecdotes, as well as planning the formation of a Texas Bankers Association museum. Both projects are set for completion shortly before 1985, the Centennial year of the Association. Gene Edwards, as chairman of the Historical Committee, has done an outstanding job in getting these two projects 'off the ground,' and he will be contacting Texas bankers soon to encourage the offering of historically interesting photographs of Texas banking memorabilia or artifacts to our Association," he said.

The research and documentation for the narrative and anecdotal history began immediately. It involved interviews with numerous Texas banking leaders in various regions, thorough research of the TBA archives and the *TBR* volumes since 1911. The Historical Committee, meeting regularly, had substantive input in the manuscript preparation and the planning of a TBA museum. Fortunately, provision for museum space in the TBA headquarters building was provided at the time of its construction.

The history and museum plans were coordinated by EVP Sam Kimberlin and Mrs. Mary Ellen Simpson, TBA director of administration and finance. Mrs. Simpson, a veteran professional staff member of the association, has worked closely with the TBA membership since September 12, 1966, when she became secretary to the executive vice president.

The TBA Centennial plans revolved around the association's 1985 convention in Austin.

Pride in the association, coupled with its effective voluntary leaders and professional staff, was a good reason for Texas bankers to turn aside for a time from their pressing responsibilities to take a look at their goodly heritage as they rounded out the first century of the TBA and moved boldly into the second. Crises strewed the paths of their predecessors; they prevailed; and so will their descendants as a good organization of first-rate bankers in the Lone Star State. It was a time to look at the record.

A man who had been a part of the TBA since 1939, Milton Boswell, editor of the *TBR*, retired September 30, 1981. Said President Young: "It is noted with some regret but yet with deep appreciation and admiration that Editor Milton Boswell will retire from that position. . . . Mr. Boswell joined the *Record* as Associate Editor in 1939 and was elevated to Editor in 1964. His dedicated efforts to produce the finest monthly publication of any banking association in this country have brought well-deserved recognition to him, his small (but highly productive) staff and the Association as a whole. Our warmest regards and best wishes are extended to Anne and Milton for the years ahead!"

Seldom does an editor possess the competence and durability of Milton Boswell. In 1939, as war threats were spreading, the young Plainview native received his diploma in business and journalism at The University of Texas in Austin. He was not absolutely certain that he should go to work for the TBA, but he did, and that was his career, a remarkable career of highly professional publishing and editing standards. He was well trained from the outset by William A. Philpott, Jr. He had the capacity to get acquainted with bankers and advertisers. He knew and understood the pressures of publishing deadlines, and to be certain that all members were treated fairly was his guiding star. Editing is demanding work; Milton Boswell met the challenge without flinching. As Philpott said in 1939 of Boswell: "He can chop adjectives to one in a hill."

The TBA lost no time in securing editorship succession. In the same announcement of Boswell's retirement, President Greer advised the membership: "We are pleased to announce that George Seagert has joined the Texas Bankers Association as Editor to succeed Milton Boswell. Mr. Seagert received a BBA degree from The University of Texas in 1948, majoring in advertising with special studies in public relations and business writing." He was with the Austin Chamber of Commerce, 1952–1972, was the first editor of *Austin Magazine* and later marketing director for a financial firm. Editor Seagert began his service August 1, 1981.

Another long time staffer of the *TBR* retired in 1981—Mrs. Annette Pannell, editorial assistant. Carla Mathews joined the staff as associate editor, March 26, 1982.

As the plans were going ahead for the centennial of the association, the *TBR*, which had documented so much of the early history of banking and the association, was now moving ahead with new faces to continue as the ultimate in state banking association journals.

4

FRONT-BURNER ISSUES
and the DEREGULATORY SPLASH

I think we are driving bankers up the wall.
WILLIAM ISAAC, FDIC chairman

CONGRESS TOOK UP BANKING MATTERS in 1982. The Garn Bill, often referred to as the "expanded powers" bill and the "financial reorganization" bill, moved to the front burner. TBA board members, in Washington in late January for the annual conference with governmental and regulatory officials and the ABA staff, sought equity in any banking legislation enacted. They also wanted to impress officials of the Depository Institutions Deregulation Committee (DIDC) with the concern in Texas banking over the slowness of the deregulation process. The group was the first to be briefed by C. Todd Conover, the new Comptroller of the Currency.

At a series of eight district meetings, President Greer presented his views on what might be the dramatic changes "for the banking industry for the coming decade." Said he: "Technology, government and competition" were the influences "dictating the course of our present banking lives."

Banking leadership, both in Texas and the nation, emphasized to DIDC the necessity for action on the agenda of change. Greer said in March 1982 that DIDC should act on its "commitment to 'get on with its mandate' for orderly phaseout of Regulation Q." Congress had left the matter up to DIDC, and bankers viewed the action as woefully slow.

Meanwhile, the economy turned downward, and the deep recession continued throughout the year, only to recover at the beginning of 1983. Happily, the rate of inflation decreased markedly. Also, the prime rate began a downward curve which continued to bolster hopes that the economy would soon shake off the doldrums. The Texas economy was damaged by the lower demand for oil and gas, and the Fed held to its policy of monetary control—tight money—to reduce inflation. Too, the Reagan tax proposals had been approved by Congress, a phased reduction of income tax.

On March 22 DIDC adopted a phaseout schedule for total elimination of Regulation Q by May 1, 1982, with time ceilings eliminated on savings accounts with maturities of three and one-half years or more. Also authorized was a new deposit instrument, a 91-day savings certificate with a minimum balance of $7,500, a change from the existing $10,000 for the six-month money market certificate.

President Greer applauded part of the DIDC action, but felt the failure was in establishing a $5,000 minimum balance, limited transaction account. He saw the action as a step in the right direction, but not significant enough to pull back to banking some of the deposit losses to money market mutual funds that largely operated without regulations and ceilings. It was like fighting with one arm tied, the bankers argued.

217

At the TBA convention in Dallas in May, Greer reflected on a year of many changes. Membership increased from 1,485 to 1,540 banks. The association, approaching the century mark, had reached new performance peaks after its reorganization in 1964. Its elected officers and leadership family, along with the professional staff, reflected the new emphasis. The results were impressive.

Robert B. Lane of Austin was elected president; Glen E. Lemon of Booker, vice president. Vernon S. Marett, Jr., San Antonio, was elected treasurer. His father had been TBA treasurer when he was a banker in Gonzales.

Picking up the presidential duties early, President Lane held organizational meetings to set the TBA agenda. A legislative consensus was developed for banking associations in the state to follow: capital shares tax, "sunset review" of Texas Department of Banking and branching options for Texas banks, among the matters for the 1983 legislature.

Reporting on the meeting, President Lane urged bankers to contact their legislators to inform them of the significance of the issues. He said: "Trade association groundwork is effective, but there is no substitute for contact by local bankers with their elected officials."

As the year progressed the TBA Historical Committee continued to meet and to preview and develop plans for a history of the association and a TBA museum. Chairman Gene Edwards reported the projects on schedule in time for the association's centennial in 1985, with the publication of the history planned for 1984.

Meanwhile, in Washington Congress was involved in the Garn-St Germain depository institutions legislation. Many feared that no action would be taken because the election year was at hand. That was, however, an incorrect assessment of the mood of Congress. The issue had been around too long to put off action.

The TBA board endorsed the view of the ABA to link new thrift asset powers "with establishment of a money market deposit account for banks," Lane informed the TBA membership. "The heart of the ABA proposal would direct by statute that the DIDC establish a new money market deposit account with access, liquidity, and denomination features that are directly equivalent to and competitive with those features offered by consumer money market mutual funds," he said.

The association warned "that this proposal to deregulate banking is timely but will require the exercise of good management skills should this deposit account be authorized by Congress."

"Deregulation is the most serious issue to confront our industry since the end of World War II," President Lane said.

After a long summer Congress passed the Garn-St Germain legislation as amended. It necessitated conference committee action to iron out the two versions. During the Labor Day recess bankers stressed to their elected officials the importance of the "level playing field" concept. Money market fund leaders, stockbrokers and investment bankers "joined the fray to preserve their turf," Lane pointed out. He observed that politicians were "caught in the middle in a no-win situation."

A big day for bank deregulation was September 30, 1982. Congress agreed on the final bill. On the Senate side the bill managers were Jake Garn, John Tower,

218

Dick Lugar, Don Riegle and Alan Cranston; for the House, Fernand St Germain, Henry S. Reuss, Frank Annunzio, J. W. Stanton and Chalmers P. Wylie.

A key factor in winning the victory was unity of the associations. The conference report received quick approval by both Senate and House, and the legislation was sent to the White House for approval. As Texas bankers were assembling in Atlanta for the 1982 ABA convention, President Reagan signed into law on October 15 the Garn-St Germain Depository Institutions Act of 1982.

Now the nail-biting period began as bankers awaited final action on deregulation by DIDC as provided by the law—and they had 60 days to do it.

The statute established a new deregulated market rate account to compete with the money market mutual funds, the speeding up of the phaseout of existing interest rate differentials to be eliminated by January 1, 1984. Thrifts were given power to invest up to 5 percent of their assets in commercial loans.

The glamour part of the new law was the money market account, described as "a deregulatory splash," for commercial banks and other depository institutions.

Keeping ahead of the Congressional time frame mandate, DIDC decided in mid-November what the account would be: minimal initial denomination, and maintenance balances of no less than $2,500; no interest limitation unless the average falls below a $2,500 balance; no minimum maturity period; transfers permitted, up to six per month, and so on.

Had Santa Claus arrived before Christmas? Some thought so, but others wondered what would happen in an entirely different banking and financial climate. FDIC Chairman William Isaac, groping with the dilemma of rapid change, commented: "I think we are driving bankers up the wall."

While the act was being studied—just eight days before the effective date of the new money rate deposit—DIDC made additional changes, including the creation of a super-NOW account, permitting third-party drafts.

With the coming of 1983 Texas bankers were considering the impact of deregulation on the year's earnings. As time passed the earnings picture was generally good; there was a strong effort by banks to go after the huge investments in the money market mutual funds and to bring them back to commercial banking. Reports showed that the outflow back to traditional financial institutions was successful.

As was pointed out by President Lane, "We are struggling to determine the amount of deposit migration within our banks and aggressively competing with unregulated money market funds."

In August 1982 the stock market began a long upturn to new records; it was the era of the bull market. Early in 1983 signs appeared that an economic upturn was under way, a trend that rapidly gained momentum. President Reagan reappointed Paul Volcker as chairman of the Federal Reserve, taken as further evidence of monetary control, and he was promptly confirmed by the Senate. Volcker, concerned over the mounting federal deficit, helped to keep the pressure on Congress for restrained spending. In early 1983 the prime reached the lowest point since 1978, down to 10½ percent in late February. It remained at that point until a slight uptick in August. Housing starts had rebounded; automobile sales were impressive. But the problem of

The glamour part of the new law was the money market account.

219

unemployment, also turning down in midsummer, remained a stubborn problem. It was a major problem to Texas and the nation, along with the mounting national deficits of astronomical proportions. Drought, widespread in the nation—bad in west Texas—reduced the agricultural production in many states.

Another issue fretting bankers and consumers alike was the law to begin withholding tax on interest and dividends, passed as a part of the Reagan tax program in August 1982. Bankers joined other groups in opposition to withholding as an expensive and time-consuming nightmare for financial institutions. Many felt, in the words of an old-timer, that it would "raise more hell than revenue." As a consequence, a major legislative struggle developed in Congress. Over the strong opposition of President Reagan and Senator Robert Dole, the Senate postponed interest and dividend withholding; the House voted to repeal it. After review by a conference committee, both Senate and House voted to repeal the provision in a bill that gave the White House one of its special requests. So President Reagan signed the repeal legislation into law on August 5, 1983; the unpopular law was removed from the books, but many banks had already spent vast sums to prepare for it.

Writing in the TBR, Professor William R. Carden, director, Center for Banking, Baylor University, observed: "If Rip Van Winkle had been a Texas banker who began his slumber in 1963 in the Texas Hill Country and awakened in 1983, he would undoubtedly have had feelings of dismay similar to those the original Rip experienced. During the past 20 years, the United States Banking Industry has undergone a virtual revolution in appearance, product size, and philosophy."

Along with others, he noted the development of a new industry, the financial services industry. "A changing legislative and economic environment created the idea, new consumer demands created the need, and new technology made it possible," Professor Carden wrote.

In July 1983 the United States Supreme Court, by a vote of 6–2, struck down a Texas law that permitted counties and cities to tax the value of stock of commercial banks. The case was brought by 52 commercial banks in Dallas County that had paid the tax for their shareholders. The court held that the Texas law conflicted with federal law, which prohibits the states from taxing federal securities, directly or indirectly. It was a decision that the TBA had been vitally interested in since the association opposed the capital shares tax.

When the TBA convened in San Antonio in May 1983, President Lane completed the presidency and was succeeded by Glen Lemon of Booker.

"Deregulation has been the focal point of our 1982–1983 program of work. Bankers, regulators and legislators continue to search for ways to define the rules of the game and develop the illusive 'level playing field,'" he said. He and the TBA leadership had gone a long way in preparing the bankers of Texas for "operating in a deregulated marketplace," Lane concluded.

Incoming President Lemon turned to the development of a "product committee . . . to study and recommend specific product and service lines for Texas bankers to utilize in a deregulated environment." Referring to the TBA deregulation study, President Lemon began the effort to put the study in perspective. "It is my feeling that in 1993, one decade after the deregulation study, Texas bankers will be able to look back at the changes which transpired as a result of the study, and we will take special notice of the foresight and wisdom that went into recognizing the need for such a study," he observed. Lemon named Lowell Smith, Jr., Rio Vista, chairman, and Allen M. Burt, Tyler, vice chairman of the committee.

To head a task force to study the TBA structure, Lemon selected Charles E. Cheever, Jr., San Antonio. Brownsville's R. M. Duffey, Jr., was named vice chairman. Working with them were subcommittee chairmen Robert G. Greer, Houston; Robert B. Lane, Austin; and Vernon S. Marett, Jr., San Antonio.

Lemon, a Panhandle small-town chief executive, knowing the value of being customer-oriented, brought the same innovative ideas to the presidency of the TBA. Said he, "I extend an open invitation to any of our 1,639 member banks to contact us with your suggestions and ideas for improving the Texas Bankers Association."

Elected on the officer team with Lemon were A. W. Riter, Jr., vice president, Tyler, and David E. Sheffield, treasurer, Victoria. As pointed out by Lemon, TBA member banks represent nearly 12 percent of the banks in the United States.

When Texas bankers speak, others listen, so President Lemon made it clear that all opinions expressed and directions taken "can have an important role at the national level."

As President Lemon finished his term at the 1984 convention in Fort Worth, the association had made a significant leap forward, and the TBA had moved to the threshold of its centennial convention in Austin in 1985.

The propelling forces that produced financial deregulation in the last decade of the first TBA century in many instances ran ahead of the Congress and the regulators.

As has been pointed out, non-bank entities got the jump on the traditional financial institutions, including banks. It appeared that the competition would be minimal at the beginning, in the early 1970s. But the trickle became a torrent as money market mutual funds, not restrained by interest ceilings, created a serious outflow of deposit dollars from banks. Necessity caused the bankers to fight for equity and for new powers to compete. As was true with the TBA, other state associations and the ABA launched forces to protect their turf. Not every battle was won—but the concept of deregulation and its application buoyed bankers to compete aggressively in a manner not seen in 50 years. Even banks began to move from the restrictions imposed on them to prohibit their activities in equities. Also, the concept of banking across state lines has come out of the deregulatory climate for more diverse banking activities. In short, the free environment is fairly new for banks, and the decisions made today will set the financial services for years to come.

The TBA, seasoned by 100 years of experience, supported by the membership and a younger generation of bankers, is positioned to enter a second century of recognized banking trade association performance.

In Lampasas 100 years ago 31 bankers produced the first state banking association in the nation. But they actually created more than a banking association. They established a tradition for ethical, efficient and productive performance in peace and war, in boom and depression, and in all things, large and small. The TBA led the way; others followed. The bankers of Texas nourished their association by unselfish support and have always been willing to stand in the place where their predecessors

The propelling forces that produced financial deregulation in the last decade of the first TBA century in many instances ran ahead of the Congress and the regulators.

221

stood, a place that is alive with a rich heritage in every respect. Their story is worth the telling.

The Texas Bankers Association is ready to launch the Second Century. They know history—they make it!

PART FOURTEEN

The Gallery of Presidents of the Texas Bankers Association

James F. Miller
1885–86

N. B. Sligh
1887

Ed. J. L. Green
1888

J. Z. Miller
1889

Nicholas Weeks
1890

G. A. Levi
1891

J. W. Blake
1892

A. P. Woolridge
1893

T. J. Groce
1894

A.S.Reed
1895

J.N.Brown
1896

C.C.Hemming
1897

J.E.Longmoor
1898

M.B.Loyd
1899

George E.Webb
1900

F.F.Downs
1901

H.P.Hilliard
1902

J.E.McAshan
1903

A. V. Lane
1904

W. H. Rivers
1905

J. L. White
1906

C. A. Beasley
1907

Edwin Chamberlain
1908

T. C. Yantis
1909

O. E. Dunlap
1910

W. H. Fuqua
1911

W. R. Hamby
1912

H.R. Eldridge
1913

Nathan Adams
1914

J.A. Pondrom
1915

Joe Hirsch
1916

J.W. Butler
1917

Howell E. Smith
1918

W.W. Woodson
1919

F.M. Law
1920

Eldred McKinnon
1921

Warren P. Andrews
1922

M. C. Driscoll
1923

A. M. Graves
1924

R. L. Thornton
1925

F. H. Welch
1926

Charles A. Fisk
1927

W. M. Massie
1928

W. A. Williams
1929

A. A. (Buck) Horne
1930

Jno. Q. McAdams
1931

J. W. (Fred) Hoopes
1932

Melvin Rouff
1933

D. E. Blackburn
1934

Sam R. Greer
1935

Fred F. Florence
1936

T. H. Nees
1937

J. E. Woods
1938

Oral Jones
1939

Dan E. Lydick
1940

Walter P. Napier
1941

P. R. Hamil
1942

P. B. Doty
1943

J. O. Gillham
1944

M. C. Ulmer
1945–46

DeWitt Ray
1947

W. A. Kirkland
1948

John T. Yantis
1949

Tom E. Acker
1950

C. E. McCutchen
1951

A. E. Dabney, Jr.
1952

W. Guy Draper
1953

W. Neal Greer
1954

John M. Griffith
1955

P. B. (Jack) Garrett
1956

Joe A. Clarke
1957

Roy Selby
1958

Howard Hambleton
1959

W. A. Pounds
1960

Thomas C. Patterson
1961

L. S. Goforth
1962

V. P. Patterson
1963

D. R. Blackburn
1964

James W. Aston
1965

Jeff Austin
1966

Walter F. Johnson
1967

S.R. (Buddy) Jones, Jr.
1968

John F. Geis
1969

Derrell Henry
1970

Tom Frost
1971

Oscar Lindemann
1972

Leon Stone
1973

C. Truett Smith
1974

Gene Edwards
1975

J. B. Wheeler
1976

S.R.(Ross) Greenwood
1977

Charles L.Childers
1978

Charles E.Cheever, Jr.
1979

R.M.Duffey, Jr.
1980

Sam D.Young, Jr.
1981

Robert G.Greer
1982

Robert B.Lane
1983

Glen E.Lemon
1984

PART FIFTEEN

Traditions, Bankers and Nostalgia

1

THE FLYING SQUADRON—
PILGRIMS in the CLUB CAR

As soon as we all got aboard, we all headed for the club car . . . .
The poker game started promptly.
BILL KIRKLAND of Houston, recalling the fun

THE STORIES OF THE FLYING SQUADRON live in the banking folklore of Texas.

Beginning in 1908 and ending in 1957, an annual and successful activity of the TBA in February was the operation of the popular Flying Squadron train. Scheduled at the time of the round of TBA district meetings, the train carried high-powered bankers from Texas and "foreign" places such as the major money market centers of the United States, numbering on occasion more than 100 and requiring special trains and many Pullman cars. The train departed from Dallas and made stops in several of the major cities of the state, always winding up in Fort Worth, generally following the district meetings. On the way were layover days, time for golf, attendance at the meetings, and as some described the tour—"a continuous poker game with liberal amounts of good food and drink."

Many old-timers still speak in glowing terms of the good fun and excitement of the pilgrim bankers on the TBA Flying Squadron.

In announcing the termination of the Flying Squadron because of changing times and conditions, William A. Philpott, Jr., long a participant and "den mother" of the unique event, wrote:

"There was not much gnashing of teeth, bitterness or lamentation when the Administrative Council, Texas Bankers Association, recently announced that the Flying Squadron Trip, the Group Swing, the special train movement of the TBA District

Many old-timers still speak in glowing terms of the good fun and excitement of the pilgrim bankers on the TBA Flying Squadron.

235

Meetings, had been discontinued. Naturally a score of potent reasons entered into the Council's decision to abolish the train trip to the different meetings. Russian sputniks, integration, inflation, the recent silly antics of the Dow Jones averages, the Asian flu, or the President's health had nothing whatever to do with it.

"You former pilgrims should not shed tears—except for flutters of sentiment. The dates are so placed this year a fellow can attend all the meetings by car or by plane comfortably, sleep in a *still* bed each night, get in at least eight extra rounds of golf, and much, much more poker playing."

Known for maintaining a prompt schedule for departure and operation of the special train, Philpott always joined in the levity of the trip, but he was a teetotaler and abstained from imbibing and smoking all his life. To ensure the health of the group, he always placed a juicy apple on the pillow of each berth "to keep the doctor away."

As the fame of the Flying Squadron spread across the country, bankers clamored for space on the special train. It was a haven for correspondent bankers. Lapel pins of the total number of trips were worn proudly. Usually lasting ten days, the trip often produced unexpected excitement for the uninitiated.

One of these great moments took place on Monday morning, February 20, 1939. An "extra" edition of the *San Angelo Morning Times* reported the event in a bold front page streamer: OUTLAWS HOLD-UP BANKERS' TRAIN. The subhead read: Flying Squadron Special Is Captured A Short Distance From San Angelo at 7:30.

Reported the story: "The Old West lived again in the early hours of Monday morning when approximately 100 of the roughest and toughest outlaws east of the Pecos ganged together to hold-up the San Angelo-bound "Flying Squadron Special," bringing this city more than 80 officials representing leading financial institutions from all sections of the United States. The daring hold-up, engineered at Crow's Nest Creek crossing about 13 miles east of San Angelo, was typical of those in earlier days when lone bandits selected that very spot at which to rob stagecoaches."

The truth was that the "hold-up" was staged, unknown to some of the neophytes from outside Texas aboard the special Santa Fe train, by masked men wearing bands around their 10-gallon hats reading, "Welcome—San Angelo Junior Chamber of Commerce."

With the full cooperation of local bankers and law enforcement officials, the realistic hold-up caused pandemonium aboard the sleeping cars. One banker from New York, believing the hold-up to be the real thing, fled in his pajamas across a field, pursued by a mounted Jaycee. Captured, he was brought back and suffered the indignity of jeers at his unsuccessful attempt to escape.

The "outlaws" carefully searched the cars for bankers "wanted" in connection with special, official-looking posters, which included a photograph and fingerprints. When the "wanted" banker was located, he was escorted to San Angelo for entertainment and a luncheon at the Cactus Hotel by his "outlaw" Jaycee. J. E. Woods of Temple, TBA president, was described as "Fish Eye" on his "wanted" poster issued by the "Hell-Raising Department, Old Scratch in Charge."

This hospitality hold-up lives in the vivid memory of many Texas bankers, victims of this well-staged event in 1939, including P. B. (Jack) Garrett, S. Marcus Greer, Virgil P. Patterson, DeWitt T. Ray and William A. Kirkland.

The famed Flying Squadron began its tour of TBA district meetings in Dallas. Many of the 1938 group paused long enough before departing on special cars that February 13th evening. William A. Philpott, Jr., seated at the far right, insisted that the train move on schedule.

The 2,500-mile train tour tested the stamina of all aboard. The late John M. Griffith of Taylor, a veteran of many tours, always chuckled when recounting the rigors of the round of meetings. On one occasion, he remembered that at the end of the ten-day tour he returned home, thoroughly tired from loss of sleep. He found that Mrs. Griffith had arranged for them to attend the movies to see the epic production, *Gone with the Wind.* Said John, "I went with Kate, but I slept through the entire movie."

Houston's Bill Kirkland recalls the Flying Squadron as a saga of immense proportion. The tour began with the annual meeting in Dallas. At the conclusion of the district meeting, the Flying Squadron group were at the railroad station by 9 p.m., ready to leave on the special train. Says Kirkland, a former TBA president who made many tours, "As soon as we got aboard, we all headed for the club car, and it was a miracle if we got any sleep the first night." The poker game started promptly.

"It was all in good fun," Kirkland says, noting the many exciting experiences awaiting the travelers in San Angelo. The Jaycees, with the support of the local bankers, never missed an opportunity to greet the visitors with some form of memorable excitement, such as the train robbery. On another occasion, Kirkland pointed out, the touring bankers were "captured" and put in the cattle auction area, and each banker was "auctioned off" for the fun of the audience.

In a way, it was dangerous to fail to take the Flying Squadron trip if you were expected to participate. For instance, in 1914 at the Westbrook Hotel Grill in Fort Worth, a clever plan was executed to make absentees foot the bill for an elegant dinner. Planning for this chicanery began in Temple where a quantity of draft blanks was procured. These drafts were made payable to "Ourselves," and the endorsing began. Soon the reverse side of the draft bore a conglomeration of signatures, every man on board being represented. The amount of each draft was $10. Each was honored, so the account goes.

The erosion of time has taken most of the pilgrims of the much-heralded Flying Squadron. One suggested that he hoped a reunion could be arranged in the Great Beyond—he'd like to hear some of the good stories and somehow rejoin the perpetual poker game.

One suggested that he hoped a reunion could be arranged in the Great Beyond—he'd like to hear some of the good stories and somehow rejoin the perpetual poker game.

2
THE "MEMWAS" of PREACHER KNIGHT

PASCHAL BRANTLEY KNIGHT IS HIS NAME—but most Texans know him as Preacher Knight.

He retired February 24, 1979, as a national bank examiner in the Dallas region. In addition to his long and highly respected career as an examiner, Preacher became a legend in his own time for his ability to experience and tell a good story, a reputation that spread throughout the state. When he announced his forthcoming retirement, Mike Doman, head of the Dallas Region, suggested that Preacher sit down and write his memoirs. "Hell," Preacher retorted, "I don't even know how to spell it!" So it was, he says, that he sat down at his typewriter ("Old Blessed") and wrote in fluent, salty and flowing style his "Memwas" which were published in booklet form, fully titled: *The Next to the Last Old Time National Bank Examiners in Texas.*

Upon retiring, Preacher became vice president of the First City Bank of Dallas.

"When I finally hang up my suit, I will go to my ranch in Bosque County," Preacher said in 1981. The Ponder, Denton County, native has "Rainbow" cattle—they are

238

every color in the rainbow, he chuckles—a goat herd, and will keep busy in activities he enjoys.

Preacher (he got his name as a child by imitating the Methodist preacher who served his family) in his book—a collector's item—reviewed his entire career, the moves throughout Texas, and the bankers and people he got to know. The story is liberally sprinkled with humor, salty but not demeaning.

When he began as examiner December 17, 1947, the salary was $2,694.96, with per diem at $6 per day. "You could stay all night in the Mayfair Hotel in Dallas for $1.75, provided you stayed two to a room," he observed. Automobiles sold for $1,750. He wore out 17, served under five Chief Examiners (Regional Administrators)—W. A. (Doc) Sandlin, Reed Dolan, Clarence Redman, Norman Dunn and Mike Doman.

"Old Blessed," Preacher's faithful typewriter, had a case to carry it around in. On it were pasted one-liner sayings that bankers and others gave him, in addition to a generous sprinkling of ones he collected for "Old Blessed's" box.

"It has always been the first thing that bankers want to see after we have gotten in the bank and all settled down to work," he noted. On examination trips bankers would drop in the directors' room when Preacher was working to check on what new had been added on the box. It all began with one big bold print saying in the middle of the typewriter case: BLESSED IS HE WHO HAS COLLATERAL FOR HE SHALL BE PAID. But there were many other one-liners, and a few are listed here:

> Two things I don't want to miss—a free meal and a bad loan. (Preacher says this was his trademark.)
> Every day is judgment day. Use some today.
> Borrowing money is like drinking whiskey—both are good if you don't overdo it.
> Sometimes it takes a lot of scratching around to get you out of a situation you were itching to get into.
> When you are feeling "Tolible" it means you feel well enough to eat but you don't feel like working.
> Taking the easy path is what makes rivers and people crooked.

Preacher had developed some pretty straight-talk views on management and examiners.

On management: "I judge management on the results they produce and not on some resume they keep in a drawer for inspection."

On examiners: ". . . a good examiner should have a little earthy and human touch. . . . Judgment is a two-way street. . . . Furthermore, it is my strong conviction and belief that the worst thing in the world the government can do is send a bank examiner with no common sense through the front door of a bank with a big thick book under his arm," he wrote.

Preacher believes that his appreciation for people helped his career. He admits that he met a lot of "characters" along the way, but he enjoyed them, tried to bring out the best for banking by being firm but understanding human nature.

He said some of the banks he examined in the early years of his career were so small that it was said of him that he could drive up, leave his car's engine running,

Preacher's sayings: Borrowing money is like drinking whiskey—both are good if you don't overdo it.

239

examine the bank, get back in his car and be on the way in a few minutes.

Stationed in many Texas places in his career, Preacher Knight developed a lot of fishing and hunting buddies who still remember and laugh at some of his great stories, including how much a goat is worth as bank collateral.

In so many ways he represented the wit, wisdom and philosophy of the one-liners on "Old Blessed's" box.

3
NAIL UP the PASSAGEWAY
to the SALOON

Rule in a bank's minute book, 1884

BACK IN 1954 the *TBR* had an article that glanced back at some of the rules applicable to a bank's employees in 1884. Here is the story:

"Recently, President C. R. Hallmark of the First National Bank, San Angelo, looked back in an old minute book of the Concho National Bank, original name of the First National, and came up with a laughing item or two. The time was January 21, 1884, and the directors set down a few rules for employee conduct—regulations which sound strange today. Here are the suggestions drawn up as resolutions in the minute book: 'Employees shall be held responsible for any shortage in cash; employees are required not to bet at cards in any way whatever; the Bank's back door leading into the saloon of Fitzpatrick and Little must be securely nailed up so that there will be no passage from the Bank to this saloon in that way.' Evidently the Concho National's employees did not have the coffee drinking habit in those faraway days, else there would have been a resolution on that."

4
HURRAH for a LIVING WAGE!

The Department of Labor announced a wage scale of 40 cents an hour
for bank employees, 1944

THINGS HAVE CHANGED since 1944, to be sure, such as wages and bank deposits. That year the administrator of the Wage and Hours Division of the U. S. Department of Labor announced a wage scale of 40 cents an hour for bank employees.

Considering the dramatic increases of the past 40 years in postage, the cost of living—you name it—there was relativity in the bank deposit structure in Texas. As of the June 30, 1944, call, there were only five banks in Texas having totals of $100,000,000 or more. They were located in Dallas, Houston and Fort Worth.

5
CARTER GLASS and HIS TWO-MINUTE SPEECH

A new deal relates itself somehow to playing cards.
SENATOR GLASS, 1935

SENATOR CARTER GLASS OF VIRGINIA, the venerable godfather of many banking acts, including the Federal Reserve System, was a newspaper publisher in Lynchburg in the Old Dominion. A political conservative, he began to have serious doubts about the New Deal of President Franklin D. Roosevelt. As a consequence of his political views, he often kicked out of the traces of the Democratic Party and its smiling leader in the White House.

Speaking to the graduating class of Tufts College in June 1935, he said: "A *new deal* relates itself somehow to playing cards. Cards, as you very well know, are largely used for gambling purposes. So, when you have a *new deal*, you should make certain too many cards are not passed to the players on one side of the table and too few to those on the other side."

Period. End of graduating address. His entire remarks took only two minutes!

Senator Glass dominated banking law until his death.

6
THE LAST ROUNDUP of a LOSER

THE LAST BANK BANDIT KILLED while robbing a Texas bank, and for whose killing the TBA paid a reward of $5,000, was one of two brothers who successfully robbed the Bremond State Bank on December 23, 1948, according to the record. The amount taken was $12,350. The Robertson County Sheriff shot one of the robbers as the escape car sped away. The surviving brother at the wheel, the TBR said, pushed his dead brother to the street and fled to freedom. Later, he was captured and much of the money recovered.

7
TEXAS RANGER OPENS a BANK— SHOTGUN BASIC EQUIPMENT

W. W. COLLIER was born December 2, 1863, in Cherokee County, Texas. After graduating from high school he sought an active and exciting life, so he joined the Texas Rangers. His grandson, S. H. Collier, Jr., McAllen banker, described the rough and ready life of a Ranger, camping out, in hot or freezing weather. He served four years and was leader of his company. Then he located in Uvalde and opened a private bank in the late 1800s. No charter was required for a private bank. Securing a small space, he had a sign painted on the front glass, "W. W. Collier, Banker," acquired a desk, chair, shotgun and a safe—and he was in business. The shotgun, pretty basic equipment, was to ward off any would-be robbers.

He was elected treasurer of Uvalde County and held that office many years. Meanwhile, he had secured a national charter. In 1908 he moved to San Antonio, engaged further in banking and was urged by Governor Colquitt to accept appointment as Commissioner of Banks, effective July 28, 1913.

The shotgun, pretty basic equipment, was to ward off any would-be robbers.

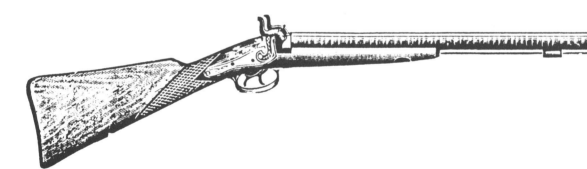

8
WHO CAN PLAY the ARITHMOMETER?

SHADES OF THE GOD OF TECHNOLOGY!

In 1901 a new adding machine, called an "arithmometer," was being advertised in Texas as a machine that "will list and add—saving time, worry, work, and money—doing all the hard part—doing away with the drudgery of accounting work—and used by at least 10,000 banks."

(You know the old story about the church committee wanting to buy a chandelier and the dear old deacon observing that he opposed the proposition because it was unnecessary and even if purchased nobody in the congregation could play it.)

The arithmometer. To the interested Texas bank, one of the machines was offered on "30 days free trial."

Does anybody remember what happened to the newfangled machine?

How did it work on a roll-top desk which didn't go out of style until about 1920?

Incidentally, through the efforts of Vernon S. Marett, Sr., of Gonzales, former TBA treasurer, a roll-top desk used by James F. Miller, first TBA president, was placed in the association's headquarters in Austin a few years ago. It is typical of the type of desk used by most banking executives of that day.

9
IS an AUTOMOBILE NECESSARY?

IN 1918 A BURNING QUESTION with Texas bankers was: "Should a bank lend a farmer (or anyone, for that matter) money to purchase an automobile?" The *TBR* reported that Gib (Rabbit Twister) Poteet, the "sage of Roxton," said, "Washington authorities should pass a federal law prohibiting any man from buying an automobile on credit."

Installment credit hadn't caught on.

It was said that one banker felt so strongly against automobile loans that, upon making the loan, he would hold the keys in his desk drawer until the borrower paid off the loan!

Times have changed. The parking lots and highways are full of autos financed by banks to help consumers.

10
HOTEL RATES in SAN ANTONIO

ALONG WITH EVERYTHING ELSE, hotel rates have increased through the years. The TBA delegates at the convention in San Antonio in May 1921 were charged the following hotel rates: St. Anthony, $2.50 single, $4 double; Gunter, $2 single, $3 double; Menger, $1.50 single, $2.50 double. At the St. Anthony the presidential suite, consisting of parlor, two bedrooms and two baths was quoted at $12 per day.

Some delegates thought the rates too steep and fussed at the inflationary prices— but that did not keep them from attending the annual convention.

11
GOODBYE to CIRCULATION

NATIONAL BANKS ENJOYED THE PRIVILEGE of note circulation from the Civil War days to early 1935. Treasury Secretary Henry Morgenthau called in all Panama Canal bonds and Consols for redemption on July 1, 1935. It was goodbye to bank notes and circulation privileges which national banks prized for 70 years.

12
AN "ITCHY RASH"—
RATION COUPONS

BANKERS HAVE BEEN ASKED TO DO many things for the government through the years. The response has been positive. But bankers and depositors balked successfully at the imposition of withholding of interests and dividend tax in 1983. Congress repealed the law.

Ration banking gave every banker a headache in 1943. The Office of Price Administration (OPA) saddled this job on the patriotic bankers in World War II. Texas bankers received the bulky manual of operation on Ration Banking, described as an "itchy rash if there ever was one."

Every ration coupon had to be collected, counted and credited. But Texas bankers cooperated, thinking of victory. One banker sounded this prewar note, however; "So far as I know, history affords no example of a people, situated as we are at this time, drunk with a temporary and wholly artificial prosperity, created and sustained solely by the lavish and reckless expenditure of our own money, most of it borrowed at that." And he predicted dark days ahead with mounting deficits. Many leaders, including Mariner Eccles, were saying that the time to stop inflation was then. The dollar was worth about 80 cents. As early as 1941 Jesse Jones of Houston had warned that a national debt of $90 billion or more was probable. At the time he was head of the RFC.

244

13
PIONEER WOMAN BANKER
BROUGHT HER BANK through
the DEPRESSION

FANNIE DAVIS (MRS. R. E. L.) UPCHURCH of Bedias, Grimes County, president of the First State Bank, died at age 92 on October 29, 1982. The obituary account credited her with having served actively as a bank president longer than any other woman banker in Texas "and probably in the United States." She also found time to manage her vast ranch acreage and to serve her church.

During the depression of the 1930s she brought the bank through the dark economic times and expanded other interests to become a "legend in her own time." Born in 1890, she was one of the few women of her generation to hold a college degree, a major in mathematics in 1910 from the University of Texas. She never took medication of any kind until she was 90, the report said. The first time she was admitted to a hospital was when she broke her hip at home a few days before her death.

14
ANOTHER FIRST for TEXAS—
TRANSIT NUMBERS

THE FIRST ISSUE OF THE TEXAS BANKERS RECORD, September 1911—the first page of volume one, number one—was headed "The Numerical System." It referred to the adoption by the ABA of a universal numerical system to provide every bank in the United States with a transit number, being assigned by Rand, McNally & Company.

A numbering system had been working smoothly in Texas for three years. The system was perfected by two men of the old American Exchange National Bank, Dallas—C. J. Grant and F. C. Pondrom. Grant headed the ABA committee which finally installed the system nationally. As was written in the TBR later, "Like the Russians, Texas claims everything, even the universal numerical system for banks." Why not? It's the daddy-rabbit of all.

15
REGIONAL BANKERS ASSOCIATIONS
and the TBA—
PANHANDLE ORGANIZED in 1904

In those early days, pioneer bankers themselves made the banks safe.
J. C. PAUL, 1937

Texas has had many regional or area banking associations, all working closely with the TBA.

The most visible is the Panhandle Bankers Association, organized June 8, 1904, in the office of C. T. Ware "in the rear of the Amarillo National Bank Building," according to Duane F. Guy, West Texas State University, in his history of that association.

When the TBA was organized in 1885 there were no banks listed in the Panhandle, Guy points out. But banking developed with the coming of the railroad in 1886. The first banks were in Canadian, Panhandle and Amarillo. By 1904 banks had been established in other places such as Dalhart, Claude, Hereford, Memphis and Quanah, reflecting the rapid growth of the region.

J. E. Ledbetter of Quanah is credited with the first move to organize a regional banking association. His suggestion struck responsive bankers as a good idea, so a meeting was held in Amarillo to launch the association on June 8, 1904. J. C. Paul of Panhandle was elected its first president. The first meeting had 14 bankers present, including W. H. Fuqua of Amarillo's First National Bank, a bank founded in 1889. Fuqua later became TBA president.

To attend a meeting or convention of the TBA posed a heavy travel burden. But bankers needed the advantages of an organization to provide a meeting ground to discuss common interests without much emphasis on the social side of the meetings.

The TBA applauded the organization and welcomed it enthusiastically. It has continued to be one of the regional organizations. From its bankers have come many of the top TBA leaders, including, in recent years, Gene Edwards of Amarillo and Glen Lemon of Booker.

A world of stamina was required to start a banking business in the Panhandle before the turn of the century. The story of J. C. Paul, a pioneer Panhandle banker, typifies the trials and tribulations of bank development in a remote region of Texas. He left Wichita, Kansas, in 1888 and followed the new railroad to Panhandle, where he began at once the construction of a two-story bank building "in which his family and the Panhandle Bank were housed for years." As cashier he drew $40 per month salary. To augment his income he was treasurer of the railroad, insurance agent and real estate dealer. But it was difficult to build deposits. At the end of the first year the

246

bank had aggregate deposits of only $3,336. There was little cash available in the Panhandle then.

Interest rates in those early days were 10 percent to 18 percent, and "on small loans the rate was two percent per month."

The 1893 depression, followed by a disastrous drought the next year, tested the survival of many business institutions. Writing to a friend in New York on March 30, 1894, Paul told of the severe conditions in the wheat crop. "I never saw a finer prospect than I had up to a month ago, but lack of moisture is killing the wheat outright. We are losing some settlers and shall lose some more right along. Nearly every man here is giving up. But I hope the cloud may soon show its silver lining."

Frank A. Paul, son of the pioneer Panhandle banker, spoke at a meeting of the Panhandle Bankers Association in 1937 and recounted the early days of banking and the experiences of his father and other early bankers. J. C. Paul had a customer with whom he had interesting business dealings. The customer operated a grain and coal business at Panhandle. He came to Paul for funds to finance the purchase of a carload of corn. The banker observed that times were hard, but the customer quickly retorted: "Mr. Paul, when I want more corn I order more corn; when you want more money you order more money." The customer got the money.

"My father had a farm two miles south of Panhandle on which he decided to plant oats, and he sent a wagon to J. E. Southwood's store for a load of seed oats," the pioneer banker's son recalled. "Southwood came rushing into the bank with the bill. My father suggested that the first of the month was the time to present the bill, but Southwood said: 'If anybody is damn fool enough to plant oats in this country, I want to collect my money from him right away.'"

Concluding his 1937 address, Paul listed the names of many of the Panhandle pioneer bankers who "neither closed nor went into bankruptcy. They were ruggedly honest; they had all the essential qualifications that dependable and successful men must have in every age and place," he said. "In those early days, pioneer bankers themselves made the banks safe; today, our system of laws and banking regulations provide the measure of safety that our social and business order demand."

As pointed out in Guy's history, the genius of banking is not in making the loan but in collecting it. "One banker said that if the potential borrower was a farmer, he looked at his shoes first. If they were shiny he was suspicious," according to Guy.

The *TBR* reported in 1930 that there were a number of other regional banking associations as well as many county associations. They included the Gulf Coast, Hill County, North Texas, South Plains, Southwest, Valley, Central Texas and Four-County associations.

Several years ago the First National Bank of Amarillo published a brochure to honor the living bankers of the Panhandle who had each given 50 years or more to banking: "The greatest tribute to these exceptional bankers cannot be printed on any page; it appears in the admiration and the respect they have earned wherever they are known."

Those honored were Orlin Stark, Quitaque; C. A. Gibner, Spearman; V. P. Patterson, Amarillo; F. E. Imel, Pampa; C. L. Culver, Groom; Marvin Carlile, Tulia;

The customer got the money.

A. R. Bort, Gruver; Ben Parks, Memphis; C. T. Hubbard, Wellington; Raymond L. Thompson, Vega; and C. E. Bedwell, Sunray.

Old Archimedes, were he privileged to look at the founders and developers of banking in Texas, would still stand by his famous saying, "Give me a place to stand, and I will move the earth."

Bankers from all sections and from all sizes of institutions have provided Texas the leverage to move the earth in their day.

16
STATE BANKING DEPARTMENT ORGANIZED in 1904—TO DATE, TWENTY-SIX COMMISSIONERS

WHEN THE VOTERS OF TEXAS amended the Constitution to permit the state to charter banks in 1904, the legislature created the State Banking Department as a consequence of the mandate from the people. It was at first under the Department of Agriculture, Insurance, Statistics and History, headed by the commissioner of that department. Several changes developed along the way, but it was in 1923 that the divorcement of insurance and banking functions took place by the creation of an independent Department of Banking.

From 1905 until 1943 the Commissioner of Banks was appointed by the Governor of Texas. In the latter year the legislature created a Finance Commission, appointed by the Governor on staggered terms of six years each. The power of appointment of the commissioner was given to the new Finance Commission. In 1961 the Building and Loan Division was divorced from the Banking Department by the creation of the Savings and Loan Department.

Since 1905, 26 men have served as Texas Banking Commissioners. They are as follows, along with the beginning year of service: W. J. Clay, 1905; R. J. Miller, 1907; Thomas B. Love, 1907; William E. Hawkins, 1910; Frederick Von Rosenberg, 1910; B. L. Gill, 1911; W. W. Collier, 1913; John S. Patterson, 1915 (killed in line of duty examining a bank in 1916); Charles O. Austin, 1916; George Waverly Briggs, 1919; J. C. Chidsey, 1920; J. T. McMillin, 1920; Ed Hall, 1921; J. L. Chapman, 1922; Charles O. Austin (second period of service), 1925; James Shaw, 1927; E. C. Brand, 1933; Irvin McCreary, 1935; Zeta Gossett, 1935; Fred Branson, 1939; Lee Brady, 1940; John Q. McAdams, 1941; H. A. Jamison, 1944; L. S. Johnson, 1945; J. M. Falkner, 1947; Robert E. Stewart, 1970; and James L. Sexton, Pampa native and FDIC Director of Supervision, was named Commissioner of Banking on November 7, 1983, following the retirement of Commissioner Stewart.

PART SIXTEEN

The Second Century

1

THE TBA in a WORLD of CHANGE: HOW the ASSOCIATION WILL LEAD in a NEW CENTURY

By GLEN E. LEMON
President
Texas Bankers Association
1983–1984

A S THIS 100-YEAR STUDY of the Texas Bankers Association is concluded, and with an unprecedented level of change taking place within the banking industry, quite a few Texas bankers have begun to ask the question: "What will be the role of our states' trade association in the new and revolutionized financial services industry?" Certainly, the question addresses a legitimate concern.

Changes within any respective industry most often have a clear-cut impact on the bottom line of the professional association which attempts to serve that industry. As anyone who has ever been involved with the TBA will admit, there can be no doubt that the Texas Bankers Association has been changing just as its member banks have been changing. The adjustments in each case are determined and driven by the marketplace.

While some may be troubled and concerned with the idea of altering what has been a proven and consistent state association, there are also a few who accept and welcome the opportunity to upgrade and adapt the TBA at the newly positioned marketplace. The TBA will continue to face questions similar to those which are affecting its member banks. Our Association is struggling internally to meet the needs of its customers just as we bankers have struggled to meet the needs of our customers.

Quickly looking back, the TBA has in the past served an industry which (1) was regulated and protected by law, legislation and custom; and (2) was highly transaction-oriented, with a large amount of its focus directed at the routines of serving the transaction-based customer. Then, within the past few years, all of this changed.

For example, technology is no longer the big-ticket item that it once was. The minicomputer and the microcomputer, when combined with the increased availability of computer software, have brought an exciting degree of technology into even the smallest banking institutions in the state.

Banking executives in both small and mid-sized institutions have discovered that the ground on which their industry rests still commands an enormous advantage in the marketplace environment. The challenge that lies before us is one of molding the new ideas, new techniques, new technologies, and new laws and regulations into a strong and resilient financial services provider. Our member banks must recognize the need and the responsibility for change.

As an association that seeks to serve its industry and state, the Texas Bankers Association must, in the future, assist our member banks while they are adapting to the effects of change. Yes, we will be responding to our members' needs—the need to compete, the need to survive and the need to have the management tools which will be necessary to serve our customers in the future.

As long as the *financial services* industry exists, there will always be a need for a trade association like the TBA. We must understand the need for, and the importance of, the volunteer efforts which are put forth by hundreds of Texas's bankers each year. In order for the TBA to maintain its quality and excellence within the deregulated environment of the financial services industry, these volunteer efforts must continue. They will have an even greater role in helping our state's banking association in the future.

2

THE CENTENNIAL YEAR—a BENCHMARK HISTORY and a PERMANENT MUSEUM

By A. W. (DUB) RITER, JR.
President, Texas Bankers Association
1984–1985

A century has passed since a small group of bankers, motivated and inspired to action, formed the Texas Bankers Association, an innovation that others quickly embraced.

Moved to action by the urgent necessity to remove the shackles of prejudice against banking institutions in Texas, they sought a dual banking system to serve Texas on a broad and large scale not limited to the few commercial centers of that day. Incredible as it may seem, they had to fight for two decades before the dramatic change was approved by the voters of Texas.

Now we are at the end of the first century and the beginning of the second. It is an appropriate time to review the issues, leaders, conditions, successes and failures that formed a strong link in the banking chain for economic development in Texas.

The solid accomplishment of the TBA Historical Committee, chaired by Gene Edwards, former TBA president, and supported by the association membership, has provided this benchmark history and a permanent museum in the TBA Headquarters in Austin. They are appropriate features of the TBA Centennial and serve as vivid reminders of the colorful first century and the beginning of the new, dramatically told in the lives and services of men and women in the Texas banking community. Today's dedicated bankers will recognize their valuable legacy.

Within recent years we have observed the increased interest in news and history of finance and business. This volume reinforces the banking history of Texas and underlines the fact that history is timeless.

As president of the Texas Bankers Association in the year of the TBA Centennial—a very important milestone in our history—I urge all bankers to read this history and visit the TBA museum. I also commend the volume to the general public as a valuable source of important information about Texas banking and the TBA, the organization that has contributed to banking's growth and service to the people of this state.

As we mark the 100th anniversary of the TBA at the 1985 convention in Austin, we are deeply indebted to all who have served to mark this important year in a meaningful and lasting way.

A.W.(Dub) Riter, Jr.

Appendix

PRESIDENTS OF THE TBA

Each President is dated by the year of the convention
at which he presided, at the end of his term of office.

Year Presided	Name	City	Site of Convention
1885 and 1886	James F. Miller	Gonzales	Lampasas
1887	N. B. Sligh	Galveston	Galveston
1888	Ed. J. L. Green	San Marcos	Galveston
1889	J. Z. Miller	Belton	Dallas
1890	Nicholas Weeks	Galveston	Houston
1891	G. A. Levi	Victoria	Austin
1892	J. W. Blake	Mexia	Waco
1893	A. P. Woolridge	Austin	San Antonio
1894	T. J. Groce	Galveston	Fort Worth
1895	A. S. Reed	Fort Worth	Galveston
1896	J. N. Brown	San Antonio	Dallas
1897	C. C. Hemming	Gainesville	Belton
1898	J. E. Longmoor	Rockdale	Austin
1899	M. B. Loyd	Fort Worth	San Antonio
1900	George E. Webb	San Angelo	Fort Worth
1901	F. F. Downs	Temple	Houston
1902	H. P. Hilliard	Austin	Galveston
1903	J. E. McAshan	Houston	Wood Lake
1904	A. V. Lane	Dallas	El Paso
1905	W. H. Rivers	Elgin	Dallas
1906	J. L. White	McKinney	San Antonio
1907	C. A. Beasley	Houston	Corpus Christi
1908	Edwin Chamberlain	San Antonio	Fort Worth
1909	T. C. Yantis	Brownwood	Houston
1910	O. E. Dunlap	Waxahachie	El Paso
1911	W. H. Fuqua	Amarillo	Dallas
1912	W. R. Hamby	Austin	San Antonio

1913	H. R. Eldridge	Houston	Galveston
1914	Nathan Adams	Dallas	Fort Worth
1915	J. A. Pondrom	Texarkana	Waco
1916	Joe Hirsch	Corpus Christi	Houston
1917	J. W. Butler	Clifton	El Paso
1918	Howell E. Smith	McKinney	Galveston
1919	W. W. Woodson	Waco	Galveston
1920	F. M. Law	Houston	Galveston
1921	Eldred McKinnon	Austin	San Antonio
1922	Warren P. Andrews	Fort Worth	Fort Worth
1923	M. C. Driscoll	Yoakum	Dallas
1924	A. M. Graves	Clarksville	Austin
1925	R. L. Thornton	Dallas	Houston
1926	F. H. Welch	Taylor	Galveston
1927	Charles A. Fisk	Amarillo	El Paso
1928	W. M. Massie	Fort Worth	San Antonio
1929	W. A. Williams	San Antonio	Galveston
1930	A. A. (Buck) Horne	Galveston	Fort Worth
1931	Jno. Q. McAdams	Winters	San Angelo
1932	J. W. (Fred) Hoopes	Dallas	Austin
1933	Melvin Rouff	Houston	Mineral Wells
1934	D. E. Blackburn	Victoria	Dallas
1935	Sam R. Greer	Tyler	Galveston
1936	Fred F. Florence	Dallas	Houston
1937	T. H. Nees	Beaumont	San Antonio
1938	J. E. Woods	Temple	Fort Worth
1939	Oral Jones	Wichita Falls	Dallas
1940	Dan E. Lydick	Fort Worth	Galveston
1941	Walter P. Napier	San Antonio	Houston
1942	P. R. Hamil	Bay City	San Antonio
1943	P. B. Doty	Beaumont	Fort Worth
1944	J. O. Gillham	Brownfield	Dallas
1945 and 1946	M. C. Ulmer	Midland	Galveston
1947	DeWitt Ray	Dallas	Houston
1948	W. A. Kirkland	Houston	San Antonio
1949	John T. Yantis	Brownwood	Fort Worth
1950	Tom E. Acker	Jacksonville	Fort Worth
1951	C. E. McCutchen	Wichita Falls	Dallas
1952	A. E. Dabney, Jr.	Corpus Christi	Galveston
1953	W. Guy Draper	Temple	Houston
1954	W. Neal Greer	Houston	San Antonio
1955	John M. Griffith	Taylor	Fort Worth
1956	P. B. (Jack) Garrett	Dallas	Dallas
1957	Joe A. Clarke	Fort Worth	Galveston
1958	Roy Selby	Ganado	Houston

TBA PRESIDENTS (cont'd.)

Year Presided	Name	City	Site of Convention
1959	Howard Hambleton	Waco	San Antonio
1960	W.A.Pounds	Tyler	Fort Worth
1961	Thomas C.Patterson	El Paso	Dallas
1962	L.S.Goforth	Comfort	Galveston
1963	V.P.Patterson	Amarillo	Houston
1964	D.R.Blackburn	Victoria	San Antonio
1965	James W.Aston	Dallas	Fort Worth
1966	Jeff Austin	Frankston	Austin
1967	Walter F.Johnson	Abilene	Dallas
1968	S.R.(Buddy) Jones, Jr.	Pasadena	San Antonio
1969	John F.Geis	Beaumont	Houston
1970	Derrell Henry	Odessa	Fort Worth
1971	Tom Frost	San Antonio	Dallas
1972	Oscar Lindemann	Dallas	San Antonio
1973	Leon Stone	Austin	El Paso
1974	C.Truett Smith	Wylie	Fort Worth
1975	Gene Edwards	Amarillo	Houston
1976	J.B.Wheeler	Plainview	El Paso
1977	S.R.(Ross) Greenwood	Temple	Dallas
1978	Charles L. Childers	Tyler	San Antonio
1979	Charles E.Cheever, Jr.	San Antonio	Fort Worth
1980	R.M.Duffey, Jr.	Brownsville	Houston
1981	Sam D.Young, Jr.	El Paso	El Paso
1982	Robert G.Greer	Houston	Dallas
1983	Robert B.Lane	Austin	San Antonio
1984	Glen E.Lemon	Booker	Fort Worth
1985	A.W.(Dub) Riter, Jr.	Tyler	Austin

TREASURERS OF THE TBA

W. A. Kelsey	1885	Martin McCain	1933
J. Caro Russell	1886–1887	A. B. Childs	1934
Carey W. Shaw	1888–1889	V. W. Robertson	1935
W. S. Gibbs	1890	Henry W. Warden	1936
Walter Nolte	1891	W. Guy Draper	1937
E. O. Tenison	1892	Jno. D. Mitchell	1938
W. Goodrich Jones	1893	E. L. Noble	1939
J. G. Lowden	1894–1895	V. P. Patterson	1940
George E. Webb	1896	J. Edd McLaughlin	1941
J. W. Butler	1897	H. W. McGoldrick	1942
H. P. Hilliard	1898	V. S. Marett	1943
Edward Rotan	1899	M. M. Galloway	1944–1945
Ewing Norwood	1900	W. A. Pounds	1946
H. C. Davis	1901	Jas. F. Smith	1947
T. C. Yantis	1902	George W. Baines	1948
Samuel Webb	1903–1904	Walter W. Housewright	1949
George S. Berry	1905	W. B. Russell	1950
A. W. Wilkerson	1906–1907	Clyde A. Northington	1951
T. W. Slack	1908–1909	Jno. J. Faubion, Jr.	1952
Thomas F. Rodgers	1910–1911	John A. Hughes	1953
Rufus Coy	1912	Doyle W. Taylor	1954
T. B. Benson	1913	J. Autrey Walker	1955
George D. Campbell	1914	C. D. Acker	1956
Chas. A. Fisk	1915	J. O. McCaskill	1957
C. E. McCutchen	1916	H. K. Allen	1958
H. M. Hart	1917	George H. (Jack) Neill	1959
Jno. Q. McAdams	1918	E. R. Gregg	1960
Paul G. Taylor	1919	C. B. Keeland, Jr.	1961
Melvin Rouff	1920	Ray M. Keck, Jr.	1962
F. E. Chamberlain	1921	T. Gilbert Adams	1963
Ford Seale	1922	Wilson E. Guest	1964
Chester Harrison	1923	Wilson E. Guest	1965
F. C. Pondrom	1924	Leon Stone	1965–1966
Owen W. Sherrill	1925	James T. Denton, Jr.	1966–1967
R. K. Mims	1926	A. W. (Dub) Riter, Jr.	1967–1968
F. E. Hendricks	1927	C. Truett Smth	1968–1969
J. Edwin Brown	1928	Ernest R. Esch	1969–1970
D. E. Box	1929	J. B. Wheeler	1970–1971
Irvin McCreary	1930	Max A. Mandel	1971–1972
E. L. Boston	1931	Jeff E. Bell, Jr.	1972–1973
J. E. Woods	1932	Bookman Peters	1973–1974

Harold M. Luckey	1974–1975	Glyn Gilliam	1979–1980
W.F. Smith, Jr.	1975–1976	W.R. Collier	1980–1981
R.M. Duffey, Jr.	1976–1977	Kenneth T. Murphy	1981–1982
E.W. Williams, Jr.	1977–1978	V.S. Marett, Jr.	1982–1983
Robert B. Lane	1978–1979	David E. Sheffield	1983–1984

TEXAS BANKERS ASSOCIATION

General Officers–Executive Committee

PRESIDENT–Glen E. Lemon, *Booker*
VICE PRESIDENT–A. W. Riter, Jr., *Tyler*
TREASURER–David E. Sheffield, *Victoria*
EXECUTIVE VICE PRESIDENT–Sam O. Kimberlin, Jr., *Austin*
IMMEDIATE PAST PRESIDENT–Robert B. Lane, *Austin*

Board of Directors

Bookman Peters, *Bryan*; Ernest Deal, *Houston*; C. Linden Sledge, *San Antonio*;
Walter L. Roots, Jr., *Taft*; Larry Franks, *San Marcos*; Dan Haynes, *Burnet*; Gordon
Gardner, *McGregor*; Willard J. Still, *Cranfills Gap*; Rick L. Palmer, *Sulphur Springs*;
Ridley Briggs, *Paris*; Tom G. Hussman, *El Paso*; William J. Multhauf, *El Paso*;
Gary W. Schur, *Munday*; Don Maples, *Abilene*; Ted Davis, *Amarillo*;
Jay Godwin, *Canadian*

District Chairmen

Michael G. Murphy, *Houston* (1); Jim Price, *Corpus Christi* (2); Gerald W. McCoy,
Austin (3); Craig McSpadden, *Teague* (4); Gene P. Catalano, *Plano* (5); John R.
Childers, *San Angelo* (6); Elwood McKinney, *Fort Worth* (7); Ronnie Paulger,
Idalou (8)

Divisions and Chairmen

ADMINISTRATION, AUDIT AND AUTOMATION, Angie De Los Santos, *San Antonio*; AGRICULTURAL AND RURAL AFFAIRS, Jay Dycus, *Pecos*; CORRESPONDENT AND CORPORATE BANKERS, H. F. (Hal) Means, Jr., *Tyler*; COMMUNITY BANKERS, Gene Garrison, *Alice*; CONSUMER BANKING, Hershel Kime, *Amarillo*; MARKETING, James T. Cockrell, *Temple*; NATIONAL BANK, Charles C. Brinkley, *Fort Worth*; REAL ESTATE AND MORTGAGE FINANCE, Kenneth E. Pulley, *Houston*; STATE BANK, C. Ivan Wilson, *Corpus Christi*; TRUST, Karen J. Cole, *Houston*

Administrative Staff

Sam O. Kimberlin, Jr., *executive vice president*; James C. Lederer, *counsel*; Christopher L. Williston, *director, banking and professional activities*; Mary Ellen Simpson, *director, administration and finance*; Iris Walker, *assistant to the director of administration and finance*; Deborah Sperry, *secretary to the executive vice president*; Josephine Roche, *administrator, insurance trust*; Carlisle Pearson, *special services coordinator*; Lenelle Bright, *executive secretary to counsel*; Don Cavness, *legislative consultant*; Jane Holstien, *assistant administrator, insurance trust*; George Seagert, *editor, Texas Bankers Record*; Carla Mathews, *assistant editor*; Scott Blech, *executive director, trust division*; Bebe Smith, *executive assistant, trust.*

MANAGING OFFICERS OF THE TBA

William A. Philpott, Jr., SECRETARY, May 11, 1916–January 1, 1964
Milton Boswell, ACTING SECRETARY, January 1, 1964–September 15, 1964
Sam O. Kimberlin, Jr., EXECUTIVE VICE PRESIDENT, September 15, 1964 ———.

NOTE: Prior to 1916, the office of TBA Secretary was held by an active banker. Mr. Philpott began his employment with the TBA as editor of the *Texas Bankers Record* in 1913 and continued as secretary-editor until his retirement. Mr. Boswell served as associate editor from 1939 until he succeeded Philpott in 1961. He retired as editor in 1981.

HISTORICAL COMMITTEE
OF THE
TEXAS BANKERS
ASSOCIATION

Gene Edwards, CHAIRMAN, *Amarillo*
Jeff Austin, Sr., *Frankston*
S. R. Greenwood, *Temple*
Derrell Henry, *Odessa*
John Griffith, *Taylor* (deceased)
S. R. Jones, Jr., *Pasadena*
C. Truett Smith, *Wylie*
J. B. Wheeler, *Plainview*
Leon Stone, *Austin*
R. M. Duffey, Jr., *Brownsville*
Robert G. Greer, *Houston*
Robert B. Lane, *Austin*
Glen E. Lemon, *Booker*

Index

Acker, Tom E., 163
Adams, Jack, 181, 183
Adams, Nathan, 101, 111, 115, 118,
   124, 158
Aday, Iva M., 125
Aldrich, Sen. Nelson W., 100, 110
Alexander, J. S., 20, 21, 24
Alexander, Willis, 183
Allen, Annie L., 106
Allen, H. K., 171
Andrews, Warren P., 128
Annunzio, Rep. Frank, 219
Ansley, Dick, 128
Armin, E. A., 20
Aston, James W., 170, 171, 179, 180
Austin, Charles O., 129, 248
Austin, Jeff, 180, 181, 183
Austin, John Franklin, Jr., 153
Austin, Stephen F., 5, 32, 34

Babson, Roger, 140
Bachman, Mary (*See* Mrs. William A.
   Philpott, Jr.), 174
Bain, J. H., 191
Ball, F. D., 19, 20, 21
Ball, George, 43
Barney, F. R., 155
Baxter, E. F., 20
Bayersdorffer, W. J., 114
Beasley, C. A., 91, 92
Bedwell, C. E., 248
Bennett, Samuel Burk, 50
Bentsen, Sen. Lloyd M., 161, 162,
   214
Bentsen, Lloyd M., Sr., 161
Betts, I. Frank, 166
Binkley, Christopher C., 18
Blackburn, David E., 151, 152, 169
Blackburn, David R., 168, 169, 170
Blake, J. W., 66
Blech, Scott A., 213
Blough, Roger, 183
Bollaert, William, 32
Bort, A. R., 248
Boswell, Milton, 104, 154, 155, 158,
   163, 165, 170, 174, 179, 216
Boyd, Bob, 194

Boykin, Robert H., 214
Brady, Lee, 248
Brand, E. C., 248
Branson, Fred, 248
Breck, Edward C., 25
Briggs, George Waverly, 248
Briscoe, Gov. Dolph, 162, 206, 207,
   210
Brooks, Fred T., 188
Brown, J. N., 18, 69
Bryan, Guy M., Jr., 20
Bryan, William Jennings, 24, 110,
   139
Bullock, Mr. (hotelkeeper), 38
Burleson, Albert S., 114
Burt, Allen, 221
Butler, John P., 149
Butler, J. W., 70, 80, 81, 88, 91, 92,
   97, 121, 122, 123
Byrd, Richard E., 139
Byrnes, James, 159

Cameron, William, 20, 21
Camp, A. C., 51
Camp, William B., 181, 183
Campbell, Gov. Thomas M., 95, 134
Carden, William R., 220
Cariker, Robbie, 106
Carlile, Marvin, 247
Carlson, Avery Luvere, 45, 47
Carter, Pres. Jimmy, 162, 211, 213
Castaneda, C. E., 34
Chamberlain, Edwin, 94, 95
Champion, George, 183
Chapin, Gordon, 27
Chapman, J. L., 248
Chase, Salmon P., 5
Cheatham, D. W., 20, 21
Cheever, Charles E., Jr., 206, 211,
   212, 214, 221
Chidsey, J. D., 248
Childers, Charles, 165, 189, 206,
   211
Clark, Gov. Edward, 45
Clark, George, 66
Clark, L. A., 141
Clarke, Joe A., 165

Clay, W. J., 90, 248
Clements, Gov. William, 162, 212, 214, 215
Cleveland, Pres. Grover, 9, 68
Cody, William F. (Buffalo Bill), 11
Coggin, Mrs. S. R., 106
Cohan, George M., 165
Coke, Gov. Richard, 51
Coleman, Alan B., 214
Collier, Shelly H., Jr., 212, 242
Collier, W. W., 114, 242, 248
Collins, C. B., 19, 25
Colquitt, Gov. O. B., 115
Comfort, H. F., 141
Connally, Gov. John M., 161, 181, 186
Conover, C. Todd, 217
Cooke, Jay, 50
Coolidge, Pres. Calvin, 134
Corbitt, Leffler, 106
Cranston, Sen. Alan, 219
Crum, Lawrence L., 34, 47, 89, 94, 126, 211
Culbertson, J. J., 115
Culver, C. L., 247

Dabney, A. E., Jr., 163, 169
Dallas, George M., 42
Daniel, Gov. Price, 161
Davis, E. J., 51
Dealey, G. B., 114
de Iturbe, Augustin, 33
Denson, W. B., 57, 58
de Saligny, M., 38, 39
de Tocqueville, Alexis, 8
Dewey, Thomas E., 160
Dobie, J. Frank, 174
Dolan, Reed, 239
Dole, Sen. Robert, 220
Doman, Mike, 238, 239
Dorsey, Frank, 69
Doty, P. R., 158
Doughton, Rep. R. L., 152
Downs, F. F., 77
Draper, W. Guy, 164
Driscoll, M. C., 128
Duffey, R. M., Jr., 209, 212, 213, 221
Dunlap, O. E., 97, 98
Dunn, DeWitt C., 114
Dunn, Norman R., 182, 239
Dunn, T. C., 114
Dyer, Isador, 20, 47

Edwards, Gene, 183, 184, 187, 189, 191, 193, 206, 209, 212, 215, 218, 246
Eisenhower, Pres. Dwight D., 161, 167
Eldridge, Herbert R., 111
Elkins, James A., Sr., 159, 188
Ellis, William E., 20
Elzner, Jonnie Ross, 13
Emerson, T. T., 20, 21
Evans, W. J., 155
Exall, Col. Henry, 1, 19, 56, 59

Falkner, J. M., 168, 182, 187, 248
Fall, Albert, 47
Faltin, August, 48
Ferguson, Gov. James E., 115, 116, 149
Ferguson, Gov. Miriam A., 145, 147, 148, 149
Fisher, S. W., 97
Fisk, Charles A., 134
Florence, Fred F., 153, 164, 165, 168
Ford, Pres. Gerald, 162, 214
Ford, Henry, 139
Fowlkes, J. S., 20
Franklin, Ben, 8
Frost, T. C., 27, 114
Frost, Tom C., Jr., 169, 170, 185, 186, 187
Fuqua, W. H., 98, 99, 100, 101, 246

Garn, Sen. Jake, 218
Garner, Vice Pres. John N., 145
Garrett, P. B. (Jack), 153, 165, 168, 180, 184, 236
Gaston, W. H., 51
Geiss, John F., 183, 184
Gibbs, Charles, 141
Gibner, C. A., 247
Gidley, Andy, 141
Gill, B. L., 104, 248
Gillham, J. O., 158
Glass, Sen. Carter, 110, 241
Godfrey, Berle E., 168
Goforth, Lawrence S., 167
Gossett, Zeta, 248
Grant, C. J., 245
Grant, Joseph M. (Jody), 34, 47, 89, 94, 126, 211
Grant, Pres. Ulysses S., 9, 24, 51
Graves, A. M., 129
Green, Ed J. L., 19, 20, 21, 57, 58
Greenwood, S. Ross, 189, 191, 193, 194, 206, 207, 210

Greer, Marcus, 148, 236
Greer, Mrs. Marcus, 148
Greer, Robert G., 215, 216, 217, 218, 221
Greer, Sam R., 152, 153
Greer, W. Neal, 164
Gresham, Sir Thomas, 31
Griffith, John M., 147, 148, 154, 155, 164, 237
Griffith, Mrs. John M. (Kate), 237
Groos, Frederick, 43
Grose, T. J., 68
Guy, Duane F., 246

Hale, Ronald E., 214
Hall, Charles B., 25
Hall, Ed, 248
Hallmark, C. R., 240
Hambleton, Howard, 166
Hamby, William R., 91, 100, 105, 106
Hamer, Frank, 135
Hamil, P. R., 158
Hamilton, Alexander, 109
Hamilton, Charles, 166
Hammond, Bray, 46
Harding, William P., 111
Harris, Roger, 165
Harriss, F. M., Jr., 153
Hawkins, William E., 248
Heller, Walter, 182
Hemming, C. C., 69
Henry, Derrell R., 184, 185, 214
Henry, O., 123
Henry, Robert L., 110
Hester, Minnie, 106
Hickman, Tom, 130
Hilliard, H. P., 77, 78, 83, 162
Hirsch, Joe, 117
Hitler, Adolph, 157
Hobby, Gov. William P., 124
Hogan, William Ransom, 32
Hogg, Gov. James Stephen, 66
Holton, John, 182
Hoopes, J. W. (Fred), 92, 95, 99, 100, 101, 104, 111, 112, 115, 116, 122, 142, 163
Hoover, Pres. Herbert, 140
Hope, C. C., Jr., 212
Horne, A. A. (Buck), 140, 141, 148
House, Charles S., 20
House, Edward M., 12, 105, 110, 111, 114
House, Thomas W., 105
Houston, David, 112, 114
Houston, Sam, 6, 10, 33, 37, 40, 42, 45

Howenstein, James T., 25
Hubbard, C. T., 248
Hubbard, John Barry, 182
Humphrey, Sen. Hubert H., 162
Hutchings, John Henry, 43, 47
Hutchings, Sealy, 43

Imel, F. E., 247
Ireland, Gov. John, 12
Isaac, William, 219

Jackson, Pres. Andrew, 33, 35, 40, 42, 109
Jamison, H. A., 248
Jefferson, Pres. Thomas, 109
Jester, Gov. Beauford H., 161
Johnson, L. S., 248
Johnson, Pres. Lyndon B., 161, 162, 181, 182, 186
Johnson, Richard B., 165, 183, 214
Johnson, Walter F., 181, 182, 191
Jones, Pres. Anson, 38
Jones, Jesse H., 128, 151, 152, 162, 244
Jones, Oral, 154
Jones, S. R. (Buddy), 182, 183
Jones, W. Goodrich, 59, 63
Joplin, Scott, 11
Joseph, Tom, 168

Kayser, E. W., 114
Kell, Frank, 115
Kelsey, W. A., 18, 19, 20, 21, 24, 54
Kennedy, Pres. John F., 161, 169
Kimberlin, Alison (Mrs. Sam O., Jr.), 206
Kimberlin, Sam O., Jr., 2, 95, 116, 127, 134, 168, 179, 180, 183, 210, 213, 215
Kirkland, W. A. (Bill), 149, 162, 235, 236, 237, 238
Knight, Paschal B. (Preacher), 238, 239, 240
Knox, John Jay, 10
Korth, Fred, 165
Kyger, Murray, 159, 181

Labatt, J. H., 57
Lafferty, J. Lewell, 155
Lamar, Pres. Mirabeau B., 38
Lane, A. V., 84, 87
Lane, Robert B., 218, 219, 220, 221
Lanham, Gov. Samuel W. T., 81, 88
Law, F. Marion, 125, 134, 151, 152, 153, 164
Lawrence, Dewey, 167
Ledbetter, J. E., 246

Lederer, James C., 213
Lemon, Glen E., 218, 220, 221, 246
Levi, G. A., 65
Lincoln, Abraham, 5
Lindbergh, Charles A., 139
Lindemann, Oscar, 187
Lipscomb, J. W., 123
Lobit, J., 20
Longcope, E. M., 1, 14, 16, 25, 60,
    61, 66, 70, 95, 158
Longmoor, J. E., 20, 70
Love, Thomas B., 88, 93, 94, 95, 96,
    114, 248
Loyd, M. B., 49, 50, 70
Lugar, Sen. Richard, 219
Lydick, Dan E., 155

McAdams, John Q., 141, 142, 248
McAdoo, William G., 110, 112, 113
McAshan, Harris, 164
McAshan, J. E., 59, 62, 80, 81, 82
McAulay, George W., 210
McCaleb, Walter Flavius, 101, 115
McCracken, James P., 137
McCreary, Irvin, 248
McCutchen, C. E., 163
McCutcheon, W. A., 20
McGovern, Sen. George, 162
McIlhenny, Ned, 114
McKinney, B. A., 114
McKinney, James R., 114
McKinney, Thomas F., 35, 37, 38
McKinnon, J. Eldred, 122, 125, 127
McMahan, T. H., 46
McMillin, J. T., 248
McNary, J. G., 114
McPeters, Liddon, 211
Malone, Frank R., 1, 14, 16, 18, 19,
    20, 21, 25, 27, 54
Marett, Vernon S., Jr., 218, 221
Marett, Vernon S., Sr., 243
Markley, Clyde P., 49
Martin, Anna, 129
Martinez, Felix, 115
Mason, Paul, 49, 182, 183, 214
Massie, William M., 135, 136
Mathews, Carla, 216
Matkin, George G., 149
Mertz, C. W., 20
Metcalf, Irby, Jr., 189
Miller, James Francis, 4, 19, 20, 21,
    24, 25, 26, 54, 63, 66, 81, 162,
    243
Miller, J. Z., Sr., 59, 60, 68, 69
Miller, R. J., 248
Mills, Robert & David G., 40, 43
Mitchell, John D., 143, 144
Mitchell, Kate, 106

Moody, Gov. Dan, 96
Moody, W. L., 46
Morgan, J. P., 92
Morgenthau, Henry, 244
Morris, Alf, 141
Morrison, Samuel Eliot, 13
Morrow, R. E., 151

Napier, Walter P., 157
Nees, Theodore H., 154
Nees, Tom, 97
Neilan, Edwin Peter, 153
Newberry, O. P., 142
Newton, G. R., 18
Newton, Joe, 137
Nimitz, Chester W., 12
Nixon, Pres. Richard M., 161, 186
Noble, Earl, 157

Oakley, Annie, 11
O'Connor, J. F., 18
Oppenheimer, D. & A., 43
Oppenheimer, Dan, 166
Oppenheimer, J. D., 152
Owen, Robert, 110

Page, Paul D., 134
Pannell, Annette, 216
Parks, Ben, 248
Passmore, Leonard, 180, 210, 213
Patman, Rep. Wright, 154
Patterson, John S., 121, 248
Patterson, Thomas C., 167
Patterson, Virgil, 148, 149, 159, 167,
    168, 169, 170, 236, 247
Patterson, W. J. B., 100
Patton, James A., 65
Paul, Frank A., 247
Paul, J. C., 246, 247
Perry, Marcella, 188
Peters, Bookman, 188
Phillips, C. W., 20
Phillips, Nelson, 141
Philpott, Bill, 175
Philpott, William Albert, Jr., 12, 14,
    54, 101, 104, 116, 117, 127, 130,
    134, 163, 165, 169, 170, 171,
    173–177, 184, 235
Philpott, Mrs. William A., Jr. (See
    Mary Bachman), 128
Pistor, Charles, 214
Polk, Pres. James K., 42
Pondrom, F. C., 245
Pondrom, J. A., 115, 116

Poteet, Gib (Rabbit Twister), 243
Pounds, W. A. (Abe), 167
Price, Frank, 166
Pujo, Rep. A. P., 110

Querbes, Andrew, 114

Randall, K. A., 182
Raphael, E., 16, 18, 20, 21
Ray, DeWitt T., 158, 162, 165, 169, 236
Rayburn, Rep. Sam, 161
Reagan, Pres. Ronald, 219, 220
Redman, Clarence, 239
Reed, A. S., 68
Reuss, Rep. Henry S., 219
Riddle, Lena (Mrs. Edgar L. Steck), 104, 106
Riegle, Sen. Don, 219
Riter, A. W., Jr., 221
Rivers, W. H., 87, 90, 93
Rockefeller, John D., 92
Rodes, O. H., 141
Roemer, Ferdinand, 32
Rogers, Nat S., 182, 183, 184, 186
Roosevelt, Pres. Franklin D., 141, 145, 146, 150, 152, 153, 158, 160, 241
Root, Elihu, 110
Rose, J. K., 18, 19, 20, 21
Rosenberg, Henry, 47
Rouff, Melvin, 144, 150
Runge, H., 43
Rushing, J. N., 19, 20, 21, 56
Russell, J. C., 20
Russell, John Caro, 58

Sandlin, W. A. (Doc), 187, 239
Sandmeyer, E. J., 20
Sanford, F. E., 19
Sansom, Marion, 115
Santa Anna, 37, 42
Sass, Reed, 166
Sayers, Gov. Joseph, 80
Saxon, James J., 181
Schreiner, Charles, 48, 98
Schreiner, L. A., 186
Seagert, George, 104, 216
Sealy, John, 43
Selby, Joe, 210
Selby, Roy, 165, 210
Sexton, James L., 248

Shaw, Carey, 20, 21, 60
Shaw, James, 136, 248
Sheffield, David E., 221
Shepherd, B. A., 43, 162
Shepherd, Phillip, 194
Shepherd, R. E., 153
Sheridan, Gen. Philip, 51
Shivers, Gov. Allan, 161, 183
Simpkin, William R., 214
Simpson, A. D., 134
Simpson, Mary Ellen, 206, 213, 215
Sligh, N. B., 16, 18, 19, 20, 21, 24, 25, 54, 56, 58
Smith, A. B., 58
Smith, C. Truett, 168, 181, 187, 188, 189, 191, 206
Smith, Howell, E., 101, 122, 123
Smith, Lowell, Jr., 221
Smith, R. G., 141
Spencer, A. C., 189
Stanton, Rep. J. W., 219
Starke, Orlin, 247
Stephenson, Gilbert T., 182
Sterling, Gov. Ross, 145
Stevenson, Adlai, 161
Stevenson, Gov. Coke, 158
Stewart, Robert E., 248
Stewart, Robert H., III, 188
St Germain, Rep. Fernand, 219
Stone, Leon, 188, 206

Taft, Pres. William H., 105
Tandy, William L., 153
Taylor, Bobbye, 186
Tennison, E. O., 115
Thompson, Raymond L., 248
Thornton, R. L., 127, 129
Tower, Sen. John, 161, 162, 182, 218
Trespalacios, José Felix, 33, 34
Truman, Pres. Harry, 160, 167
Tyler, Pres. John, 42
Tyler, Mrs. J. O. (Lillian), 104, 165
Twain, Mark, 11

Ulmer, Marvin C., 158, 159, 162
Upchurch, Fannie Davis (Mrs. R. E. L.), 245

Van Zandt, Khleber Miller, 48
Van Zandt, R. L., 115
Viertel, Hubert B., 214
Volcker, Paul, 212, 219
Von Rosenberg, Frederick, 248

Walker, Charls, 182, 183
Ware, C. T., 246
Watson, J. E., 122
Watson, T. R., 122
Watson, W. R., 122
Webb, George E., 70, 77
Webb, Sam, 88, 91
Webster, Daniel, 53
Weeks, Nicholas, 19, 22, 54, 62, 65
Weems, B. F., 18
Welch, Francis H., 129
Wells, H. G., 4, 5
Wells, Oscar, 115
Wester, R. H., 90
Wheeler, J. B., 193, 206, 210
White, J. L., 91
White, Gov. Mark, 162
Wiggins, Norman A., 182
Wilborn, Lee, 182, 211
Wiley, Bell Irvin, 45
Williams, E. W., 206
Williams, John Skelton, 114
Williams, Samuel May, 35, 36, 37,
  38, 44
Williams, W. A., 140
Willis, H. Parker, 110

Williston, Christopher L. (Chris),
  213
Wilmont, E. P., 124
Wilson, Pres. Woodrow, 98, 105,
  110, 111, 114, 139
Windom, W. W., 92
Withers, Col. John, 18
Wood, Ed, Jr., 189
Woods, J. E., 154, 236
Woodson, W. W., 124, 125
Woolridge, A. P., 65, 66, 68, 81, 82
Wooten, Ben, 166, 167
Word, J. P., 184
Worthington, William Floyd, 153
Wright, John A., 189
Wylie, Rep. Chalmers P., 219

Yantis, John T., 163
Yantis, T. C., 96
Yarborough, Sen. Ralph, 161
Young, D. J., 70
Young, Sam, Jr., 165, 213, 214
Yopp, Edward A., 210, 213
Yturri, D., 43

Ziegler, Jesse A., 43